西安交通大学
XI'AN JIAOTONG UNIVERSITY

U0719644

研究生"十四五"规划精品系列教材

Quality Graduate Teaching Materials for the 14th Five-Year Plan of Xi'an Jiaotong University

中华才艺实践教程

Practice Coursebook on Chinese Cultural Skills

主　　审　陈向京
主　　编　靳　蓉
副 主 编　杨　芳
参　　编　（按姓氏笔画）
　　　　　杨　扬　沈　妍　宋天悦　张丽娟
　　　　　邵　娟　庞云青　赵晓英　俞程成
视频音乐创作　宋天牧

西安交通大学出版社
XI'AN JIAOTONG UNIVERSITY PRESS

图书在版编目（CIP）数据

中华才艺实践教程 : 汉文、英文 / 靳蓉主编.
西安：西安交通大学出版社，2025.8. --ISBN 978-7
-5693-4016-7

Ⅰ . K203
中国国家版本馆CIP数据核字第20255C77B2号

中华才艺实践教程
Practice Coursebook on Chinese Cultural Skills

主　　编	靳　蓉
责任编辑	庞钧颖
责任校对	李　蕊
数字编辑	宋庆庆
装帧设计	伍　胜

出版发行	西安交通大学出版社
	（西安市兴庆南路1号　邮政编码710048）
网　　址	http://www.xjtupress.com
电　　话	（029）82668357 82667874（市场营销中心）
	（029）82668315（总编办）
传　　真	（029）82668280
印　　刷	西安五星印刷有限公司

开　　本	787 mm×1092 mm　1/16	**印张**	13.75	**字数**	300千字
版次印次	2025年8月第1版　　2025年8月第1次印刷				
书　　号	ISBN 978-7-5693-4016-7				
定　　价	52.00元				

如发现印装质量问题，请与本社市场营销中心联系。
订购热线：（029）82665248　（029）82667874
投稿热线：（029）82668531　（029）82665371

前 言
Preface

　　在奔流不息的历史长河中，中华才艺如熠熠生辉的明珠，散发着独特而迷人的魅力。它们不仅凝聚了中华民族的智慧与创造力，更是传承千年文化的关键所在。中华才艺在传播中华文化的过程中发挥着至关重要的作用。首先，中华才艺具有直观的吸引力。如精美的剪纸、绚丽的京剧脸谱等，能以独特的视觉效果迅速抓住人们的眼球，激发人们对中华文化的兴趣。其次，中华才艺富有参与性。像编中国结、编串珠手工艺品、包饺子等活动，能让人们在亲身体验中感受中华文化的魅力。再者，中华才艺是文化的生动载体。它们蕴含着丰富的历史、哲学、价值观等内涵。例如，传统的中国结及串珠手工艺品常常反映了特定时期的审美和社会风貌；在国际舞台上展示中华才艺，也能够打破语言和地域的限制，促进不同文化之间的相互理解和尊重。最后，中华才艺能够激发情感共鸣。中华才艺所体现的精湛手工技艺和深厚文化底蕴，容易触动人们的心灵，促使人们对中华文化产生深切的认同感与由衷的喜爱之情。总之，中华才艺以其独特的魅力和方式，在传播中华文化方面发挥着不可或缺的作用，有效提升了中华文化的影响力和吸引力。

　　《中华才艺实践教程》的编写目标与国家教育方针中的德智体美劳要求相契合，即通过实践活动促进学习者的全面发展。教材致力于为读者开启一扇通向中华才艺宝库的大门。在琳琅满目的中华才艺中，编写者遴选在海外汉语教学课堂中受欢迎程度高、可操作性强和易学的中华才艺作为教材的核心内容，包括中国结编制、剪纸制作、京剧脸谱绘制、串珠手工艺品制作、中华美食制作及中国画绘制，内容丰富，各高校"中华才艺"课程的授课教师可根据学生的具体情况进行取舍。教材还包含生动的插图和切实的范例，旨在助力学习者更加直观地了解中华才艺作品所承载的美学意义，领略中华才艺背后深厚的文化和历史底蕴。此外，教材编写者也注重培养学习者的动手能力，才艺技法步骤一步一图，更有录制的视频指导学生掌握各项中华才艺，切实做到边学边用，学中用，用中学，学用结合，学以致用。如此系统的教学安排，不仅有助于学习者熟练掌握中华才艺技能，更能为学习者未来讲好中国故事、弘扬中华优秀传统文化筑牢语言与才艺的双重根基。

具体而言，教材特色主要体现在以下几方面。

1. 以 POA 教学理念为理论指导

POA（Production-Oriented Approach）是基于产出导向法的外语教学理念。产出导向法指出，教学要让学习有效发生，并且"学""用"无缝衔接，让学生学会用英语做事，真正做到学有所用。本教材的编写以 POA 教学理念为指导，力图通过实践性训练，让学生在学习中华才艺的实际任务中反思自身跨文化交际能力和语言转换能力的不足，从而激发学生学习兴趣，同时着重培养学习者对中华优秀传统文化的认同感和自豪感。POA 提倡"学用一体"，因此教材采用中英双语，深度挖掘各项中华才艺源远流长的历史及其所蕴涵的中国传统文化元素，不仅仅是单纯地"学才艺"，而是将中国传统文化有机融入中华才艺学习中，有效地规避"母语文化缺失"。用中英双语介绍各项中华才艺的渊源和发展历史也能为学生提供有关"中国元素"的英文储备，提升用英语表述中华文化的能力，最终消除"中华文化失语症"，增强文化自信，提升中华文化展示力和传播力。

2. 教材中融入思政元素

本教材积极响应国家教育方针，致力于培养德智体美劳全面发展的社会主义建设者和接班人，在传授中华才艺技能的同时，帮助学生树立正确的世界观、人生观和价值观，将思想品德培养有机融入中华才艺实践教学中。

3. 注重实践性和实操性

本教材的编写团队成员均为资深教师，不仅精通英语，还在中华才艺领域有着多年的深耕。他们在长期的教学实践中积累了丰富的英语教学经验，并对各项中华才艺的学习过程有细致的观察和深刻的理解，因而能够精准把握才艺学习过程中的难点，并总结出切实可行的攻克方法。此外，编者们也充分利用现代教学手段和网络环境帮助学习者达成课程目标。作为一本中华才艺实训教材，本书尤为注重实践性与实操性。教材中才艺学习的各个步骤清晰完整、图文并茂，并配有教学视频，读者可扫描二维码获取。

《中华才艺实践教程》适用于国际中文教育专业以及本研一体化体美劳研修课程，也适用于来华交流的各国留学生以及对中华文化和才艺感兴趣的中外人士，可作为手工艺类课程或公选课程的教学用书，也可作为继续教育、素质教育、美育教育等培训的参考用书。无论您是热衷于探寻中国艺术之美的爱好者，还是期望丰富自身才艺的学生，这本书均是珍贵的资源，会在您探索和实践中华艺术的旅程中为您带来启迪和引导。

在教材编写过程中，编者们全力以赴，始终秉持精益求精的态度，但因自身水平有限，加之编写时间仓促，教材中难免存在一些疏漏与不足，在此恳请专家、学者及广大使用者提出宝贵意见，帮助我们不断改进完善。同时，本教材在编写过程中参阅了大量国内外相关文献资料和同类教材，在此向所有相关作者致以诚挚的谢意。

编　者

2025 年 4 月

目 录
Contents

v

Chapter 1

中国结
Chinese Knots

中国结是中国传统手工艺品。它是以线、绳等材料为载体，通过手工编绾而成的绳结装饰品。中国结历史源远流长，文化内涵独具一格，制作工艺精巧，样式丰富多样且寓意深远，尽显独特的东方神韵。它不仅是精美的装饰之物，更是中华民族智慧与文化传承的象征。2021 年，中国结传统编织技艺被列入山东省省级第五批非物质文化遗产代表性项目。

The Chinese knot is a traditional handicraft in China made with threads, ropes, and other materials by hand. The Chinese knot boasts a long history and distinctive cultural connotations. Its manufacturing process is elaborate, and the patterns and styles are numerous and diverse, carrying profound meanings and fully showcasing the unique oriental charm. It is not merely a beautiful adornment but also a symbol of the wisdom and cultural inheritance of Chinese nation. In 2021, the traditional weaving technique of Chinese knot was enlisted in the fifth batch of representative items of provincial-level intangible cultural heritage in Shandong Province.

Section 1

中国结概况
An Overview of Chinese Knots

中国结渊源久远，它始于上古，兴于唐宋，盛于明清，复兴于今，其所展示的情致与智慧是古老中华文明的一个缩影。经过数千年的演变，它从一种实用的绳结演变成现代精美绝伦的装饰性艺术品。

The Chinese knot boasts a long history which started from ancient time, prospered in the Tang and Song dynasties, flourished in the Ming and Qing dynasties and revives at the present day. The appeal and wisdom displayed by Chinese knots are the epitome of ancient Chinese civilization. After thousands of years of evolution, it has transformed from practical knotting into the present-day exquisitely decorative works of art.

中国人使用结的历史可以追溯到旧石器时代。远古时期，采集和渔猎是人们主要的衣食来源。原始人用草、藤、麻、棕、竹、葛、枝条等线形材料，采用拧扭、交叉的方法用于穿系、捆扎果实和猎物，形成最原始的绳编。

The history of using knots by Chinese people can be traced back to the Paleolithic Age. In ancient times, people got their food and clothing mainly from gathering, fishing and hunting. Primitive people twisted and intersected natural material such as grass, rattan, hemp, palm fiber, bamboo, kudzu vine and branches to bind around their clothing and strap the fruit and prey. They could be prototypes of the knots.

北京周口店龙骨山山顶洞人生活在约 18000 年前。考古学家发现山顶洞人不仅会制作许多精美的装饰品，如石头吊坠和沟槽骨管等，还会用骨针和骨锥缝制兽皮衣服。骨针是迄今中国发现的旧石器时代最早的缝纫工具，在当时用于缝制鹿皮裙。在山顶洞人的遗址中发现的骨针以及各种带孔的骨类和贝类饰品，表明旧石器时代晚期已出现用于缝纫和穿连的人为加工的绳线。当人们用绳线穿骨、贝壳等作为装饰物及缝制衣物时，必然会产生原始的、简单的绳结。可以说，绳结的历史几乎与人类文明的历史一样悠久。

The Upper Cave Man lived in the caves of the Longgu Hill, Zhoukoudian, Beijing about 18,000 years ago. Archaeologists found the Upper Cave Man could not only make many fine and beautiful ornaments, such as stone pendants and grooved bone tubes. They also made animal-skin clothing with bone needles and bone awls. The bone needle is the earliest Paleolithic sewing tool discovered in China to date, and was used to sew deer skins into skirts. Bone needles and various bone and shell ornaments with drilled holes found in the remains of the Upper Cave Man indicate the appearance of man-made thread and rope for sewing and threading in the late Paleolithic Age. Therefore, the primitive and simple knots were bound to be made when the Upper Cave Man threaded bone and shell ornaments and engaged in sewing. It is believed that the history of knots is as old as the history of human civilization.

除了绑缚功能外，绳结还被充满智慧的先民们赋予了另一种实用的功能——记事。有考古文献证明，在文字产生之前，人们用绳索打结的办法来记事、协助治理天下。

中国的几部经典文献都提到了绳结。例如，《道德经》第八十章提到"使民复结绳而用之"。《周易·系辞下》中也有记载"上古结绳而治，后世圣人易之以书契"，意思是说，上古时代没有文字，人们用结绳记事的办法来治理天下。后来有杰出人物发明了文字，于是人们不再结绳记事，改用文字。只不过那时纸张还未发明出来，人们用刀将文字刻在陶器或龟甲兽骨上。东汉学者郑玄为《周易》作注，他写道："事大，大结其绳，事小，小结其绳。"这是说用不同的结形来记载各种事情，重要的事情就结一个大的绳结，不太重要的事情就结一个小的绳结。从历史记载中，我们可以了解到上古时的绳结除了最简单的捆扎、系、绑缚功用外，还有记载历史的文化功能，在当时人们的生活中起着重要的作用。

In addition to the practical use for binding and fastening, the ingenious ancient Chinese people endowed knots with another vital function, which was to keep records. Archaeological evidence confirms that before the advent of written language, knotted cords were used to document events and even aid in governance. This practice is well-documented in classical Chinese texts. For example, *Dao De Jing* alludes to it in Chapter 80: "Let the people return to the use of knotted cords." Similarly, *The Book of Changes* ("Appended Remarks, Part II") states: "In ancient times, governance was carried out successfully through knotted cords. Later sages replaced them with written characters and bonds." This suggests that in preliterate societies, knot-keeping served as an administrative tool until written language emerged. At that time, since paper had not yet been invented, people carved characters onto pottery, tortoise shells, or animal bones instead. Zheng Xuan, an Eastern Han Dynasty scholar, elaborated in his commentary on *The Book of Changes*: "Major affairs were recorded with large knots, and minor ones with small knots." This indicates that different knot sizes encoded varying levels of importance, functioning as an early archival tool. Thus, in ancient times, knots were not merely used to tie, fasten and bind items, they also served as a cultural medium for preserving history, playing a vital role in people's lives at that time.

在已出土的新石器时期彩陶上有花纹样式各异的装饰纹样，其中包括绳结纹。这表明在远古时期，人们对绳结有着特殊的感情，并将绳结之美通过器物装饰展现出来。

There were different decorative patterns on the unearthed painted potteries in the Neolithic Age, among which there were twisted rope pattern. These patterns demonstrated that people in ancient times held a special affection for knots and were eager to show the beauty of the knot through the pattern decoration on the artifacts.

新石器时代大溪文化彩陶上的绳结纹
Twisted rope patterns on painted pottery of Daxi culture in the Neolithic Age

随着文字的形成和发展，绳结的记事功能渐渐隐退，但实用功能继续保留，装饰功能不断发展。

With the invention and development of written language, tying knots to keep records disappeared step by step, but the practical function of the knots continued to be retained and the decorative function gradually developed.

从西周（公元前 1046 年—公元前 771 年）开始，结在人们的生活中被广泛使用，绳结常用于器物的装饰，如车篷伞盖上的装饰结、青铜器上的络绳纹装饰、汉代瓦当上的结纹，以及铜镜、砖刻、石雕上的结饰等。络绳纹是青铜器纹饰之一，由并连的绳索相连或套结，连成菱形或长方形的网格状。络绳纹在器皿上较为常见。绳子或绳结通过较为写实的浮雕手法装饰在壶、瓮之类的器物上，制作出的器物看起来如同用绳子套住一般。

Since the Western Zhou Dynasty (1046 BCE–771 BCE), knots have been widely used in people's daily lives and for the decoration of utensils as well. For example, there were ornamental knots adorning carriage canopies and ceremonial parasols, the rope-net pattern embellishing ritual bronze vessels, knot patterns on Han Dynasty roof tiles as well as knot ornaments on bronze mirrors, brick carvings, and stone carvings. The rope-net pattern was one of the decorative patterns on bronze wares which was made by connecting ropes with knots, creating the pattern of diamond or rectangular grids. This design appeared most frequently on ceremonial vessels. Through relatively realistic relief techniques, ropes or rope knots were used to decorate utensils such as pots and urns, making these utensils appear to be physically bound by actual ropes.

春秋时期错红铜络绳纹壶，山西博物院藏
Knot pattern on copper pot in the Spring and Autumn period, kept in Shanxi Museum

战国早期络绳纹罍，山西博物院藏
Knot pattern on copper wine vessel Lei in the early Warring States period, kept in Shanxi Museum

　　绳结不仅用于器物的装饰，也用于衣服上的配饰，从出土文物和古代绘画作品中均能找到服饰上结饰的影子。例如，陕西西安秦始皇兵马俑博物馆中将军俑的胸前和肩头有结饰，射手俑从肩膀到前胸处也有结饰。在东晋顾恺之的绘画作品《洛神赋图》中，也能看见洛神所着服饰上装饰有中国结。

Besides being used for decoration of objects, knots were also tied on clothes as accessories. Knots on the clothes can be found both in unearthed cultural relics and ancient paintings. For example, in the Museum of Terracotta Warriors and Horses of Qinshihuang in Xi'an, Shaanxi Province, knot ornaments can be found on the chest and shoulders of the general and also from the archer's shoulder to his front chest. In Gu Kaizhi's painting *The Goddess of the Luo River* in the Eastern Jin Dynasty, it can also be seen that the Goddess of Luo's clothing is decorated with Chinese knots.

《洛神赋图》（局部），（东晋）
顾恺之，故宫博物院藏
Part of Gu Kaizhi's painting *The Goddess of the Luo River* in the Eastern Jin Dynasty, kept in the Palace Museum

　　印绶制度是汉代（公元前 202 年—公元 220 年）服饰的一大特点。依汉制之规定，汉代的帝王及百官外出时必须随身携带官印，官印上系束着丝织的绦带，此即为绶。一印一绶，合称为印绶。汉代的官印尺寸较小，被称作方寸之印。印绶由朝廷统一颁发，是区分官阶的重要标识。佩戴时必须将官印置于腰间的皮质鞶囊里，同时将绶带垂于外边。印绶多穿过身前身后的腰带，自然地垂挂而下。从皇帝至各级官员所佩的绶带，在尺寸、颜色以及织法上均因等级差异而有所不同，使人一眼望去便知佩绶者的身份。佩戴过程中，因绶带很长，还需打成花结用作装饰。

The practice of wearing seals with silk ribbons (Yinshou) constituted a distinctive element of the Han Dynasty (202BCE–220CE) official attire. Under Han court regulations, the emperor and all government officials were required to carry their official seals when traveling. These seals, secured with specially designated silk fasteners called "Shou," formed a complete set known as "Yinshou" (seal and ribbon). Han Dynasty official seals, characteristically compact in size, were commonly referred to as "square-inch seals." The imperial court uniformly issued these Yinshou sets, which served as crucial visual indicators of officials' practical rank. Officials wore them by placing the seals in leather pouches at their waists while allowing the ribbons to drape visibly. The ribbons typically passed through the wearer's front and back belts, hanging naturally in elegant folds. From the emperor down through the entire bureaucracy, these silk ribbons varied significantly in sizes, colors, and weaving techniques according to the wearer's status, enabling immediate identification of rank. Given their considerable length, the ribbons needed to be tied into flower knots for decoration.

中国人佩玉的风尚拥有很长的历史，《礼记》中有记载"君子无故玉不去身""君子必佩玉"。佩玉标志着一个人的身份地位、道德修养、品格情操。几件或成组列的美玉需要借助绳结相连接才能系在衣服上，而且必须靠穿绳打结才能佩戴。早在战国时期就已经存在较多样的佩玉绳结，如河南信阳楚墓出土的彩绘木俑，上面清晰地描绘了当时人们佩玉打结的情形。另外，那些单耳结和下端的带饰，除了系扎、固定玉璜及玉环外，更有陪衬和装饰的作用。

Wearing jade accessories has a long history in China. As recorded in *The Book of Rites*, a gentleman "never parts with his jade without proper reason" and "must always wear jade." Jade ornaments served as markers of social status, ethical attainments and moral character. Several pieces or groups of jades required intricate rope knotting for secure attachment to garments, making the knotting technique essential for the proper wearing of jade. This practice dates back to the Warring States period, when various specialized knotting methods for jade suspension were already well-developed. Evidence from painted wooden figurines excavated from Chu tombs in Xinyang, Henan Province vividly illustrates the jade-wearing customs and knotting techniques of that era. Those single-ear knots and decorative tassels at the lower ends not only helped to tie jade Huang (semicircular jade pendants) and jade rings but also enhanced their aesthetic appeal through complementary decoration.

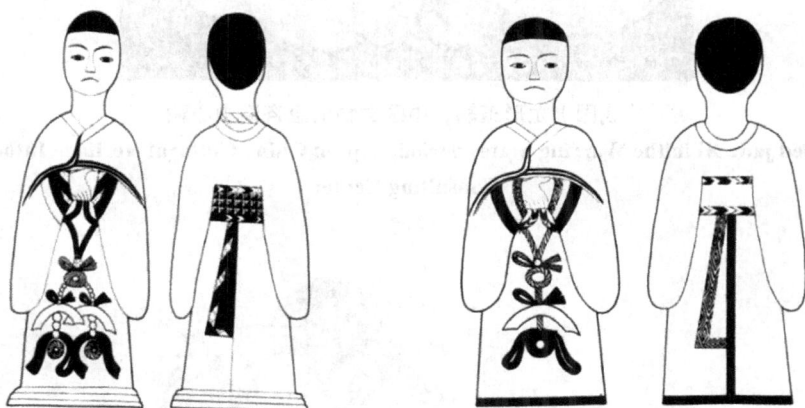

河南信阳楚墓出土的彩绘木俑身上组玉佩佩戴情况
The arrangement of the sets of jade pendants on the painted wooden figurines unearthed from the Chu Tomb in Xinyang, Henan Province

古人的服装特点为"宽衣博带"。要想使衣服贴体、保暖，就要用带子扎系起来。由于需要经常打结和解结，人们常常佩戴"觿"。觿是一种角形器，最初是一种随身携带的解结工具，后演变为佩饰。对于"觿"，《说文解字》中有这样的解释："觿，佩角，锐端，可以解结也。"最早的玉觿见于新石器时代，流行于商周至汉代，魏晋以后则少见。

The clothes in ancient times were characterized by loose costumes with straps. To make clothes fit and keep warm, people had to tie and knot the strap. Because of the need of tying and untying the knot frequently, it became the custom for men to wear Xi. As for Xi, the book *Shuowen Jiezi* has such an explanation: "Xi, pendant horn, with tapering tip, is used for untangling the knots." With the time going by, Xi developed from the tool to untie the knot to a kind of ornament. The jade Xi appeared in the Neolithic Age, popularized in the Shang, Zhou and Han dynasties, barely used after the Wei and Jin dynasties.

（战国）龙形玉觽，中国文物信息咨询中心藏
Dragon-shaped jade Xi in the Warring States period, kept in China Cultural Heritage Information and Consulting Center

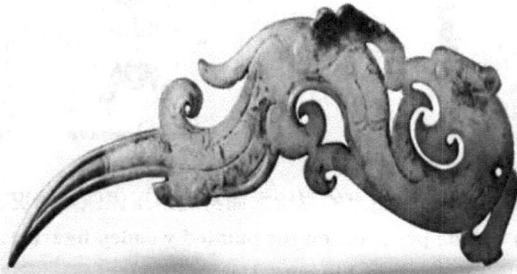

（西汉）龙形玉觽，故宫博物院藏
Dragon-shaped jade Xi in the Western Han Dynasty, kept in the Palace Museum

在汉代时期，中国结中的一些基本结已初具雏形。例如，在湖南省长沙市马王堆1号汉墓出土的漆棺彩绘二龙穿璧图中，有一块悬挂着的璧，其上下都系着由丝带绾成的雀头结。新疆尉犁营盘墓地15号墓出土的东汉时期的红黄绢地香囊，其系带两端有反向编织的吉祥结，耳翼和尾线呈花卉状，具有极强的装饰性。

In the Han Dynasty, some basic knots in Chinese knots began to take shape. For example, there was a suspended jade disk in the colored drawing of two dragons passing through a jade disk on the lacquered coffin unearthed from the No.1 Han Tomb in Mawangdui, Changsha, Hunan Province. The magpie-head knots formed by silk ribbons were tied to both the upper and lower parts of the jade disk. Moreover, the red and yellow silk sachet from the Eastern Han Dynasty unearthed from Tomb No.15 in the Yingpan Cemetery in Yuli, Xinjiang, had auspicious knots woven in reverse at both ends, and its ear wings and tail lines were in the shape of flowers, presenting a highly decorative effect.

（西汉）漆棺彩绘二龙穿璧图
Colored drawing of two dragons passing through a jade disk on the lacquered coffin from the Western Han Dynasty

（东汉）红黄绢地香囊
Red and yellow silk sachet from the Eastern Han Dynasty

　　唐代（618 年—907 年）迎来了中国结发展历史的重要时期，在这一时期，编结工艺分工极为细致，还出现了专门的编结作坊。结作为一种艺术装饰，被广泛运用在服饰和器物之中。例如，唐代永泰公主墓和章怀太子墓壁画中的宫人，多着单色裙，裙腰下两侧各开一衩口，露出其内所穿的细密间裙，并以一条环绶结带从腰衩内伸出垂下，或在腰衩下端打一花结。

　　The Tang Dynasty (618–907) witnessed an important period in the development history of Chinese knots. During this era, the knotting craft was highly detailed in its division of labor, and specialized knotting workshops emerged. Knots were widely used as an artistic decoration in clothing and utensils. For example, palace attendants in the murals of Princess Yongtai's tomb and Prince Zhanghuai's tomb of the Tang Dynasty mostly wore single-colored skirts. On both sides below the waist of the skirt, there was a slit each, exposing the fine interwoven skirt worn within. A looped and knotted ribbon hung down from within the slit at the waist or formed a flower knot at the lower end of the slit.

　　在唐代的双鸾衔绶纹铜镜上，鸾鸟昂首展翅，口中衔着系有同心结的绶带，优雅地翩翩起舞。同心结因两结相连的特点，常被用来象征男女之间的爱情，取恩爱情深、永结同心之意。而"绶"与长寿的"寿"同音，因此，双鸾衔绶图案整体蕴含着幸福、长寿、爱情美满等美好含义，将人们对美好生活的追求展现得淋漓尽致。

　　On the bronze mirror decorated with the pattern of two mythical birds holding ribbons tied with truelove knots in their beaks in the Tang Dynasty, the mythical birds hold their heads high, spread their wings, and dance gracefully with ribbons tied with truelove knots in their beaks. The truelove knot is often employed to symbolize the everlasting deep love between men and women due to its feature of two connected knots. The Chinese character "绶" has the same pronunciation as the character "寿" which means longevity. The overall pattern of two mythical birds holding ribbons tied with truelove knots in their beaks implies meanings such as happiness, longevity, and a perfect love, vividly demonstrating people's pursuit of a wonderful life.

（唐）双鸾衔绶纹铜镜，陕西历史博物馆藏

Bronze mirror decorated with the pattern of two mythical birds holding ribbons tied with truelove knots in their beaks in the Tang Dynasty, kept in Shaanxi History Museum

唐代鎏金舞马衔杯纹银壶是中国首批禁止出国（境）展览文物，1970 年于陕西西安南郊何家村出土，现藏于陕西历史博物馆。此壶仿契丹族皮囊壶制作而成。银壶的两面各有一匹马，马颈系绶带，象征长寿，绶带在马背系成团锦结样式，寓意锦绣前程、团圆、团结等。马的奔跑姿势飘逸洒脱，口中衔杯欲跪拜祝寿，生动再现了唐玄宗生日庆典上舞马衔杯祝寿场景。

The gilt silver pot with pattern of dancing horses holding goblets in their mouths of the Tang Dynasty is among the first batch of cultural relics forbidden from exhibition abroad. It was unearthed in Hejiacun which is located in the southern suburbs of Xi'an, Shaanxi Province in 1970, and is currently housed in

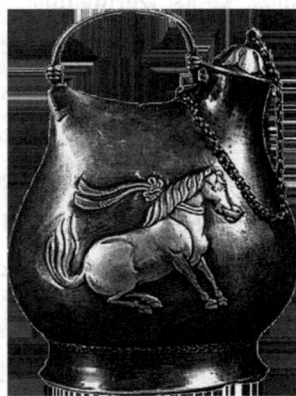

（唐）鎏金舞马衔杯纹银壶，陕西历史博物馆藏

Gilt silver pot with pattern of dancing horses holding goblets in their mouths of the Tang Dynasty, kept in Shaanxi History Museum

the Shaanxi History Museum. This pot was made in imitation of the leather bag pot used by the Khitan people, a northern nomadic ethnic group in China. There is a horse on each side of the silver pot. The necks of the horses are adorned with long ribbons, symbolizing longevity. The ribbons are tied on the backs of the horses in the form of round brocade knot, which implies a prosperous future, reunion and unity, etc. The horse has an elegant and unrestrained galloping posture and holds a cup in its mouth as if it is about to kneel and offer birthday blessings, which vividly recreates the scene of the dancing horse presenting a cup to offer birthday wishes at Emperor Xuanzong of the Tang Dynasty's birthday celebration.

在唐朝时期，中国结进入宫廷并深受王公贵族的青睐，其结饰的应用极为广泛。例如，《宫乐图》描绘了唐代宫廷贵妇聚会奏乐饮茶的日常生活场景。图中后宫妃嫔十多人围坐在一张巨型的方桌四周，有的在品茗，有的在弹奏乐器，而她们所坐的椅子上均挂有精美的中国结用作装饰。与此同时，经由大量中外文化交流活动，中国结编制艺术也传至海外，在日本和朝鲜半岛尤为流行。

During the Tang Dynasty, Chinese knots made their way into the imperial court and were extensively used as the decoration and were highly favored by the nobility. For example, the painting *Entertainment in Palace* depicts the daily life scenes of noblewomen in the Tang Dynasty's imperial court gathering, playing music and drinking tea. In the painting, more than ten imperial concubines were seated around a huge square table. Some were enjoying tea, while others were playing musical instruments. The chairs they sat on were all adorned with exquisite Chinese knots for decoration. Meanwhile, through numerous cultural exchange activities between China and foreign countries, weaving art of Chinese knot was spread overseas, particularly to Japan and the Korean Peninsula.

在宋代（960年—1279年），中国结饰开始商业化，出现了专门出售结饰的生意。北宋苏汉臣的《货郎图》便生动地表现了当时结饰售卖的场景。画中一株梅花树下，货郎手推货车，车上货物琳琅满目，其中就有各类结饰艺术品。此外，这一时期结饰的应用范围有所扩大，已经被应用于战士的盔甲中。宋代战士的头盔、胸前、腰间、剑柄、鞋面等都布满了造型不同、功能各异的结。

The Song Dynasty (960–1279) witnessed the commercialization of Chinese knot ornaments, and businesses specializing in selling them emerged. The painting *The Peddler* by Su Hanchen of the Northern Song Dynasty vividly portrays the scene of selling knot ornaments at that time. Under a plum tree in the painting, a peddler pushed a cart laden with a dazzling array of goods, among which were various kinds of knot artworks. Moreover, during this period, the application of knot ornaments expanded and they were used in the armors of soldiers. The helmets, chest plates, waists, sword hilts and shoe surfaces of the soldiers in the Song Dynasty were all adorned with knots of diverse shapes and functions.

　　明清时期是中国结艺发展的鼎盛阶段，从众多日常用品中皆能看到式样丰富、配色精美的结饰。至清代（1644年—1911年），构思巧妙的结俨然成为衣兜。《红楼梦》第三十五回里有宝玉请莺儿为他打络子的情节。所谓络子，指的是以线绳编织而成的有各式花样的小网袋，通常系于腰间，用以系挂各类坠饰或装汗巾、香囊、扇子等随身小物件。络子花样繁多，有一炷香、朝天凳、方胜、连环、梅花、柳叶等多种样式。此外，结饰还被应用于纽扣之上。除了由金玉等材质制成的纽扣外，还有用丝绸或布料编制的盘扣，就是将狭窄布条卷成圆形或扁圆形盘条，再盘成各种花样，一端制成球形用作扣子，另一端制成环套，而后用针线固定在衣襟上。在中国民间，关于盘扣的编制方法众多，如蜻蜓扣、孔雀扣、凤凰扣、梅花扣、琵琶扣，等等。

The Ming and Qing dynasties witnessed the peak period of the development of Chinese knot art, with intricately designed and vibrantly colored decorative knots adorning a wide variety of everyday objects. By the Qing Dynasty (1644–1911), these ingeniously crafted knots had served as pockets. A notable example appears in Chapter 35 of *Dream of the Red Chamber*, where Baoyu asks Ying'er to weave a Laozi for him. The so-called Laozi was a small, exquisitely knotted net pouch made from threaded cords. Worn at the waist, the Laozi served as holders for pendants, handkerchiefs, sachets, folding fans, and other personal items. They came in various patterns, such as single incense stick, upward stool, interlocking lozenge, chain links, plum blossom, and willow leaf. Beyond Laozi, knots were also incorporated into clothing fasteners. In addition to buttons made of gold, jade, or other materials, there were Pankou— ornamental knotted buttons crafted from silk or fabric strips. These were made by rolling narrow fabric strips into round or flat cords, then shaping them into intricate patterns. One end formed a spherical knob, while the other looped into a fastening ring, both sewn onto garments. In Chinese folk traditions, there were a rich variety of Pankou styles, such as dragonfly button, peacock button, phoenix button, plum blossom button, and pipa button.

　　20世纪80年代以来，随着人们对传统文化符号越来越重视，中国结重焕生机。在中国的许多重要节日和庆典活动中，人们都会使用中国结来装饰场所，增添喜庆和热闹的氛围。现如今，人们更加注重中国结的装饰功能，同时融入现代元素，令其造型愈发多变。中国结伴随北京2008年申奥成功蜚声海内外，成为现代设计中重要的装饰应用元素。中国结所彰显的情致与智慧，恰是古老中华文明中的一个文化切面，它代表着质朴的人生，蕴含着天地的哲学，是中华儿女心连心的象征，也表达了对全人类携手向未来的美好期许。在 2022 年北京冬奥会闭幕式上，91 个国家和地区的运动员伴随着《欢乐颂》的旋律，在地屏呈现的彩色中国结中穿梭，与荧屏上借助 AR 技术呈现的空中巨型中国结交相辉映。中国结代表的美好祝福，联通世界各国人民的心灵，更加体现了人类命运共同体的理念。中国结，让我们与祖先思绪相连；中国结，使我们与世界情意相通。

Since the 1980s, as people pay more and more attention to traditional cultural symbols, Chinese knots have regained their vitality. In many important festivals and celebratory events in China, people always use Chinese knots to adorn venues, thus enhancing a festive and bustling atmosphere. Nowadays, people attach greater importance to its decorative function, and incorporate modern elements to make Chinese knots more diversified in shape. Chinese knot became famous at home and abroad with the success of Beijing's bid for the 2008 Olympic Games and have become important decorative elements applied in modern design. The appeal and wisdom manifested by Chinese knots precisely constitute a cultural aspect of ancient Chinese civilization. It represents a plain and simple life, embodies the philosophy of heaven and earth, is a symbol of the unity among the sons and daughters of the Chinese nation, and expresses the good expectations for all mankind to move towards the future hand in hand. At the closing ceremony of the 2022 Beijing Winter Olympics, athletes from 91 countries and regions weaved through the colorful Chinese knots displayed on the ground screen to the melody of "Ode to Joy," corresponding to the giant Chinese knot presented on the screen with the aid of AR technology. The good wishes represented by the Chinese knot connect the hearts of people from all over the world and profoundly embody the concept of a community with a shared future for mankind. The Chinese knot links our thoughts to our ancestors', and the Chinese knot makes our affection resonate with the world.

Exercises

1 **Answer the following questions.**

(1) On what occasions are Chinese knots often used in Chinese culture?

(2) How does the making process of a Chinese knot reflect traditional Chinese craftsmanship?

(3) What role does the Chinese knot play in promoting cultural exchanges between different countries?

❷ Choose the best answer to each of the following questions.

(1) When did Chinese people begin to use bone needles to do the sewing?

A. In the early Paleolithic Age.   B. In the late Paleolithic Age.

C. In the early Neolithic Age.   D. In the late Neolithic Age.

(2) Who had used the technology of drilling to make fine and beautiful bone and shell ornaments?

A. Yuanmou Man.   B. Upper Cave Man.

C. Peking Man.   D. Wushan Man.

(3) How did people record the events before the invention of written language in the late Paleolithic Age?

A. They drew the pictures on the rocks and trees.

B. They tried hard to use their brains to memorize.

C. They tied the knots with some natural materials.

D. They passed down the events orally.

(4) What's the function of Xi?

A. It was used to untie the knot.

B. It was used to help to pass a thread through the eye of a needle.

C. It was used as the hairpin to do up the hair.

D. It was used to clear up the dust in the crevices.

(5) Which of the following is the symbolic meaning of round brocade knot?

A. Everything goes well and smoothly.

B. Have good fortune as one wishes.

C. Good things come in pairs.

D. Have a prosperous future.

中国结编制基本技法
Basic Techniques of Threading Chinese Knots

编制中国结的主要材料是线材，常用的线材有中国结编织线、玉线、五色线、股线等。初学编结时可以用粗一点的线，以便于观察线的走向。当然，越粗的线材能做出的中国结也越大。

The main material for tying Chinese knots is thread. Commonly used types of thread include string of the Chinese knot, jade cord, five-color cord, and stranded cord. When beginners start learning to make knots, they can use thicker thread as it is easier to observe the movement of the thread. Certainly, the thicker the thread is, the larger the Chinese knot that can be crafted.

中国结编织线带有丝质光泽，光滑柔软。若被锐物勾到容易出现起毛现象。接头处可用打火机烧灼黏接。编织中国结常用的线有中国结 5 号线、6 号线、7 号线，号数越大，线越细。这类线颜色很多，并有加金线和不加金线的区别。其中，中国结 1 号线的直径为 9 毫米，中国结 2 号线、3 号线、4 号线、5 号线、6 号线、7 号线的直径分别为 6、4.5、3、2.5、2、1.5 毫米。

The string of the Chinese knot is smooth and soft with silky sheen. If snagged by a sharp object, it is prone to fuzzing. Its loose ends can be sealed by melting them with a lighter. Commonly used strings for weaving Chinese knots are No.5, No.6, and No.7 string of the Chinese knot. The higher the number is, the thinner the string is. These strings come in many colors and there is also a distinction between those with gold thread and those without. Among them, No.1 string of the Chinese knot has a diameter of 9 millimeters. No.2, No.3, No.4, No.5, No.6, and No.7 strings have a diameter of 6, 4.5, 3, 2.5, 2, and 1.5 millimeters respectively.

玉线织法紧密，表面有交织的花纹，结实耐磨，不容易出现起毛现象。接头处可用打火机烧灼黏接。常用型号有 A 玉线、B 玉线、71 号玉线、72 号玉线和 73 号玉线。在台湾，71 号玉线称为 AA 线，72 号玉线称为 AB 线。玉线常用来串编珠饰，是珠宝店常用的线材之一。A 玉线、B 玉线、71 号玉线、72 号玉线和 73 号玉线的直径分别为 1、1.5、0.4、0.8 和 0.6 毫米。

Jade cord is tightly woven with interlaced designs on its surface. It is sturdy, wear-resistant, and not likely to become frizzy. Its ends can be fused together using a lighter.

Commonly used types of cords include A jade cord, B jade cord, No.71 jade cord, No.72 jade cord, and No.73 jade cord. In Taiwan Province, No.71 jade cord is called AA cord and No.72 jade cord is known as AB cord. Jade cord is frequently used for threading bead ornaments and is one of the commonly used cords in jewelry stores. The diameters of A, B, No.71, No.72, and No.73 jade cords are 1, 1.5, 0.4, 0.8, and 0.6 millimeters respectively.

五色线的织法和材质与玉线类似，由红、黄、白、青、黑五种颜色编织而成。五色线和玉线使用同样的型号标记，但一般同型号的五色线比纯色玉线要稍粗一些，常用型号有 A 线和 72 号五色线。就颜色而言，有偏红、偏黄的五色线，此外还有加金线的五色线。

The weaving technique and material of the five-color cord are similar to those of the jade cord. It is woven with five colors: red, yellow, white, cyan, and black. The five-color cord and the jade cord utilize the same number to mark its size. Generally, the five-color cord of the same size is slightly thicker than the jade cord in pure-color. Commonly used cords include A cord and No.72 cord. In terms of color, there are five-color cords that are reddish or yellowish, and there is also a type with gold thread added.

股线是用数股丝线搓拧而成的，织法相对松散，线体柔软，线头容易散开。线头可用小火加热烧粘，但火烧后容易变黑。常用型号有 12 股、9 股、6 股、3 股。股数越少，线越细。较粗的股线可直接编手绳，特别细的股线常用于绕在别的线上作装饰。

Stranded cord is made by twisting several strands of silk thread into one. Woven loosely, the stranded cord is soft and its end is prone to disperse. The cord end can be heated with a small flame to be fused together, but it easily turns black after being burned. Commonly used models include 12-strand, 9-strand, 6-strand, and 3-strand. The fewer the number of strands is, the thinner the cord is. Thicker stranded cords can be directly used to thread bracelets. Extremely thin stranded cords are often used to wind around other strings for decoration.

编制中国结主要依靠灵巧的双手来完成。然而，当编制结构较为复杂的结饰时，常需借助合适的工具。常用的工具包括卷尺、泡沫板或软木板、珠针、弯嘴镊子、打火机及剪刀。

Chinese knots are mainly made by dexterous hands. Nevertheless, when it comes to making more complex knot ornaments, appropriate tools are frequently required. The commonly used tools consist of tape measure, foam board or cork board, pins, curved-tip tweezer, lighter and a pair of scissors.

编制中国结时常用两种基本手法。一种为"挑"，即将线 1 从线 2 的下面穿过，也就是把线 2 "挑"起来，使线 1 处在线 2 的下方。另一种是"压"，即将线 1 压在线 2 的上面。

Two fundamental techniques are frequently used when threading Chinese knots. One is called the "Under" move, where string 1 goes under string 2, raising it so that string 1 lies beneath. The other is called the "Over" move, where string 1 crosses over string 2, making string 2 lie beneath.

在编制中国结的过程中，需要保持耐心，切不可急躁。要多观察，勤练习，才能够越做越好。

During the process of threading Chinese knots, one needs to be patient and stop being irritable. Observe more and practice diligently. Only in this way can one make Chinese knots better and better.

1 | 双联结、吉祥结、凤尾结、纽扣结
Double Connection Knot, Auspicious Knot, Phoenix Tail Knot, and Button Knot

双联结、吉祥结、凤尾结和纽扣结均是中国结中的基本结，初学者往往从这些基本结开始学习编制中国结。

Double connection knot, auspicious knot, phoenix tail knot (leaf knot), and button knot are all basic knots in Chinese knots. When learning to make Chinese knots, beginners tend to start from making these basic knots.

双联结是常用的基本单结之一。在汉语中，"联"与"连"同音，因此双联结的寓意为联合、连绵不断、连年有余等。双联结由两个单结相套连而成，故名双联。双联结小巧牢固，不易变形，非常实用，常用于固定主结的上下部分，或作为组合结的开头或结尾，也常用来制作腰带、手链、项链等。

Double connection knot is one of the basic knots. Connection is homophonic in Chinese with "continuousness." Therefore, double connection knot has the symbolic meaning of being connected, continuous and having a surplus year after year. The double connection knot is threaded by combining two single knots, hence the name "Shuanglian." The double connection knot has the characteristics of being small and firm, not easy to deform and very practical. It is frequently used to fix the upper part and lower part of the main knot or serves as the beginning or the end of the combined knot. It is often used to thread belts, bracelets, necklaces and so on.

扫描二维码获取双联结
制作方法与教学视频
**Scan the QR-code to
get the methods and
teaching video of tying
double connection knot**

所需材料：一根长 45 厘米的中国结 5 号线。

Material needed: one 45-centimeter-long No.5 string of Chinese knot.

吉祥结非常受人们欢迎，其结形美观，变化多端，应用广泛。吉祥结代表着祥瑞、美好、吉祥如意，它表达了人们对福、禄、寿、喜、财、安、康的期盼。吉祥结的耳圈恰好有 7 个，所以吉祥结又称"七圈结"。在古代，此结常用于祈福类饰品，常出现在僧人的袈裟及庙堂的饰物上。吉祥结在现代家居装饰中也很常见。

The auspicious knot is highly popular due to its intricate beauty, versatile variations, and wide applications. Symbolizing auspiciousness, beauty, and good fortune, it embodies people's hopes for prosperity, wealth, longevity, joy, fortune, peace, and health. The auspicious knot is also known as the seven-loop knot because it has exactly seven ear loops. In ancient times, it was commonly used in ornaments for praying for blessings, adorning monks' robes and temple decorations. Nowadays, it is also frequently seen in home decorations.

扫描二维码获取吉祥结制作方法与教学视频
Scan the QR-code to get the methods and teaching video of tying auspicious knot

所需材料：一根长 1 米的中国结 5 号线。

Material needed: one 1-meter-long No.5 string of Chinese knot.

凤尾结因其形状如传说中凤凰的尾羽而得名。该结在编缉时要绕 8 字，又称为 8 字结；因其形状也像一片树叶，所以也可称为树叶结。此结寓意龙凤呈祥，财源茂盛。凤尾结多用绳头的一端编制，其结形小巧紧实，常用于结饰的收尾和装饰，也可编制成盘扣、手链、项链等。

The phoenix tail knot got its name because its shape resembles the tail feather of the legendary phoenix. When tying this knot, one needs to thread in the shape of the number "8," so it is also known as the figure eight knot. Moreover, as its shape also looks like a leaf, it can also be called the leaf knot. This knot symbolizes the union of the dragon and the phoenix as well as abundant wealth. Mostly made with one end of a string, the phoenix tail knot has a small and compact shape. It is frequently used for the ending and decoration of knot ornaments. It can also be crafted into Pankou, bracelets, necklaces and the like.

扫描二维码获取凤尾结制作方法与教学视频
Scan the QR-code to get the methods and teaching video of tying phoenix tail knot

所需材料：一根长 40 厘米的中国结 5 号线。

Material needed: one 40-centimeter-long No.5 string of Chinese knot.

纽扣结是流传最广的基本结之一，其结形犹如钻石。纽扣结最初用在中国古代的服饰中，因长期用于衣物纽扣而得名，是一种既实用又有装饰性的结式。纽扣结不易松散，且结心可藏线头，所以常用于编制项链、手链等饰品。

The button knot is one of the most widely spread basic knots which has a diamond-like shape. Initially utilized in ancient Chinese clothing, it got its name as it was long employed as a clothing button. It is a knot ornament that is both practical and decorative. The button knot is not prone to coming loose, and its center can hide the end of the string. Thus, it is frequently used in making accessories like necklaces and bracelets.

扫描二维码获取纽扣结制作方法与教学视频
Scan the QR-code to get the methods and teaching video of tying button knot

所需材料：一根长 80 厘米的中国结 5 号线。

Material needed: one 80-centimeter-long No.5 string of Chinese knot.

Exercises

1 Answer the following questions.

(1) If you want to make a bracelet that is both stylish and strong, which two knots would be the best combination?

(2) If you want to make a decorative keychain with a knot that is both beautiful and sturdy, which one would be the best choice among double connection knot, auspicious knot, phoenix tail knot, and button knot?

2 Decide whether each of the following statements is true (T) or false (F).

(1) The quality of the thread used for making Chinese knots has no impact on the durability of the final product.

(2) A pair of curved-tip tweezers is the only tool that can be used to adjust the position of the thread during the knotting process.

(3) In Chinese culture, certain colors have specific meanings and are often chosen for Chinese knots based on their symbolic value.

(4) If a person is skilled enough, he/she can make any complex Chinese knot without using any tools.

(5) The number of pins needed depends on the complexity of the knot and personal preference.

❸ Choose the best answer to each of the following questions.

(1) Which of the following is true about the auspicious knot?

A. It is known for its symmetrical and beautiful shape, symbolizing good fortune.

B. It has the symbolic meaning of being connected, continuous and having a surplus year after year.

C. It is a knot ornament that is both practical and decorative.

D. It is not very popular among knot enthusiasts.

(2) Which knot is often used for the ending and decoration of knot ornaments and has a shape like a phoenix tail?

A. Double connection knot.   B. Auspicious knot.

C. Leaf knot.   D. Button knot.

(3) Which knot resembles a button and is often used in clothing or accessories?

A. Double connection knot.   B. Auspicious knot.

C. Leaf knot.   D. Button knot.

(4) Which knot is frequently used to fix the upper part and lower part of the main knot or serve as the beginning or the end of the combined knot?

A. Double connection knot.   B. Auspicious knot.

C. Leaf knot.   D. Button knot.

(5) Why do people usually choose auspicious knot as the centerpiece in a large wall hanging?

A. Because it is made of the cheapest materials and is cost-effective.

B. Because it symbolizes good fortune and has an eye-catching design.

C. Because its shape is very common and blends well with any background.

D. Because it can be made quickly and requires less effort.

2 蛇结手链和金刚结手链
Snake Knot Bracelet and Dorje Knot Bracelet

蛇结手链与金刚结手链的编制是以掌握蛇结和金刚结的编制为前提条件的。蛇结与金刚结的编制存在共同之处。学会蛇结的编制方法后再去编制金刚结会相对容易一些。

The threading method of snake knot bracelet and dorje knot bracelet is based on mastering the techniques of threading snake knot and dorje knot. There are certain similarities in the making of snake knot and dorje knot. Once you have learned the method of threading snake knot, it will be comparatively easy to thread dorje knot.

蛇结因形如双蛇相缠而得名，同时又因其形状如鱼鳞而被称为鱼鳞结。此结有缠绵不断、相依相随之意，多用于手链和项链的编制，也可在组合结中作结与结的间隔。

The snake knot gets its name as it resembles two intertwined snakes. It is also called fish scale knot because its shape is like fish scale. This knot carries the connotation of being unceasingly intertwined and staying together in dependence. It is mostly used in the making of bracelets and necklaces and can also serve as the spacing between knots in combined knots.

在编制蛇结手链时，需将一个蛇结紧挨着一个蛇结进行编制，直至达到与手腕周长相符的尺寸。其中，至关重要的是要确保每个蛇结的大小和紧密度保持一致，只有这样，才能编制出美观的蛇结手链。

In the process of threading a snake knot bracelet, one snake knot should be threaded closely after another until it reaches the corresponding circumference of your wrist. It is essential to ensure that each snake knot is consistent in size and tightness. Only by doing so can a beautiful snake knot bracelet be crafted.

所需材料：两根中国结 5 号线；一根 18 厘米长的中国结 7 号线；皮尺；剪刀；打火机。两根中国结 5 号线的长度需测量腕围后再确定。举例来说，若腕围为 17 厘米，则需两根各 1.2 米长的中国结 5 号线；腕围为 16 厘米，每根中国结 5 号线各 1.15 米；腕围为 15 厘米，每根各 1.1 米；腕围为 14 厘米，每根各 1.05 米；腕围为 13 厘米，每根各 1 米；腕围为 12 厘米，每根各 95 厘米。可根据个人喜好选择线绳的颜色，两根线可以同色，也可以不同色。

扫描二维码获取蛇结手链制作方法与教学视频
Scan the QR-code to get the methods and teaching video of tying snake knot bracelet

Material needed: two No.5 strings of Chinese knot, one 18-centimeter-long No.7 string of Chinese knot, a tape measure, a pair of scissors, and a lighter. The length of two No.5 strings of Chinese knot needs to be determined after measuring your wrist circumference. If the wrist circumference is 17 cm, two pieces of No.5 string of Chinese knot are respectively 1.2 meters long. If the wrist circumference is 16 cm, two pieces of No.5 string of Chinese knot are respectively 1.15 meters long. If the wrist circumference is 15 cm, two pieces of No.5 string of Chinese knot are respectively 1.1 meters long. If the wrist circumference is 14 cm, two pieces of No.5 string of Chinese knot are respectively 1.05 meters long. If the

wrist circumference is 13 cm, two pieces of No.5 string of Chinese knot are respectively 1 meter long. If the wrist circumference is 12 cm, two pieces of No.5 string of Chinese knot are respectively 95 centimeters long. You can choose the color of the strings according to personal preference.

金刚结的外形与蛇结颇为相似，但金刚结更为牢固紧实，不易松散。金刚结有平安和吉祥的美好寓意。在当今社会中，金刚结被大量运用于手工艺品及装饰品的制作，例如编制成手链、项链等饰品。人们将这些饰品佩戴在身上，借此来表达对美好生活的向往与祝福。

The dorje knot resembles the snake knot in appearance, but it is far more sturdy and tightly woven, making it resistant to loosening. The dorje knot carries beautiful meanings of peace and auspiciousness. In today's modern society, the dorje knot is widely used in making handicrafts and decorative items such as bracelets and necklaces. People wear these accessories as a way to express their hopes and blessings for a better life.

所需材料：两根中国结5号线；一根18厘米长的中国结7号线；皮尺；剪刀；打火机。两根中国结5号线的长度需测量腕围后再确定，具体参见"蛇结手链"部分。

Material needed: two No.5 strings of Chinese knot, one 18-centi-meter-long No.7 string of Chinese knot, a tape measure, a pair of scissors, and a lighter. The length of two No.5 strings of Chinese knot needs to be determined after measuring your wrist circumference. For details, please refer to the part about the snake knot bracelet.

扫描二维码获取金刚结
手链制作方法与
教学视频
Scan the QR-code to get the methods and teaching video of tying dorje knot bracelet

Exercises

1 **Answer the following questions.**

(1) What are the main differences between the snake knot and the dorje knot?

(2) If you want to make a bracelet that can better withstand wear and tear, which knot would be a better choice, the snake knot or the dorje knot? Why?

(3) Suppose you are making a gift for a person who values cultural significance very much. Which knot should you choose for the bracelet, the snake knot or the dorje knot? Why?

3 | 圆形玉米结挂件
Circular Corn Knot Pendant

玉米结因形状酷似玉米而得名，有圆形玉米结和方形玉米结两类。圆形玉米结外观圆润饱满，犹如玉米颗粒紧密排列，寓意美好，象征着节节高升、多子多福、金玉满堂、五谷丰登、衣食无忧等。此结具有一定的稳定性与立体感，常用来编制挂件、手链、装饰彩绳等。

The corn knot gets its name from its shape that is similar to an ear of corn. It is categorized into two types: the circular corn knot and the square corn knot. The circular corn knot presents a round and plump appearance, much like tightly packed corn kernels. It has auspicious meanings and symbolizes ascending step by step, having numerous offspring and blessings, being filled with gold and jade, enjoying a bountiful harvest of all grains, having no worries about food and clothing, etc. The circular corn knot has a certain level of stability and three-dimensionality and is frequently used to thread pendants, bracelets, decorative colored cords, and so on.

编制圆形玉米结挂件时，可以选用同色绳、双色绳或者四色绳。本节将介绍用四种不同颜色的线绳编制圆形玉米结的方法。在编制过程中，需始终按照一个方向（顺时针或逆时针）进行操作，只有这样才能编出规则的圆形玉米结花型。同时，要注意每一步中线的位置和走向准确无误，并且均匀用力拉紧线绳，以确保玉米结紧密且整齐。

When threading circular corn knot pendant, one can select strings of the same color, two different colors or four different colors. In this section, strings of four different colors are employed for threading circular corn knot pendant. During the making procedure, it is necessary to keep threading in one consistent direction, either clockwise or counterclockwise. Only by doing so can a regular circular corn knot pattern be created. Meanwhile, be attentive to the position and direction of the strings in each step to ensure accuracy, and apply force evenly to tighten the strings to guarantee that the corn knot is tight and orderly.

扫描二维码获取圆形玉米结挂件制作方法与教学视频
Scan the QR-code to get the methods and teaching video of tying circular corn knot pendant

所需材料： 一根 40 厘米长的红色中国结 5 号线；红色、黄色、蓝色和绿色中国结 5 号线各一根，每根 78 厘米长；一根 18 厘长的红色中国结 7 号线；皮尺；剪刀；打火机。

Material needed: one red 40-centimeter-long No.5 string of Chinese knot; four No.5

strings of Chinese knot in red, yellow, blue and green respectively, each measuring 78 centimeters in length; one red 18-centimeter-long No.7 string of Chinese knot; a tape measure; a pair of scissors; a lighter.

Exercises

1 **Answer the following questions.**

(1) What are the possible variations in the pattern of circular corn knots when different colors of strings are used?

(2) What are the mathematical principles underlying the formation of circular corn knots? Can you analyze the geometry and symmetry involved?

(3) What innovative designs or modifications can you think of to make the circular corn knot pendant more unique and appealing?

2 **Choose the correct answer(s) to each of the following questions.**

(1) What are the typical shapes of a corn knot?
A. Circle.   B. Square.
C. Triangle.   D. Hexagon.

(2) Which of the following colors might be commonly used for circular corn knots?
A. Neon green   B. Gray.
C. Brown.   D. Red.

(3) What tool might be helpful when making circular corn knots?
A. Hammer.   B. Scissors.
C. Screwdriver.   D. Pliers.

(4) Which of the following is NOT a characteristic of a well-made circular corn knot?
A. Tight knots.   B. Even spacing.
C. Loose strings.   D. Symmetrical shape.

(5) Which of the following is NOT a benefit of making circular corn knots?
A. It can relieve stress.   B. It can improve creativity.
C. It can increase physical strength.   D. It can enhance patience.

4 | 五色吉祥金刚结挂件
Five-Color Auspicious Dorje Knot Pendant

五色吉祥金刚结挂件通常用白、绿、蓝、红、黄这五种颜色的线编制。其中，绿色可以用青色替换，蓝色可以用黑色或灰色替换，红色可以用紫色或粉色替换，黄色可以用咖色替换。在中国传统文化中，这五种颜色对应金、木、水、火、土，也就是常说的五行。这些颜色组合不但赋予挂件独特的视觉魅力，还承载着深刻的文化内涵和积极的象征意义。

The five-color auspicious dorje knot pendant is usually threaded with strings in five different colors, namely white, green, blue, red and yellow. Among these, green may be substituted with cyan, blue with black or gray, red with purple or pink, and yellow with brown. In traditional Chinese culture, these five colors correspond to metal, wood, water, fire, and earth, which is commonly known as the Five Elements. These color combinations not only bestow distinctive visual appeal upon the pendant but also carry profound cultural significance and positive symbolic meanings.

五色吉祥金刚结挂件色彩绚丽、造型精巧，既可用作装饰品提升审美品位，又能作为礼物传递美好祝福。

The five-color auspicious dorje knot pendant is vivid in color and exquisitely shaped. It can serve as an adornment to enhance aesthetic taste and also as a gift to convey good wishes.

所需材料： 一根 40 厘米长的红色中国结 5 号线；一根 40 厘米长的白色中国结 5 号线；红、蓝、黄、绿色中国结 5 号线各一根，每根长 80cm；一根 18 厘米长的红色中国结 7 号线；皮尺；剪刀；打火机。

Material needed: one 40-centimeter-long red No.5 string of Chinese knot; one 40-centimeter-long white No.5 string of Chinese knot; four No.5 strings of Chinese knot in red, blue, yellow and green respectively, each measuring 80 centimeters in length; one 18-centimeter-long red No.7 string of Chinese knot; a tape measure; a pair of scissors; a lighter.

扫描二维码获取五色吉祥金刚结挂件制作方法与教学视频
Scan the QR-code to get the methods and teaching video of tying five-color auspicious dorje knot pendant

Exercises

1 Answer the following questions.

(1) How does making a five-color auspicious dorje knot pendant contribute to one's spiritual growth?

(2) In which way can the five-color auspicious dorje knot pendant be used as a medium to promote cultural exchange and understanding between different cultures?

2 Choose the best answer to each of the following questions.

(1) What do the five colors of the dorje knot pendant represent in traditional Chinese culture?

A. Five directions (East, South, West, North, and Center).

B. Five celestial bodies (Venus, Jupiter, Mercury, Mars, and Saturn).

C. Five virtues (Benevolence, Righteousness, Propriety, Wisdom, and Trustworthiness).

D. Five elements (Metal, Wood, Water, Fire, and Earth).

(2) How many No.5 strings of Chinese knot are required in total to make the dorje knot pendant?

A. 4   B. 5   C. 6   D. 7

(3) Which of the following is NOT a common color combination for the five-color auspicious dorje knot pendant?

A. White, green, blue, red, and yellow.

B. White, cyan, gray, purple, and yellow.

C. White, green, red, purple, and yellow.

D. White, green, black, pink, and yellow.

(4) What are the two primary functions of the five-color auspicious dorje knot pendant?

A. Home decoration and art collection.

B. Aesthetic enhancement and conveying good wishes.

C. Religious ceremonies and measuring lengths.

D. Agricultural rituals and medical healing.

(5) The following materials are needed for making the five-color auspicious dorje knot pendant except _____ .

A. glue   B. tape measure

C. lighter   D. scissors

5 | 盘长结挂件
Panchang Knot Pendant

盘长结的形状与佛家八宝之一的"盘长"颇为相似。盘长结的结形曲绕，编制时需来回穿压，象征着连绵长久、不断回环、永恒不灭。

The shape of Panchang knot is very similar to that of Panchang, one of the eight Buddhist treasures. The winding form of the Panchang knot requires threading, going over and under strings repeatedly during the making process, which symbolizes continuity and longevity, endless looping, and eternal immortality.

盘长结的应用十分广泛，比如人们常把它装饰在新婚帐钩上，寓意着一对相爱的人永远相依相随。北京 2022 年冬奥会和冬残奥会宣传海报之一——《热情连接世界》，就是以盘长结为基础造型，将奥运五环、冰雪图案等元素巧妙地融合在一起。它一方面展现出吉祥、简约、热情的中式美学，另一方面通过绳结将北京、世界、奥运紧密相连，传递出世界大家庭携手迈向未来的美好愿景。

The Panchang knot is widely used. For instance, it is often used to adorn the hooks of the bridal bed curtain, symbolizing an eternal bond between a loving couple who will remain intertwined through life. One of the promotional posters for the Beijing 2022 Winter Olympics and Paralympics, titled "Passion Connects the World," is based on the shape of the Panchang knot. It artfully integrates elements such as the Olympic five rings and patterns of ice and snow. On the one hand, it embodies a distinctively Chinese aesthetics featuring auspiciousness, simplicity, and enthusiasm. On the other hand, the interlaced cords visually link Beijing, the world, and the Olympics, conveying the beautiful vision of the global community joining hands to march towards the future.

盘长结蕴含着人们对美好生活的向往与祝福，常被当作礼物赠送给亲朋好友，以此来传递深厚的情谊和美好的祝愿。在婚礼、节日、庆典等场合，人们常常悬挂盘长结，以烘托喜庆祥和的气氛。

The Panchang knot contains people's aspiration and blessings for a better life and is frequently given as a gift to relatives and friends to convey deep affection and good wishes.

On occasions such as weddings, festivals, and celebrations, people often hang the Panchang knot to create a joyous and harmonious atmosphere.

盘长结结形优美，结构密实，不易变形。它既可以单独作为装饰品，又能够和其他绳结饰品搭配使用。盘长结在时尚配饰、家居装饰以及文化创意产品等领域应用广泛。设计师们常常从盘长结中获取灵感，将传统元素与现代理念相融合，设计出既有文化传承意义又具有市场吸引力的产品。

The Panchang knot has beautiful shape, dense structure, and is not easy to deform, which can be used either as a single decoration or in combination with other knot ornaments. The Panchang knot is usually used in fields such as fashion accessories, home decoration, and cultural and creative products. Designers often draw inspiration from the Panchang knot, integrating tradition and modernity to create products with cultural heritage meaning and market appeal.

四道盘长结是盘长结中最基础的样式。按照编四道盘长结的规律，增加缠绕线绳的圈数可编成六道、八道、十道、十二道等不同道数的盘长结。本部分将介绍四道盘长结挂件的编制方法。在编制的过程中，需要注意每一步的挑压都要正确无误，务必保持细心和耐心，切不可急于求成。

The four-loop Panchang knot is the most fundamental style among Panchang knots. According to the pattern of making a four-loop Panchang knot, by increasing the number of loops of the winding string, Panchang knots with different numbers of loops such as six-loop, eight-loop, ten-loop, and twelve-loop can be threaded. This part describes the method of threading a four-loop Panchang knot pendant. During the making process, make sure that each under move or over move is correct. Remain careful and patient, and avoid rushing for quick results.

扫描二维码获取四道
盘长结挂件制作方法
与教学视频
Scan the QR-code to get the methods and teaching video of tying four-loop Panchang knot pendant

所需材料：一根 1.3 米长的中国结 5 号线；一个 12 厘米长的流苏（流苏和线需同色）；泡沫板或软木板；珠针；弯嘴镊子；剪刀；打火机。

Material needed: one 1.3-meter-long No.5 string of Chinese knot, one 12-centimeter-long tassel with the same color as No.5 string of Chinese knot, foam board or cork board, positioning pins, a curved-tip tweezer, a pair of scissors, and a lighter.

Exercises

1 **Answer the following questions.**

(1) How does the structure of Panchang knots reflect the traditional Chinese concept of symmetry and harmony?

(2) What cultural and symbolic meanings are embedded in the complex patterns of Panchang knots?

(3) If you were to design a modern art piece based on the Panchang knot, what innovative elements could you incorporate to combine tradition with modernity while still maintaining the essence of the original knot?

2 **Choose the best answer to each of the following questions.**

(1) The Panchang knot is known for its symmetrical design. Which of the following best describes the importance of symmetry in a Panchang knot?

A. It makes the knot look more random.

B. It helps in reducing the complexity of the weaving process.

C. It gives the knot a sense of balance and aesthetic beauty.

D. It allows for easier addition of other decorative elements.

(2) Chinese knot, especially Panchang knot, is a traditional handicraft with profound cultural connotations. Which of the following is NOT a common symbolic meaning of Panchang knots?

A. Eternity and longevity.

B. Prosperity and good luck.

C. Harmony and unity.

D. Sadness and loneliness.

(3) The structure of a Panchang knot is complex. Which of the following steps is crucial in the process of making it?

A. Randomly threading the strings.

B. Following a specific threading sequence.

C. Tightly twisting the strings without any pattern.

D. Using a large amount of glue to fix the shape.

(4) In traditional Chinese culture, the Panchang knot is often used in decorations. Where is it least likely to be found in traditional settings?

A. On the eaves of ancient buildings.

B. As a pendant on a sword.

C. Inside a modern minimalist painting.

D. On the cover of an ancient book.

(5) When preserving a Panchang knot, which of the following environmental factors should be avoided the most?

A. Strong sunlight.   B. Low humidity.

C. Moderate temperature.   D. Stable air circulation.

Chapter 2

⌗⌗⌗⌗⌗⌗⌗⌗⌗⌗⌗⌗⌗⌗

中国剪纸
Chinese Paper-Cut

造纸术作为华夏文明对世界文化宝库的伟大贡献之一，其深远影响跨越时空。剪纸艺术则是中华民族智慧与创造力的又一璀璨结晶。中国民间剪纸艺术是民俗文化的一种，它将物质文明与精神文明融为一体，深深扎根于民族土壤，广泛体现在民间信仰和生活习俗中，鲜明地反映出中国广大民众的心理特征、审美情趣及价值观念。

Papermaking, as a great contribution of Chinese civilization to the treasure trove of world culture, has exerted profound influences that transcend time and space. Meanwhile, papercutting stands out as a brilliant embodiment of the wisdom and creativity of the Chinese nation. Chinese folk papercutting is a type of folk-custom culture. Deeply rooted in the national soil, it integrates material civilization and spiritual civilization, widely reflecting folk beliefs, life customs, psychological characteristics, aesthetic tastes, and values of the vast majority of Chinese people.

以纸为画布，以剪刀或刻刀为笔，剪纸艺术家创造出无数精妙绝伦、镂空见真的民间艺术瑰宝。这项技艺源远流长，其历史可追溯至约 250 万年前。早在原始社会，就已有刻痕记事、镂空装饰之迹。那时兽皮上的斑斓图腾、贝壳项链上的精巧穿孔，都是剪纸技艺朴素的前奏。陶器、玉器出现后，上面的图案和线条已与后期剪纸的纹样颇为相似。

Using paper as its canvas and scissors or carving knives as its brush, paper-cut artists create exquisite, hollowed-out treasures of folk art. This craft boasts a long and illustrious history that can be traced back to approximately 2.5 million years ago, to the primitive society, where incised markings for record-keeping and hollowed-out decorations emerged. The colorful totems on animal hides and the intricate perforations on shell necklaces from that era serve as the simple prelude to papercutting. After the appearance of pottery and jade, their patterns and lines were already similar to those of later paper-cut.

直至公元 105 年，蔡伦改良造纸术，纸张成本日趋亲民，从而广泛流通。剪纸艺术因此一跃成为中国民间艺术的璀璨明珠，绽放出前所未有的光彩。

Until 105 CE, when Cai Lun improved the papermaking process, the cost of paper gradually became more affordable, enabling its widespread circulation. Thanks to this, papercutting soared to prominence as a dazzling gem of Chinese folk art, shining with unprecedented brilliance.

在传统佳节的庆典里，剪纸不仅是装点门楣、营造喜庆氛围的精灵，更是传递文化意蕴、寄托美好愿景的使者。春节时分，家家户户以红剪纸为装饰，寓意吉祥如意、欢庆团圆；元宵之夜，灯笼之上，彩色剪纸翩翩起舞，映照出节日的温馨与欢乐；寒食清明，则见白剪纸轻展，寄托对逝者的哀思与怀念。剪纸题材广泛，涵盖自然万物之生动、历史传说之深邃、戏曲故事之精彩，无不与民众生活紧密相连，展现出深厚的人文底蕴与丰富的情感世界。

During traditional festival celebrations, paper-cut is not merely a sprite adorning door lintels and creating a festive atmosphere, but also a messenger conveying cultural implications and carrying beautiful aspirations. During the Spring Festival, families decorate with red paper-cuts, symbolizing good fortune, happiness, and reunion. On the night of the Lantern Festival, colorful paper-cuts dance atop lanterns, reflecting the warmth and joy of the festival. During Cold Food and Qingming Festivals, white paper-cuts gently unfold, embodying mourning and remembrance for the deceased. The themes of paper-cut are vast and varied, encompassing the vivacity of nature, the profundity of historical legends, and the charm of opera stories. All are closely linked to people's lives, revealing a profound humanistic heritage and rich emotional world.

尤为值得一提的是，剪纸艺术之普及，得益于其材料的平易近人。无论是纸张还是剪刀，皆是日常生活中触手可及之物。这使得剪纸成为一门门槛低、易上手、高普及的艺术形式，只要心怀热爱，人人皆可成为这方寸之间创造奇迹的艺术家，剪出属于自己的心灵之作，让传统文化在现代社会中愈加芬芳。

Notably, the popularity of papercutting stems from the accessibility of its materials. Both paper and scissors are things readily available in daily life. This makes paper-cut a low-threshold, easy-to-learn, and highly accessible art form. With passion in heart, everyone can become an artist, creating wonders within this tiny space, cutting out paper-cut pieces that resonate deeply with their souls, allowing traditional culture to become more fragrant in modern society.

中国剪纸发展概况
An Overview of the Development of Chinese Paper-Cut

说起中国剪纸的源头，人们通常会从周成王剪桐封弟之事讲起。此事最初记载于《吕氏春秋》中。西周王朝的初期，周武王的儿子周成王年幼即位，并由叔叔周公辅佐。有一天，成王与胞弟叔虞嬉戏于宫廷之中，童心未泯，竟以梧桐之叶为材，巧手剪裁，模拟古代玉圭之形，赠予叔虞，笑语间许以封地。几天后，周公进言，请择良辰吉日，正式册封叔虞为诸侯。成王初闻，以为儿戏之言，笑而应曰："余一人与虞戏也。"周公则正色以对："臣闻之，天子无戏言。天子言，则史书之，工诵之，士称之。"于是，周成王听从了周公的建议，把唐地封给叔虞，叔虞日后也就被称为"唐叔虞"了。周成王用梧桐叶剪成"圭"赐其弟，就是运用薄片材料，通过镂空雕刻的技法制成工艺品，这种方法在当时被称为"剪彩"。

The origin of Chinese paper-cut may be traced back to the story of King Cheng of Zhou, who cut a phoenix tree leaf to enfeoff his younger brother, which was originally recorded in *Lüshi Chunqiu* (*Master Lü's Spring and Autumn Annals*). During the early period of the Western Zhou Dynasty, King Cheng of Zhou, the son of King Wu of Zhou, ascended the throne at a young age and was assisted by his uncle, Duke of Zhou. One day, King Cheng and his younger brother Shu Yu, still retaining their childlike innocence, used phoenix tree leaves as material. With dexterous hands, King Cheng cut and shaped them to resemble ancient jade Gui, presented them to Shu Yu, and jokingly promised him a fiefdom. A few days later, Duke of Zhou asked King Cheng to choose an auspicious day to ennoble Shu Yu as a vassal king. Upon first hearing this, King Cheng dismissed it as a mere child's play, laughing and responding, "I was just joking with him!" Duke of Zhou, however, replied solemnly, "I have heard that the words of the Son of Heaven should not be taken lightly. Once spoken, they must be faithfully recorded by historians, sung by musicians, and disseminated by officials throughout the land." Thus, King Cheng followed the advice of Duke of Zhou and enfeoffed the land of Tang to Shu Yu, who later became known as "Tang Shu Yu." King Cheng's act of cutting the phoenix tree leaf into a jade Gui and presenting it to his brother is an example of using thin material and the technique of hollow-carving to create an artwork, which was known as Jiancai (cutting out colored paper) at that time.

在这个故事中，周成王用一片普通的树叶制作出了一个形象具体的"圭"，那么，他借助于什么工具呢？以手撕扯，以刀刻镂，还是以剪刀裁切？

In this story, King Cheng created a vivid and specific Gui by using an ordinary tree leaf. So, what tool did he use? Did he tear it with his hands, carve it with a knife, or cut it with scissors?

《古史考》的叙述明确了剪刀这一工具历史的久远："剪，铁器也，用于裁布帛。始于黄帝时。"然而，铁属于活跃金属，容易氧化，至今考古发现的最早的剪刀是战国时代的 U 形剪刀，刀刃与现代剪刀颇为相似。汉代出土的剪刀则与今日的形制大致相同。六朝沈约的《咏梧桐诗》中有诗句"微叶虽可贱，一剪或成圭"。初唐四杰之一王勃也在《常州刺史平原郡开国公行状》中写道"剪桐疏爵，分茅建社"。若将剪纸艺术之范畴略作延展，不拘泥于剪、刻、撕之技法，亦不局限于纸、布、帛、箔、叶之材质，则剪桐封弟之古韵，在更为广阔的层面上，与剪纸所蕴含的文化特性不谋而合。此中深意，不仅是对传统技艺的致敬，更是对剪纸艺术深厚文化底蕴的一次深刻领悟与启迪。

The narrative of *Research on Ancient History* makes clear the long history of scissors: "Scissors are iron tools used to cut cloth and silk. It began in the time of the Yellow Emperor." However, iron is an active metal that easily oxidizes, and the earliest archaeological discoveries to date are U-shaped scissors from the Warring States period, with blades quite similar to modern scissors. The scissors unearthed in the Han Dynasty were roughly the same shape as they are today. Shen Yue of the Six Dynasties wrote "The Poem of Chinese Parasol": "Though a tiny leaf may be humble and low, a single cut may turn it to a gem aglow." And Wang Bo, one of the four outstanding poets of the early Tang Dynasty wrote down the lines "Confer noble titles as in the ancient ceremony of cutting the phoenix tree leaves and establish feudal states by granting fiefdoms" in his "Biographical Sketch of Duke of Pingyuan, the Prefect of Changzhou and the Founder of the State." If we expand the scope of papercutting slightly, without being constrained by techniques like cutting, carving or tearing, and not limited to materials such as paper, cloth, silk, foil or leaves, then the ancient charm of "cutting phoenix tree leaves to confer a dukedom," coincidentally, shares similarities with the cultural characteristics embodied in paper-cut on a broader level. The profound meaning herein is not only a tribute to traditional craftsmanship, but also a profound understanding and enlightenment of the rich cultural heritage of papercutting.

早在纸张发明之前，人们就使用其他薄材料，如树叶、银箔甚至皮革来雕刻镂空图案。相传商代就有了把金锻打成薄片再刻镂剪裁的技术。到了汉代，锤打金片制作金箔的技艺更为圆熟。金箔在古代的用途十分广泛。采用类似的方法也可以把块状的银制作成薄片状的银箔。1951 年，中国考古工作人员在河南辉县发掘了一座战国时期的古墓，出土文物中最令人赞叹的是一件银箔刻花制品。它上面雕刻的镂空花纹极富美感，造型已与今天的剪纸十分相似。

Long before the invention of paper, people used other thin materials such as leaves, silver foil, and even leather to engrave hollow patterns. It is said that as early as the Shang Dynasty, gold forged into thin pieces was cut and carved. By the Han Dynasty, the technique of hammering gold into gold foil had become more skillful and sophisticated. Gold foil had a wide range of uses in ancient China. In a similar way, silver can also be hammered repeatedly to make flakes of silver foil. In 1951, a Chinese archaeological team excavated an ancient tomb of the Warring States period in Huixian County, Henan Province, and the most amazing unearthed cultural relics were a silver foil carved with flower patterns. The hollow patterns were exquisite, and the shapes were similar to today's paper-cut.

若周成王封弟是文献传说中剪纸的起源，那么金银箔剪片就是与剪纸在表现形式上同宗同源的实物例证。

If the fiefdom of King Cheng of Zhou is regarded as the origin of paper-cut in the documentary legend, then the gold and silver foil cutouts can be seen as physical evidence sharing the same origin in the expression form of paper-cut.

剪纸的主要材料是纸。东汉时期，蔡伦在总结前人制造絮纸的基础上，发明了用植物纤维制作的可用于书写的纸张，即蔡伦纸，这为后世剪纸的发展创造了条件。人们把雕、剪、刻等工艺技法逐渐转移到纸张上来，在蔡伦纸发明四百多年后的南北朝时期，剪纸艺术已经相对成熟。

The main material for paper-cut is paper. Based on the earlier paper-making technology, Cai Lun in the Eastern Han Dynasty invented Cai Lun paper which was made of plant fibers for writing, providing conditions for the development of paper-cut in later generations. Thus, the techniques of engraving, cutting, and carving gradually transferred onto paper, and about 400 years later, the paper-cut art became relatively mature in the Northern and Southern Dynasties.

目前中国发现的最早的剪纸实物，是 1959 年在新疆吐鲁番高昌遗址附近阿斯塔那墓葬群中出土的南北朝时期的五幅作品。这五幅剪纸采用的材质是麻料纸，形式上都是折叠型祭祀剪纸，与今天的民间团花剪纸极其相似，表现内容以植物、动物图案为主，分别刻画了"对马""对猴""菊花""金银花""八角花"等艺术形象。这些剪纸虽为随葬之物,但从技艺上来说已经相当精巧成熟,它们的发现为我国剪纸的形成提供了实物佐证。由此也可以看出,剪纸在中国至少已有 1500 年的历史。

团花剪纸,1959 年出土于新疆吐鲁番阿斯塔那墓

Paper-cut with round flowers, unearthed in the Astana Tombs in Turpan, Xinjiang in 1959

The earliest physical examples of paper-cut discovered in China are five works excavated from the Astana Tombs near the Gaochang Ruins in Turpan, Xinjiang in 1959. These tombs date back to the Northern and Southern Dynasties. The five paper-cuts are made of hemp paper and are all in the form of folded sacrificial paper-cuts, which are extremely similar to today's flower-patterned paper-cuts. They mainly depict plants and animals, including artistic images such as "paired horses," "paired monkeys," "chrysanthemums," "honeysuckle flowers," and "eight-pointed flowers." Although these paper-cuts were burial objects, the craftsmanship was already quite sophisticated and mature. The discovery provides physical evidence for the formation of paper-cut in China. This also indicates that paper-cut has a history of at least 1,500 years in China.

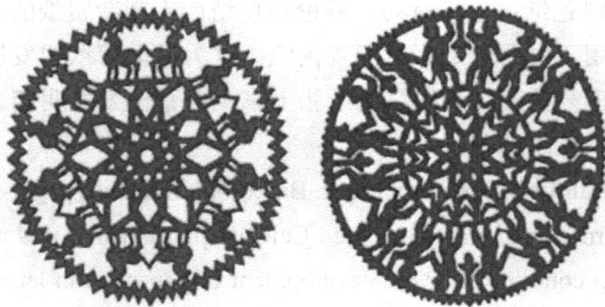

对马、对猴团花(复原图),1959 年出土于新疆吐鲁番阿斯塔那墓

Paired horses and paired monkeys patterned paper-cut (restored image), unearthed in the Astana Tombs in Turpan, Xinjiang in 1959

隋朝时,由于佛教盛行,剪彩多用作佛教法事,僧俗都刻镂锦彩来弘扬佛法,同时也推进了剪纸艺术的发展。

Paper-cut was often used in Buddhist rituals due to the prevalence of Buddhism during the Sui Dynasty. Both monks and laypeople carved and cut colorful fabrics for Buddhist teachings, which also promoted the development of papercutting.

唐代是剪纸艺术的大发展时期，剪纸活动盛行于帝王贵族之家。唐代李商隐的诗句"镂金作胜传荆俗，翦彩为人起晋风"，流传至今。

The Tang Dynasty was a period of great development for papercutting. The papercutting activity was prevalent in the households of emperor and nobles. The verses "carving gold to make auspicious decorations, spreading the customs of Jing; cutting colored paper to make human figures, arising the style of Jin" by Li Shangyin, a poet of the Tang Dynasty, have been passed down to this day.

唐代流行剪刻的小幡，又称春幡或幡胜，每逢立春日，人们便用银箔、罗彩剪成饰物或小幡，或簪于鬓发，或系于花下，用以欢庆春日的来临。唐代诗人韦庄在《立春》诗中描述："雪圃乍开红菜甲，彩幡新翦绿杨丝，殷勤为作宜春曲，题向花笺帖绣楣。"立春之日象征万物复苏，所以剪彩这一民俗活动集中在立春这天，人们剪刻各种幡胜作为节日的礼物，以此来表达美好的祝愿。

Small streamers cut out of paper, also known as spring banners or festive streamer ornaments, were popular in the Tang Dynasty. On the Beginning of Spring (the first day of the 24 solar terms marking spring's arrival) each year, people would cut silver foil and colorful silk brocade into ornaments or tiny streamers. Some were pinned in their hair, others tied beneath flowers, to celebrate the arrival of spring. The Tang poet Wei Zhuang captured this scene in his poem "On the Start of Spring": "From gardens still covered in snow, red vegetable shoots burst forth; newly cut, colorful streamers mimic the green threads of willows. With great care, I compose a song to welcome spring, inscribe it on flower-patterned paper, and paste it on the embroidered lintel." Since the start of spring symbolizes the revival of all life, this folk custom of cutting colored decorations became centered on this day. People carved various festival ornaments, using them as holiday gifts to convey their heartfelt good wishes.

现展出于大英博物馆的七层叠加剪纸制成的花朵来自唐代，出土于中国甘肃省敦煌的千佛洞。这朵纸花长 13 厘米，是保存下来的早期剪纸和拼贴画示例之一。

The flower made by seven superimposed layers of paper-cut, displayed in the British Museum, was from the Tang Dynasty. It was excavated in Thousand Buddha Caves, Dunhuang, Gansu Province, China. This paper flower, 13 centimeters long, must be among the early examples of paper-cut and collage that have been preserved.

七层叠加剪纸制成的花朵，现展出于大英博物馆
Flower made by seven superimposed layers of paper-cut, displayed in the British Museum

宋代是民间美术繁盛的时代，造纸技术发展迅速，纸张在这一时期用途扩大，品类繁多，广泛应用于印纸马、扎花灯、糊灯笼、剪窗花、刺绣花样等多种民间美术形式中，推动了剪纸在中国的发展，并开始有了专业剪纸的民间艺人。在这一时期，剪纸贴印有文字和花卉等图案，附着于陶瓷上，颇具装饰意味。宋代江西吉州窑的瓷器上就有剪纸花样，它是制作者在施釉过程中，贴上剪纸，入窑烧制而成的。

The Song Dynasty was an era of flourishing folk art, with rapid developments in papermaking techniques. During this period, paper had a wider range of uses and was available in various types. It was widely applied in various forms of folk art, such as printing paper horses, making lanterns, pasting lanterns, cutting paper window decorations, and creating embroidery patterns, which promoted the development of paper-cut in China and led to the emergence of professional folk paper-cut artists. In this period, paper-cuts with characters and flower patterns were attached to ceramics, which added a decorative touch. Examples of paper-cut patterns can be found on ceramics from the Jizhou Kiln in Jiangxi during the Song Dynasty. These patterns were created by artists applying paper-cuts during the glazing process and firing them in the kiln.

南宋时期有六瓣花纸图案装饰的茶碗，现收藏于大英博物馆
A tea bowl with decoration of paper-cut designs of six-pedaled flowers, now kept in the British Museum

元代时期，剪纸艺术继续发展，并融合了汉文化、蒙古文化及其他少数民族文化。与唐、宋两朝相比，关于这一时期剪纸艺术发展的直接文献记载较少，但可以合理推测的是，这种艺术形式在适应不断变化的文化环境的同时，作为珍贵的民间传统继续蓬勃发展，并保留了其本质。

During the Yuan Dynasty, papercutting continued to develop and integrate Han culture, Mongolian culture, and other ethnic minority cultures. Compared with the Tang and Song dynasties, there are fewer direct literary records about the development of papercutting in this period, but we can reasonably speculate that this art form, while adapting to the ever-changing cultural environment, continued to flourish as a precious folk tradition, preserving its essence.

在那时，人们会在雨季剪出一个手持扫帚的妇女形象来祈求晴天，这一形象也被称为"扫晴娘"，其中，"扫"意为清扫，"晴"意为晴天，"娘"意为女子。在元代，此习俗在北方很流行。李俊民曾在诗作中这样描述"扫晴娘"："卷袖褰裳手持帚，挂向阴空便摇手……龙公不作本分事，中间多少闲云雨。见说周人忧旱母，宁知东海无冤妇……"显然，"扫晴娘"就是民间祈求雨止天晴这一愿望的生动体现。

元代剪纸作品《扫晴娘》
Sao Qing Niang, a paper-cut from the Yuan Dynasty

In that period, people cut a woman figure out of a paper holding a broom in the rainy season to wish for a sunny day, which is called "Sao Qing Niang." "Sao" means sweep, "Qing" means sunny and "Niang" means woman. This custom was popular in the north during the Yuan Dynasty. Li Junmin once described "Sao Qing Niang" in his poem as follows: "Roll up sleeves, lift up skirt, hold a broom in hand, and hang it in the overcast sky to wave...The Dragon King neglects his duty, leaving idle clouds and rain. It is said that the people of Zhou worried about the drought, but who knows if there are any innocent women in the East China Sea..." Obviously, "Sao Qing Niang" is a vivid embodiment of the folk wish for the rain to stop and the sky to clear up.

明清两朝，剪纸艺术迎来了发展的鼎盛时期。明代的夹纱灯很有名，制作方式是将纸剪刻成花鸟、走兽或者人物形象，用颜色晕染，夹在薄纱中，用烛光映出花纹。这是剪纸在日常生活中的又一应用。这种方式增添了民俗生活之美，推动了民间美术中灯彩艺术的新发展。在明代，剪纸不仅用于彩灯上，还作为花样点缀广泛运用于折扇中。

In the Ming and Qing dynasties, papercutting experienced its peak development. The Ming Dynasty was famous for its gauze-sandwiched lanterns, which were made by cutting paper into patterns of flowers, birds, animals or human figures, dyed with colors, and sandwiched between thin gauze to cast the patterns with candlelight. This was another application of paper-cut in daily life. This method added beauty to folk life and promoted the new development of lantern art in folk art. Paper-cut in the Ming Dynasty was not only used on colored lanterns but also widely used as patterns to decorate folding fans.

在清代，剪纸艺术更成为日常装饰的一部分，甚至在皇帝大婚之时，其新房的顶棚上也要用团花剪纸来布置。这一时期，剪纸艺术与刺绣相结合，人们一般先剪出描绘的花样，以此为底样来刺绣。在清代遗留下来的剪纸品类中，以绣花样子最多，此外还有扇面装饰、窗花等，风格趋向精细秀丽，俗中求雅，题材既保有传统之风，又与时俱进。

During the Qing Dynasty, papercutting became an integral part of daily decoration. Even during the emperor's wedding, the ceiling of the newlyweds' bedroom was decorated with paper-cut flowers. During this period, papercutting was combined with embroidery, where people would first cut out the designed patterns and use them as templates for embroidery. Among the paper-cut categories left over from the Qing Dynasty, the most abundant were embroidery patterns. In addition, there were also fan decorations, window flowers, etc., with a style tending to be exquisite and elegant, seeking refinement amidst the ordinary. The themes retained traditional elements while keeping up with current events to create numerous new works.

中华人民共和国成立以来，剪纸艺人的地位也在不断提高，许多剪纸高手得到了政府机构授予的"民间工艺美术师""工艺美术师""剪纸艺术家"等光荣称号。剪纸的表现形式也在不断创新，在 20 世纪 50 年代，上海电影制片厂制作了中国第一部剪纸动画片《猪八戒吃西瓜》，在国际美术界产生了轰动性的影响。现代剪纸艺术对其他画种影响深远，与农民画、年画、木版画等互为借鉴。剪纸元素在招贴广告、包装设计、服装设计、陶瓷艺术、环境艺术设计等现代视觉传达艺术领域中，成为不可或缺的重要内容。

Since the founding of the People's Republic of China, the status of paper-cut artists has continued to improve, and many skilled paper-cutters have been awarded honorary titles such as "Folk Arts and Crafts Masters," "Arts and Crafts Masters," and "Paper-Cut Artists" by government agencies. The forms of paper-cut are also constantly innovating. In the 1950s, Shanghai Film Studio produced China's first paper-cut animated film, *Pigsy Eats Watermelon*, which had a sensational impact on the international art world. Modern papercutting has a profound influence on other painting genres, drawing inspiration from them and influencing peasant paintings, New Year pictures, woodblock prints, and so on. Paper-cut elements have become an indispensable part of modern visual communication art, such as posters, advertising, packaging design, fashion design, ceramic art, environmental art design, and so forth.

中国实行改革开放以来，国民经济进入了快车道，文化艺术领域也发生了巨大变化，剪纸艺术正以前所未有的态势继往开来、蓬勃发展。2006 年 5 月 20 日，剪纸艺术经国务院批准列入第一批国家级非物质文化遗产名录。2009 年，中国剪纸被联合国教科文组织列入《人类非物质文化遗产代表作名录》。

Since China implemented the reform and opening-up policy, the national economy has entered a fast lane, and culture and art have also undergone tremendous changes. Papercutting is developing vigorously with an unprecedented momentum. On May 20, 2006, papercutting was approved by the State Council and included in the first batch of national intangible cultural heritage list. In 2009, Chinese paper-cut was inscribed on the Representative List of the Intangible Cultural Heritage of Humanity by UNESCO.

剪纸不仅是华夏文明的传统艺术瑰宝，还在 6 世纪由僧侣传至日本，之后又传播到世界各地，在不同地区形成了自己的文化风格。

Paper-cut is not only a traditional artistic treasure of Chinese civilization, but also was brought to Japan by monks in the sixth century. Later, it spread to all over the world and formed its own cultural styles in different regions.

Exercises

1   **Answer the following questions.**

(1) How does papercutting reflect the combination of material and spiritual civilization in Chinese folk-custom culture?

(2) Explain how the development of papermaking influenced the development of papercutting.

(3) What are the different functions of paper-cut during various Chinese traditional festivals?

(4) How did the themes of paper-cut evolve across different historical periods?

(5) Discuss how papercutting has been internationalized starting from its origin in China.

2   **Choose the best answer to each of the following questions.**

(1) What materials did ancient people use to engrave hollow patterns before the invention of paper?

    A. Gold leaves.   B. Paper.

    C. Leaves and silver foil.   D. Leather and plastic.

(2) Which dynasty was known for its sophisticated technique of hammering gold sheets into extremely thin pieces?

    A. Shang Dynasty.   B. Han Dynasty.

    C. Warring States period.   D. Qin Dynasty.

(3) What was the most remarkable discovery made by the Chinese archaeological team in Hui County, Henan Province, in 1951?

    A. An ancient tomb of the Shang Dynasty.

    B. Gold leaves used for decoration.

    C. A silver foil with intricate flower patterns.

    D. An example of paper-cut from the Warring States period.

(4) How long ago was the silver foil with flower patterns unearthed in Huixian County, Henan Province?

    A. Over 1,000 years.   B. More than 2,000 years.

    C. Less than 500 years.   D. About 1,500 years.

(5) In which dynasty was paper-cut first used in Buddhist rituals?

A. Sui Dynasty.　　　　　　　　B. Tang Dynasty.

C. Song Dynasty.　　　　　　　　D. Yuan Dynasty.

(6) What was a new form of papercutting application in the Ming Dynasty?

A. On ceramics.　　　　　　　　B. In gauze-sandwiched lanterns.

C. For embroidery templates.　　　D. In emperor's wedding decorations.

(7) In the Qing Dynasty, which type of paper-cut category was the most abundant?

A. Fan decorations.　　　　　　　B. Window flowers.

C. Embroidery patterns.　　　　　D. Lantern patterns.

(8) When was the first paper-cut animated film produced in China?

A. In the 1940s.　　　　　　　　B. In the 1950s.

C. In the 1960s.　　　　　　　　D. In the 1970s.

(9) When was papercutting identified as one of the first national intangible cultural heritage items in China?

A. In 2004.　　　　　　　　　　B. In 2006.

C. In 2009.　　　　　　　　　　D. In 2010.

(10) To which country was paper-cut brought by Chinese monks in the sixth century?

A. India.　　　B. Japan.　　　C. Korea.　　　D. Vietnam.

3 **Decide whether each of the following statements is true (T) or false (F).**

(1) Papercutting in China has a history of less than 1,000 years.

(2) Cai Lun's improvement of papermaking made paper more affordable and widespread.

(3) In the Tang Dynasty, only aristocrats were allowed to engage in papercutting activities.

(4) The Song Dynasty saw the emergence of professional paper-cut folk artists.

(5) In the Ming Dynasty, paper-cut was not used for daily decoration.

(6) Since the founding of the People's Republic of China, the status of paper-cut artists has continued to improve.

(7) Papercutting has not been influenced by other painting genres.

4 **Match the following dynasties with their corresponding contributions to paper-cut.**

(1) Tang Dynasty

(2) Song Dynasty

(3) Yuan Dynasty

(4) Ming Dynasty

(5) Qing Dynasty

A. Professional paper-cut folk artists emerged

B. Popularity of gauze-sandwiched lanterns with paper-cut patterns

C. Paper-cut as an integral part of daily decoration, especially in the emperor's wedding

D. Papercutting integrated Han, Mongolian, and other ethnic minority cultures

E. Small streamers cut out of paper were popular

中国剪纸的主要流派
Main Schools of Chinese Paper-Cut

剪纸艺术在中国随处可见。由于南北地域文化存在差异，剪纸艺术也形成了不同的风格流派。这些流派各放异彩，犹如繁花盛开，使人们能真切地领略到剪纸艺术隽永的韵味。不同流派如同涓涓细流，共同汇聚并丰富着中国剪纸艺术的整体内涵。

Papercutting can be seen all over China. Due to the differences in regional cultures between the north and the south, different styles and schools have formed. These schools, like blooming flowers, are full of their own splendor, enabling us to truly appreciate the meaningful charm of papercutting. Different schools, like trickling streams, converge together and enrich the overall connotations of Chinese paper-cut.

长期以来，中国民间剪纸逐步发展出两大主要风格流派，即北方流派和南方流派。

For a long time, Chinese folk paper-cut has gradually developed into two major schools, namely the northern school and the southern school.

北方流派以陕西、山西和山东地区为代表，其剪纸风格粗犷豪放、造型简洁，展现出朴实大方的特点。

The northern school of paper-cut, represented by Shaanxi Province, Shanxi Province and Shandong Province, shows a plain and generous quality with a rough, bold style and simple shapes.

陕西地处黄河流域，这里有轩辕黄帝陵墓，有仰韶文化、龙山文化及商周文化遗址，还有众多汉代墓群。闻名遐迩的万里长城与古丝绸之路穿境而过，不同历史时期的文化在此繁荣发展，新石器时代的彩陶、汉代的画像石、唐宋时期的雕塑与绘画等，都对陕西民间艺术产生了深远影响。

Shaanxi Province is located in the Yellow River Basin. Here lies the mausoleum of the Yellow Emperor Xuanyuan. There are also ancient sites of Yangshao Culture, Longshan Culture, Shang and Zhou dynasties' cultures, as well as numerous Han Dynasty tombs. The world-famous Great Wall and the ancient Silk Road also pass through Shaanxi Province. Cultures of different historical periods once flourished here. Painted pottery in the Neolithic Age, stone reliefs in the Han Dynasty, sculptures and paintings in the Tang and Song dynasties, etc., all had a great influence on Shaanxi's folk art directly.

陕西剪纸这一民间艺术源远流长。在全国众多风格各异的剪纸流派里，陕西剪纸以古老质朴的独特魅力而广受人们喜爱。陕西剪纸造型古拙、风格粗犷、寓意有趣、形式多样，在陕西民间美术中占据重要地位。陕西剪纸被专家誉为远古文明的"活化石"，因为它完整地传承了中华民族古老的造型纹样，以及阴阳哲学思想和生殖繁衍崇拜观念，陕北剪纸中的"鹰踏兔""蛇盘兔""鹭鸶衔鱼""鱼戏莲"等便是例证。

Shaanxi paper-cut, as a form of folk art, has a long history. Among the various schools of papercutting boasting different styles and characteristics across the country, the ancient and simple Shaanxi paper-cut is loved by people for its unique charm. With its primitive shapes, rough styles, interesting implications, and diverse forms , it occupies a very important position in Shaanxi's folk art. Shaanxi paper-cut is called a "living fossil" of ancient civilization by experts because it has completely inherited not only the ancient shape patterns of the Chinese nation, but also the Chinese Yin-Yang philosophical thoughts and the concepts of reproduction and fertility worship, such as "Eagle Stepping on Rabbit," "Snake Coiling around Rabbit," "Egret Holding a Fish," and "Fish Playing with Lotus" in northern Shaanxi paper-cut.

陕西剪纸形式丰富，有窗花、窑顶花、炕围花、门画、挂帘、枕花、桌裙花、鞋花、衣物佩饰花、神龛贴花等。每逢春节，农村几乎每家每户都会在窗上糊白纸，贴上红纸剪成的窗花来迎接新年。从表现内容上看，陕西窗花可分为两类，一类是传承传统内容的窗花，另一类是贴近生活、反映现实的窗花，涵盖人物、花鸟鱼虫、飞禽走兽、戏曲故事、民间传说等，造型古朴，充满民间韵味。

The forms of Shaanxi paper-cuts are diverse and their contents are rich, including decorations for windows, kiln-tops, Kang (a heatable brick bed), doors, curtains, pillows, table-skirts, shoes, clothing-accessories, shrines, etc. Every Spring Festival, almost every household in rural areas will paste white paper on the windows and stick red window-flowers to welcome the Chinese New Year. In terms of the content of expression, Shaanxi window-flower paper-cuts either inherit traditional themes or are closely related to daily life, reflecting reality. They include figures, flowers, birds, fish, insects, beasts, as well as opera stories and folk legends, etc., with simple forms and full of folk charm.

陕西剪纸艺术风格淳朴而庄重，注重剪纸自身的文化内涵。其中，陕北民间剪纸最具代表性。陕北民间剪纸主要围绕生产、生活、生命这三大主题。陕北的"三边"地区（靖边、安边、定边）的剪纸风格别具一格，小而精致却能以小见大，剪出的线条细若发丝，对各类形象的刻画细腻入微。

The artistic style of Shaanxi paper-cut is rustic and solemn, emphasizing the cultural connotations of paper-cut itself. Among them, the folk paper-cut in northern Shaanxi is the most representative, which primarily revolves around three major themes: production, daily life, and the cycle of life. In the "Sanbian" areas (Jingbian, Anbian, and Dingbian) of northern Shaanxi, the paper-cut stands out for its distinctive style: compact in size and exquisitely carved, capable of conveying grand meanings through delicate details. The cut lines are as fine as a strand of hair, and the depiction of various images is extremely delicate and meticulous.

库淑兰是陕西剪纸杰出的代表人物之一。20世纪80年代，她的剪纸作品一经问世便广受瞩目。其作品造型夸张怪诞，色彩艳丽，充满艺术张力。海内外学者、艺术家、教育家、记者以及剪纸爱好者纷纷慕名前往咸阳市旬邑县赤道乡，只为探访这位朴实无华的乡村剪纸艺人。

Ku Shulan is one of the outstanding representatives of Shaanxi paper-cut. In the 1980s, her paper-cut works attracted widespread attention as soon as they came out. Her works feature exaggerated and vivid shapes, bright colors, and are full of artistic tension. Scholars, artists, educators, journalists, and paper-cut enthusiasts at home and abroad have flocked to Chidao Town, Xunyi County, Xianyang City out of admiration. They all came to visit this unassuming rural paper-cut artist.

1996 年，联合国教科文组织授予库淑兰"民间工艺美术大师"的称号。国家艺术学科评议组召集人张道一在撰写《剪花娘子——库淑兰》时毫不吝惜赞美之词："库淑兰的剪纸，标志着中国民间艺术的一个新高度。"享誉中外的美术家张仃也称库淑兰为"了不起的艺术家"。

In 1996, UNESCO awarded Ku Shulan the title of "Master of Folk Arts and Crafts." When Zhang Daoyi, the convener of the national art review group, wrote in *Ku Shulan, the Paper-Cut Lady*, he was not stingy with his praise at all: "Ku Shulan's paper-cuts mark a new height in Chinese folk art." Zhang Ding, a well-known artist both at home and abroad, also said that Ku Shulan was an "amazing artist."

山东民间剪纸在造型风格方面大致可分为两类。一类是渤海湾区域的剪纸，风格粗犷豪放，这种风格与黄河流域其他省份的剪纸一脉相承。另一类是山东胶东沿海地区的剪纸，这类剪纸以线为主，属于线面结合的精巧型剪纸，似乎与山东汉代画像石细微繁缛的风格一脉相承。凭借花样密集的装饰手段，这类剪纸的外形更加饱满丰富。

Shandong paper-cut can be roughly divided into two categories in terms of style. One type is the paper-cut in the Bohai Bay region, which is bold and unconstrained in style and in the same vein as the paper-cuts of other provinces in the Yellow River Valley. The other type is the paper-cut in the Jiaodong coastal area of Shandong. This type of paper-cut is mainly based on lines and is an exquisite type of paper-cut that combines lines and surfaces. It seems to inherit the elaborate and intricate style of Han Dynasty stone relief carvings in Shandong. By means of densely patterned decorative techniques, the appearance of this type of paper-cut has become more substantial and abundant.

高密剪纸在山东最具特色，在当地农舍的门窗、棚顶以及箱柜、衣橱等处常见其装饰的身影。制作高密剪纸时一般不打草稿，剪纸者即兴剪制，常将锯齿纹和挺拔的线条相结合来塑造形象。

Gaomi paper-cut is the most distinctive in Shandong Province. It can be seen for decoration everywhere in local farmhouses, such as on doors, windows, ceilings, chests, cabinets and wardrobes. Generally, no draft is made at the beginning, and it is cut improvisationally. Its characteristic is that it often combines saw-tooth patterns and straight, forceful lines to form images.

山东剪纸从古发展至今，其独特的美愈发彰显。民间艺人也因此更加注重技巧的精湛娴熟。以王继红、王雪峰为代表的一批剪纸艺术家运用创新手法创作出的作品广受好评。

Developed from ancient times to the present, the unique beauty has been increasingly shown in Shandong paper-cut. As a result, folk artists have paid more attention to the refinement of their techniques. A group of paper-cut artists represented by Wang Jihong and Wang Xuefeng have created a batch of new works with innovative techniques, which have been widely praised.

山西剪纸的题材和形式依据各地独特的民俗风情与实际需求，展现出灵活多变的面貌。其中，中阳剪纸最具代表性。中阳县位于吕梁山区，文化底蕴深厚，这也为中阳剪纸的形成和发展奠定了文化基础。

The themes and formats of Shanxi paper-cuts are flexibly arranged according to the folk customs and practical needs of different places, varying with objects and events. Among them, Zhongyang paper-cuts are the most representative. Zhongyang County is located in the Lüliang mountain area, which has a profound cultural heritage, laying a cultural foundation for the formation and development of Zhongyang paper-cuts.

目前，中阳剪纸主要在中阳县境内的南川河流域、刘家坪地区以及西山边远山区流传。鉴于各地风俗的差异，中阳不同地区的剪纸艺术呈现出不同的艺术特点。例如，南川河流域的剪纸风格细腻，是中阳剪纸文化的核心部分；刘家坪地区的剪纸风格淳朴而刚健；西山边远地区的剪纸风格粗犷。这些不同的艺术风格极大地丰富了中阳剪纸的内涵。

At present, Zhongyang paper-cuts are mainly spread in the Nanchuan River Valley, Liujiaping area, and the remote Xishan mountainous areas within Zhongyang County. Due to the differences in local customs, the papercutting in different areas of Zhongyang presents different artistic characteristics. For example, the paper-cuts in the Nanchuan River Valley are delicate in style and are the core part of Zhongyang paper-cut culture, the paper-cuts in Liujiaping area are rustic and vigorous in style, and those in the remote Xishan mountainous areas are rough in style. These different artistic styles greatly enrich the connotations of Zhongyang paper-cuts.

窗花是中阳剪纸中最为常见的类型，其大小和风格取决于窗格的形状。比如在晋北地区，窗格有菱形、圆形和多角等样式，窗花便有相应的四角、六角、八角样式的"团花"。在忻州一带，人们在庆祝春节或者操办婚事时会张贴"全窗花"，剪出柿子、如意、牡丹、莲花、桂花、笙等图案，以表达美好的祝愿。

Window-flower paper-cuts are the most common type in Zhongyang paper-cuts, and their sizes and styles depend on the shapes of window lattices. For example, in northern Shanxi, window lattices are in diamond-shaped, round and multi-angled styles, and window-flower paper-cuts have Tuanhua patterns with four, six or eight corners corresponding to each other. In the Xinzhou area, when celebrating the Spring Festival or holding a wedding, "complete window-flowers" will be pasted. Patterns such as persimmons, Ruyi (an ornamental object, regarded as a symbol of good luck), peonies, lotuses, osmanthus flowers, and Sheng (a traditional Chinese musical instrument) are cut out to express good wishes.

中阳剪纸散发着浓郁的乡土气息，蕴含着原始社会的质朴美感，折射出当地劳动妇女的审美情趣与理想追求。

Zhongyang paper-cuts exude a rich, rustic charm and contain the simple beauty of primitive society, reflecting the aesthetic tastes and aspirational pursuits of local working women.

南方流派剪纸以构图繁茂、精巧秀美闻名。不同于北方剪纸，南派剪纸剪法细腻，作品多集中于小巧玲珑的花鸟鱼虫。折纸技巧的融入也使南派剪纸作品具有立体感。

The southern school of paper-cut is famous for its lush composition, exquisiteness, and beauty. Different from the northern paper-cut, the southern-style paper-cut is cut in a delicate way. Most of the works focus on small and exquisite flowers, birds, fish, and insects. Combined with origami techniques, the southern-style paper-cut works show a three-dimensional effect.

江苏剪纸艺术以扬州剪纸为代表。扬州是中国较早流行剪纸艺术的地区之一。扬州剪纸与当地民间刺绣联系紧密。刺绣手艺人先画底样、剪纸型，将纸样粘贴于面料后再进行刺绣，因此以前扬州人称剪纸艺人为"剪花样子的"。

Jiangsu papercutting is represented by Yangzhou paper-cut. Yangzhou is one of the early areas in China where paper-cut became popular, and has an indissoluble bond with local folk embroidery. When embroidering, artisans first draw a base pattern, cut it into a paper pattern, then paste it on the fabric before starting to embroider. Therefore, in the past, people in Yangzhou always called paper-cut artists "flower-pattern cutters."

浙江剪纸注重造型的大影像轮廓，会在影像中剪出适量的阴线，让形象结构与画面风格相呼应。其中乐清细纹刻纸精妙绝伦，它随乐清龙船灯习俗发展而来。每年元宵节，乐清部分乡镇的民间艺人扎"龙船灯"时，会在灯四周贴满细纹刻纸，当地人称之为"龙船花"。因装饰龙船灯的需求，乐清民间剪纸形成了精工细巧、玲珑剔透的风格。

艺人在四寸见方的白纸上，仅凭薄竹片压出的经纬格，不用画稿就能刻出几十种复杂图案。乐清剪纸的特色主要在于图案部分，好的图案细如发丝，密而不乱，纤而不繁，工而不腻。

Zhejiang paper-cut emphasizes the large-image outline of the shape. Appropriate Yin-cut lines are cut out to make the image structure in accordance with the style of the picture. Yueqing fine-line paper-cut is extremely exquisite in Zhejiang papercutting. It has developed with the custom of Yueqing dragon-boat lanterns. On every Lantern Festival, folk artists in some towns and villages in Yueqing make "dragon-boat lanterns" and paste fine-line paper-cuts all around the lanterns, which are locally known as "dragon-boat flowers." Due to the need to decorate dragon-boat lanterns, Yueqing folk paper-cut has formed a style of exquisite workmanship and exquisiteness. Relying only on the warp-and-weft grids pressed out by thin bamboo pieces, artisans can carve dozens of complex patterns on a four-inch-square piece of white paper without any drafts. Its characteristics are mainly in the pattern part. In fine patterns, the lines are as thin as hair strands which are densely arranged yet orderly, delicate but not fussy, and exquisite without being overdone.

广东剪纸历史久远，主要分布于佛山、汕头、潮州等地。明代起佛山剪纸已实现大规模专业化生产，产品不仅售于广东省内及中南和西南各省，还远销东南亚各国。

Having a long history, Guangdong paper-cut is mainly produced in Foshan, Shantou, Chaozhou, and other regions. Since the Ming Dynasty, Foshan paper-cut has achieved large-scale specialized production, with products sold not only in Guangdong Province and in provinces in central, south, and southwest China, but also exported to various countries in Southeast Asia.

佛山剪纸依据制作原料和方法分为铜衬、纸衬、铜写、银写、木刻套印、铜凿、纯色等类别。手工艺人以本地特产铜箔、银箔为材，通过剪、刻、凿等技艺，套衬色纸并绘印图案，造就色彩浓烈、金碧辉煌且具南方特色的剪纸。佛山剪纸在表现手法上兼具纤巧秀逸与浑厚苍劲，饶宝莲是其代表性传承人，她的作品涵盖铜衬、纸衬等多种类型，华贵精美，有浮雕般的美感。

Foshan paper-cut can be divided into many types according to its raw materials and production methods, such as copper-lined, paper-lined, copper-written, silver-written, woodcut overprinting, copper-chiseled, and single-color paper-cuts. Using the locally-produced copper foil and silver foil as raw materials, and by means of cutting, carving, chiseling, and other techniques, the artisans set off various colored papers and print various patterns, forming paper-cuts with strong colors, resplendent and magnificent, and full of southern characteristics. Foshan paper-cut has both delicate and elegant, and vigorous and forceful expression techniques. Rao Baolian is a representative inheritor of Foshan paper-cut. Her works include copper-lined, paper-lined, and other types, which are magnificent and exquisite, with an aesthetic style like reliefs.

福建各地的剪纸各具特色。南平、华安等山区的剪纸多刻画山禽家畜，作品风格淳厚朴实；闽南、漳浦等沿海地区常见渔业、水产动物题材的剪纸，风格细致、造型生动；莆田、仙游一带以礼品花为主，风格华丽纤巧。

Paper-cuts in different parts of Fujian have their own characteristics. In mountainous areas such as Nanping and Hua'an, there are more works depicting mountain birds and domestic animals, and their styles are relatively simple and honest; in southern Fujian and Zhangpu areas along the coast, fishery and aquatic animals are often depicted in the paper-cuts, with a detailed style and vivid shapes; in Putian and Xianyou areas, gift-flower-themed paper-cuts are mainly produced, and they tend to be gorgeous and delicate.

闽南民间剪纸多用于礼仪礼品花、祭祀供品贴花和游神赛会灯花，目的是祈求风调雨顺、平安、丰收和安乐。其中莆田礼品花最具特色，常用于喜事或祭祀活动。

Folk paper-cuts in southern Fujian are mostly used for gift-flower for ceremonies, decal for offerings in sacrificial activities, and decorative lantern-flowers for temple-fair processions, all in order to pray for favorable weather, safe voyages, bumper harvests, and annual well-being. The most characteristic style is the gift-flower in Putian, which is often used for happy occasions or sacrificial activities.

闽北民间剪纸以浦城剪纸为代表。浦城人多在礼品上装饰剪纸，依据器物大小剪成各种纹样，装饰物大的可达盈尺，小的仅方寸。

Folk paper-cuts in northern Fujian are represented by Pucheng. Pucheng people cut out various patterns according to the size of the objects and decorate gifts with paper-cuts. The large-sized decorations can be as large as a foot in length, while the small-sized ones are only one inch.

Exercises

1 **Answer the following questions.**

(1) Compare and contrast the main characteristics of the northern-school and southern-school paper-cuts.

(2) Explain how the regional cultures in Shaanxi influence its paper-cut style.

(3) Discuss the challenges faced by Zhongyang paper-cuts in Shanxi in terms of inheritance.

(4) How does Yueqing fine-line paper-cut in Zhejiang form its unique style?

(5) Analyze the significance of the export of Foshan paper-cut in Guangdong.

2 **Choose the best answer to each of the following questions.**

(1) Which of the following regions is not typically representative of the northern-school paper-cut?

A. Shaanxi.　　　　B. Jiangsu.　　　　C. Shandong.　　　　D. Shanxi.

(2) What is the main reason for Shaanxi paper-cut being called a "living fossil" of ancient civilization?

A. It has a long history.

B. It has completely inherited ancient shape patterns and cultural concepts.

C. It is loved by people.

D. It has diverse forms.

(3) In which area of Shandong is the paper-cut more distinctive and mainly based on lines?

A. Bohai Bay region.　　　　　　　B. Jiaodong coastal area.

C. Central Shandong.　　　　　　　D. Southern Shandong.

(4) Which of the following is the most representative type of paper-cuts in Zhongyang, Shanxi?

A. Door-picture paper-cuts.　　　　B. Window-flower paper-cuts.

C. Kiln-top paper-cuts.　　　　　　D. Kang-surround paper-cuts.

(5) What is the relationship between Yangzhou paper-cut in Jiangsu and local folk embroidery?

A. They have no relationship.

B. Yangzhou paper-cut is used as a pattern for embroidery.

C. They are both declining arts.

D. They have a historical and close relationship in the production process.

(6) In Zhejiang, what is the characteristic of Yueqing fine-line paper-cut patterns?

A. Thick and simple.

B. Thin as hair strands, densely arranged yet orderly.

C. Only large-scale patterns.

D. All black-and-white patterns.

(7) Who is a representative inheritor of Foshan paper-cut in Guangdong?

A. Zhang Yongshou. B. Rao Baolian.

C. Wang Jihong. D. Ku Shulan.

(8) In Fujian, which area mainly produces gift-flower-themed paper-cuts?

A. Nanping. B. Putian.

C. Zhangpu. D. Pucheng.

(9) In Shaanxi paper-cut, which of the following themes reflects the Chinese nation's concepts of reproduction and fertility worship?

A. Eagle Stepping on Rabbit. B. Flower-bird.

C. Landscape. D. Portrait.

3 Decide whether each of the following statements is true (T) or false (F).

(1) Shaanxi paper-cuts are diverse in forms and rich in contents.

(2) Gaomi paper-cut in Shandong always requires a draft before cutting.

(3) The paper-cuts in different areas of Zhongyang in Shanxi present different artistic characteristics.

(4) Yueqing fine-line paper-cut in Zhejiang does not need any tools other than scissors.

(5) Foshan paper-cut can be divided into many types according to its raw materials and production methods.

(6) In Fujian, paper-cuts in mountainous areas and coastal areas have exactly the same style.

(7) The southern-school paper-cut is always larger in size compared to the northern-school paper-cut.

④ **Match the following regions with their corresponding contributions to paper-cut.**

(1) Shaanxi

(2) Shandong (Jiaodong coastal area)

(3) Zhongyang in Shanxi

(4) Yueqing in Zhejiang

(5) Foshan in Guangdong

A. Paper-cut related to dragon-boat lanterns custom, with extremely fine-line patterns

B. Paper-cut with ancient cultural connotations, various forms and primitive shapes

C. Paper-cut mainly based on lines, an exquisite type combining lines and surfaces

D. Window-flower paper-cut with different styles according to local customs

E. Paper-cut with various types according to raw materials and production methods, resplendent and magnificent

Section 3

剪纸的基本技法
Basic Techniques of Paper-Cut

剪刀是剪纸的主要工具，剪纸对剪刀的形制并没有特殊的要求，市面上用于裁剪衣料的普通剪刀就可用于剪纸。一般来说，选择刀尖轻巧纤细、开合松紧适度、刀刃锋利的剪刀即可。

Scissors are the main tools for papercutting, and there are no very special requirements for their shape. Ordinary scissors sold on the market for cutting fabric would be appropriate. Generally speaking, choose scissors with a sharp blade, light and slender tips, and moderate tightness when opening and closing.

纸张是剪纸的基本材料，选择合适的纸张能为剪纸带来很多方便。单色剪纸一般选用普通大红纸或者彩色电光纸。

Paper is the basic material of papercutting, and a good selection of paper can bring a lot of convenience to papercutting. Monochrome paper-cut is generally made of ordinary red paper or colored iridescent paper.

剪纸较注重原创性，不受刻刀和纸张的限制，较为自由和随意。染色剪纸和刻纸大多采用宣纸或粉连纸。刻刀的构造比较简单，自己就可以动手做。刀片用旧发条、锯条、表条均可，用砂轮打磨成所需要的形状。刀片做好后，用细线绳将其紧紧绑在小木条或竹棍上即可。

Papercutting focuses more on originality. Unconstrained by cutting knives and paper, it allows freedom and randomness. For dyed paper-cut and paper engraving, rice paper or straw-lined paper is mostly used. The cutting knife is relatively simple and can be homemade. The blade can be made from an old hairspring, saw blade or watch spring, and ground into the desired shape with a grinding wheel. After the blade is ready, tie it tightly to a small wooden stick or bamboo stick with thin strings.

配合刻刀使用的工具还有蜡板和尖锥子、钉子等。蜡板的作用是为了让刀刃刻画顺畅，且能避免损坏桌面。蜡板是用筛过的草木灰与黄蜡加热搅拌，倒入木板里压平冷却而制成的。蜡板的硬度一般跟所做的剪纸图案复杂程度有关。精致的图案应该使用较硬的蜡板，蜡板过软会使较细的线条容易断。刻制线条较粗的作品时，应采用较软的蜡板，省时省力。因此，剪纸艺人一般都有两块甚至两块以上蜡板。刻纸一般是将图样放在 20 张或者 30 张薄纸上，然后将纸放在垫板上用钉子固定，用刻刀由里到外一层层地刻，刻好花样后，刻纸就完成了。

Other tools used with the carving knife include wax plates, sharp awls, nails, etc. The wax plate is used to keep the cutting edge smooth without damaging the tabletop. The wax board is made by heating and stirring sieved plant ash and yellow wax, and then pouring the mixture into a wooden board, flattening it, and letting it cool. Generally, the hardness of the wax board is related to the complexity of the paper-cut pattern. For delicate patterns, a stiffer wax plate should be used, since too soft a wax plate may break the thinner lines. When carving works with thick lines, a softer wax plate should be used to save time and effort. Therefore, most paper-cut artists have two or even more wax plates. Paper engraving usually starts with placing the pattern on 20 or 30 sheets of tissue paper, Then, place them on the wax plate, fix them with nails, and use a carving knife to engrave them layer by layer from the inside out, and after carving the pattern, the paper engraving is completed.

剪纸手法分为阳剪法和阴镂法。阳剪法指剪去空底，留下块面和线条结构，以白纸衬出所剪图形。如果仅留下块面，即只剪出物体的外部形状，不需镂空形状内部，这种手法就叫作"剪影"，民间艺人称之为"剪大样"。剪影一般表现物象的侧面，抓住大体特征和姿态，用剪不多，概括简练，显得较为厚重。

The techniques of papercutting can be categorized into two main methods: Yang-style cutting and Yin-style carving. Yang-style cutting involves cutting away the background, leaving behind solid shapes and structural outlines, which are then contrasted against the white paper to highlight the cut-out patterns. When only the solid shapes are retained—meaning only the outer contours of objects are cut out without hollowing out the interiors—it is referred to as Jianying (profile cutting), or Jian Dayang (cutting out the overall image) by folk artists. Jianying typically depicts the side profile of objects, capturing their general features and postures with minimal cutting, resulting in a concise and solid appearance.

阴镂法，也叫镂空，指在剪影的基础上，将内部镂出空白线条结构。民间艺人称其为"抠花"或"剜花"。

Yin-style carving, also known as "hollowing out," builds upon profile cutting by cutting intricate patterns and lines within the interior. Folk artists call this process Kouhua (carving images) or Wanhua (digging out images).

剪影和镂空都讲究刀功。剪镂的基本刀工是直、曲、折。

Both profile cutting and hollow-out techniques emphasize skills in using scissors and knives. The basic skills in cutting and carving are straight cuts, curved cuts, and folded cuts.

"直"是直线，包括垂直线、水平线、对角线、斜直线、交叉线等。在民俗单色剪纸中，垂直线和水平线用得最多。民间艺人把直线统称为"钉""杠"。直线应一次剪镂而成。剪长直线是用剪口后段往前直剪，或将纸对折往前直剪。剪短直线是用剪口中段、前段往前直剪，或将纸对折往前直剪。直线应剪得笔直挺拔、刚强有力，切忌停顿或线条粗细不均。

"Straight" refers to straight lines, including vertical lines, horizontal lines, diagonal lines, oblique lines, and intersecting lines, etc. In folk single-color paper-cuts, vertical and horizontal lines are the most frequently used. Folk artists collectively refer to straight lines as "nails" and "bars." A straight line should be cut or engraved in one snip. For long straight lines, use the rear section of the scissors to cut straight forward, or fold the paper and then cut forward. For short straight lines, use the middle or front section of the scissors to cut straight forward, or fold the paper and then cut forward. It is required to cut straight, upright, and forceful, avoiding pauses and uneven thickness.

"曲"是曲线，包括弧线、波形线、飘带式曲线、旋涡式曲线、圆形线等。在民俗单色剪纸的人物、动物和植物形象中，曲线运用最为广泛。民间艺人把曲线称为"弯""弓"。剪镂曲线，左右手要协调自然，线条要流畅、顺滑、柔和，富有运动感与旋律感。

"Curved" refers to curves, including arcs, wavy lines, ribbon-like curves, vortex-like curves, and circular lines, etc. Among the figures of people, animals, and plants in folk single-color paper-cuts, curves are the most widely used. Folk artists call curves "bends" and "bows." When cutting or engraving curves, the left and right hands should be natural and coordinated. The requirements for cutting or engraving curves are that they should be smooth, gentle, and natural, full of a sense of movement and rhythm.

"折" 是折线。折线所形成的是角，包括直角、锐角、钝角，民间艺人将其统称为 "刺" 或 "尖"。若干刺排列就形成了锯齿状。锐角锯齿状被民间艺人称为 "毛"。"毛" 在民俗单色剪纸中常用于动物的羽毛、植物的花叶等。折线的剪制要求精确无误、整齐均匀，不可剪过头致使线头断裂，也不能剪不到头致使废纸屑无法掉落。

"Folded" refers to folded lines. The folded lines form angles, including right angles, acute angles, and obtuse angles. Folk artists collectively refer to them as "thorns" and "points." The arrangement of several thorns forms a serrated shape. Acute-angled serrated shapes are called "hairs" by folk artists. "Hairs" are often used in folk single-color paper-cut for the feathers of animals and the flower leaves of plants, etc. It is required to cut precisely and evenly. Do not cut too far, as this may break the fine lines or not far enough, leaving waste paper scraps.

例如，在剪一个简单的长方形边框时，就需要熟练运用长直线和短直线的剪法，保证边框的笔直和规整；剪一个花朵的轮廓，流畅的弧线和优美的波浪线能让花朵更加生动；在表现动物的羽毛时，精准地剪出锯齿状的 "毛"，能让羽毛显得更加逼真。

For example, when cutting a simple rectangular border, one needs to skillfully apply the cutting methods of long and short straight lines to ensure the straightness and regularity of the border. When creating the outline of a flower, cutting out both smooth arcs and beautiful wavy lines can make the flower more vivid. And when representing the feathers of animals, precisely cutting the serrated "hairs" can make the feathers appear more realistic.

俗话说："捉样容易打扮难。" 这里说的 "打扮" 指的就是剪纸纹样的运用。剪纸纹样又称 "剪纸语言"，它是剪纸艺术的基本构成要素。只有了解并熟练掌握这些纹样，才能灵活自如地把自己的构思通过作品展现给观者。

As the saying goes, "It's easy to catch the shape but difficult to dress it up." Here, "dressing up" refers to the application of paper-cut patterns. Paper-cut patterns, also known as "paper-cut language," are the basic components of papercutting. Only by understanding and mastering these patterns proficiently can one present his or her conception to the viewers flexibly and freely through works.

剪纸的纹样有很多，常用的纹样有月牙纹、太阳纹、云纹、柳叶纹、火纹、水纹等。人们用这些独特的符号语言作装饰，使剪纸图案内容更丰富、形式更多变。在一幅剪纸作品中，通常会运用到多种装饰纹样。

There are many patterns of paper-cut. Commonly used ones include crescent patterns, sun patterns, cloud patterns, willow leaf patterns, fire patterns, water patterns, etc. People use these unique symbolic languages for decoration, making the content of paper-cut patterns richer and their forms more varied. Usually, multiple decorative patterns are used in a single work.

月牙纹是由长短不一的弧线所组成的呈现月牙形状的纹样。月牙纹多为阴剪，常用于表现衣纹、眼眉、脊背、花卉等。月牙纹的剪制方法很简单：将剪刀插于纹样中间部分，然后沿弧线的边缘剪下即可。常规月牙纹多用于眼眉、衣纹等；弯曲月牙纹由常规月牙纹演化而来，纹样更为丰富，适用面更广，如动物背部、鱼鳞、鸟羽等。

The crescent pattern is composed of arcs of different lengths and presents a crescent shape. Crescent patterns are mostly Yin-style cuts and are often used to represent clothing patterns, eyebrows, spines, flowers, etc. The production method of crescent patterns is very simple: insert the scissors into the middle part of the pattern, then cut along the edge of the arc. Conventional crescent patterns are mostly used in eyebrows, clothing patterns, etc. The curved crescent pattern evolved from the conventional one, and the pattern is more variable and has a wider range of application, such as the backs of animals, fish scales, bird feathers, etc.

常规月牙纹（左）与弯曲月牙纹（右）
Conventional crescent pattern (left) and curved crescent pattern (right)

剪锯齿纹俗称"打毛刺""打牙牙"，它是剪纸艺术中最典型、最有代表性，也是难度最大、最能展现剪者功底的技法之一，精致的打毛刺宜剪不宜刻。锯齿纹能更好地表现物像的层次感和立体感，通常用于表现动物身上的绒毛、羽毛，以及花朵、树叶的纹理和人物的毛发等。锯齿纹的种类有很多，常见的有直线锯齿纹、扇形锯齿纹、圆形锯齿纹、篦齿纹、向心锯齿纹、轮形锯齿纹等。在同一幅作品中，锯齿纹变化不宜过多，否则会显得杂乱。

Cutting serrated patterns is commonly known as "making burrs" or "making teeth." It is one of the most typical, representative, and also the most difficult techniques in papercutting, and it can best demonstrate the skills of the cutter. Exquisite burr making is easier to do by cutting than engraving. Serrated patterns can better represent the layering and three-dimensional sense of objects. They are usually used to represent the fluff and feathers on animals, as well as the textures of flowers and leaves, and the hair of characters. There are many types of serrated patterns, commonly including straight-line serrated patterns, fan-shaped serrated patterns, circular serrated patterns, comb-shaped serrated patterns, centripetal serrated patterns, wheel-shaped serrated patterns, etc. In the same work, there should not be too many variations of serrated patterns; otherwise, it will look cluttered.

锯齿纹
Serrated patterns

圆纹在剪纸中使用很广，它既可以单独使用，如表现人物的眼睛、服饰的扣子、植物的花蕊、浪花的水珠等，又可以依靠不同的排列方式或改变直径取得各式各样的装饰效果。例如，特殊技法中的香烧法，就是由大大小小不同的圆纹完成的作品形式。

Circular patterns are widely used in paper-cut. They can be used alone, such as to represent the eyes of characters, buttons on clothing, plant stamens, and water droplets in waves. They can also achieve various decorative effects by arranging them in different ways or changing their diameters. For example, the incense burning method in special techniques is a form of work completed by using circular patterns of different sizes.

圆纹
Circular patterns

柳叶纹是由长短相同的两条弧线相对而形成的呈现柳叶形状的纹样。此纹样制作简单，多用于花卉、叶片等装饰。

Willow leaf pattern is a pattern shaped like a willow leaf, formed by two opposite arcs of the same length. This pattern is easy to make and is mostly used for decorating flowers, leaves, etc.

柳叶纹
Willow leaf patterns

云纹和水纹在剪纸作品中常表现其本意形象，通过形态上的变幻，对作品主体和气氛起到陪衬和烘托的作用。在中国文化中，"云"常被称为"祥云"。出于云在自然界中的多变性，云纹在形态上有很多种类，常见的有云钩纹、如意云头纹、行云纹、朵云纹、层云纹、气云纹，等等。

Cloud and water patterns often express their literal images in paper-cut works. Through changes in shape, they serve as a foil and enhancement to the main body and atmosphere of the work. In Chinese culture, "cloud" is often referred to as "auspicious cloud." Due to the variability of clouds in nature, cloud patterns come in many forms, such as cloud hook pattern, cloud head pattern, flowing cloud pattern, cloud bunch pattern, layered cloud pattern, and misty cloud pattern.

云纹
Cloud patterns

水纹也经常出现在剪纸作品中，它常和水鸟、鱼类、水生植物或传说人物组合，最常见的题材有"鱼戏莲""鲤鱼跳龙门""八仙过海"等。由于水在形态上是不断变化的，所以剪水纹的表现手法也不尽相同。水纹大致可分为静水纹、鱼鳞水纹、双涡水纹、卷花浪水纹、瀑布纹等。

Water patterns are frequently used in paper-cut works, often combined with waterfowl, fish, aquatic plants, and legendary figures. The most common themes include "Fish Playing with Lotus," "Carp Jumping Over the Dragon Gate," "The Eight Immortals Crossing the Sea," etc. As water constantly changes in shape, the expression techniques in paper-cuts are also different, which can be roughly divided into still water pattern, fish scale water pattern, double whirlpool water pattern, rolling wave pattern, waterfall pattern, etc.

水纹
Water patterns

在艺术表达领域里，中国剪纸可以分为两大类别："剪纸"与"刻纸"。剪纸是一门精细的艺术，完全依靠手工，用剪刀制作而成。刻纸则涉及使用刻刀进行复杂的雕刻。这些技艺进一步拓展为一系列专业技法，如单色剪纸、彩色剪纸、染色刻纸、剪贴画、"铜凿"工艺和"镶嵌式书法剪纸"，每一项都是中国剪纸艺术博大精深的有力证明。

In terms of artistic expression, Chinese paper-cut can be divided into two distinct categories: paper cutting and paper engraving. Paper cutting is a meticulous art crafted solely by hand with scissors, whereas paper engraving involves intricate incisions executed with cutting knives. These techniques further expand into a spectrum of specialized techniques, such as monochromatic paper-cut, multicolored paper-cut, dyed engraved paper, collage paper-cut, copper chisel work, and inlaid calligraphic paper-cut, each a testament to Chinese paper-cut's vastness.

单色剪纸可分为阳刻剪纸和阴刻剪纸两种。阳刻剪纸把握形状与轮廓的精髓，保留了图像的定义线条，同时精心剪去或刻去线条之外的部分。阴刻剪纸则逆转了这一原则，剪去或刻去形体轮廓本身，留下块面部分作为焦点，创造出鲜明的对比和独特的审美魅力。

Monochromatic paper-cut can be divided into Yang-style cutting and Yin-style cutting. Yang-style cutting embraces the essence of form and contour, preserving the defining lines of the image while meticulously cutting away the areas beyond these boundaries. Conversely, Yin-style cutting reverses this principle: the contours themselves are excised, leaving the solid masses as the focal point, creating a stark contrast and unique aesthetic allure.

彩色剪纸作为一门绚丽多彩的艺术形式，以其画面上交织融汇的两种乃至多种色彩而独树一帜。它涵盖了多种精妙绝伦的技法，如套色剪纸层次分明，色彩和谐共生；填色剪纸以细腻笔触为轮廓添彩，增添无限生机；染色剪纸似水墨晕染，色彩自然过渡，展现流动之美；分色剪纸的每一色块都精准分割，展现匠人之心；衬色剪纸以底色映衬主题，增添视觉深度；勾绘剪纸亦称绘色剪纸，手工艺人以线条勾勒轮廓，再以色彩填充其间，犹如画师精心绘制，每一笔都蕴含着无尽的创意与情感。

Multicolored paper-cut, as a dazzling art form, stands out for its interweaving and blending of two or more colors on the same screen. It encompasses a myriad of exquisite techniques, such as overlay color paper-cut, which boasts distinct layers and harmonious coexistence of colors; painted paper-cut, which adds vibrant hues to the contours with delicate brushwork; dyed paper-cut, resembling ink wash painting with natural color transitions, showcasing the beauty of fluidity; separated-color paper-cut, where each color block is precisely segmented, revealing the artisan's meticulous craftsmanship; contrast color paper-cut, enhancing visual depth by juxtaposing background colors with the theme; and outlined-painted paper-cut, also known as painted contour paper-cut, where the artisan first outlines the contours with lines, then fills them with colors. Akin to a painter's meticulous rendering, every stroke embodies boundless creativity and emotion.

Exercises

1 **Answer the following questions.**

(1) Briefly describe several main types of Chinese paper-cut.

(2) What are the characteristics of symmetrical paper-cut?

(3) What are the main differences between colored paper-cut and monochromatic paper-cut?

(4) Describe the functions and making methods of the wax plate in paper-cut.

(5) Compare and contrast Yang-style cutting and Yin-style carving in paper-cut.

(6) Discuss how different types of lines (straight, curved, folded) are used and their requirements in paper-cut.

(7) How do different paper-cut patterns contribute to the overall work?

2 **Choose the best answer to each of the following questions.**

(1) Which of the following is not a basic line type in paper-cut?

    A. Straight.   B. Circular.

    C. Curved.   D. Folded.

(2) What is the main difference between Yang-style cutting and Yin-style carving?

    A. Yang-style cutting uses only scissors.

    B. Yin-style carving leaves the background.

    C. Yang-style cutting cuts away the background while Yin-style carving cuts the interior of the silhouette.

    D. Yang-style cutting is for monochrome paper-cut only.

(3) Which type of paper is mostly used for monochrome paper-cut?

    A. Rice paper.

    B. Pink continuous paper.

    C. Ordinary red paper or colored iridescent paper.

    D. Black and gold paper.

(4) What is the common name for cutting serrated patterns?

    A. Making burrs or making teeth.   B. Kouhua.

    C. Wanhua.   D. Jian Dayang.

(5) Which of the following is not a type of serrated pattern?

    A. Straight-line serrated pattern.   B. Triangular serrated pattern.

    C. Fan-shaped serrated pattern.   D. Circular serrated pattern.

(6) Which pattern is often used to represent feathers in paper-cut?

    A. Serrated pattern.   B. Crescent pattern.

    C. Willow leaf pattern.   D. Sun pattern.

(7) What is the key feature of multicolored paper-cut?

    A. Using only two colors.

B. Using only natural colors.

C. Using only black and gold paper.

D. Interweaving two or more colors.

3 **Decide whether each of the following statements is true (T) or false (F).**

(1) Scissors for paper-cut need to have a very special shape.

(2) The hardness of the wax plate has no relation to the complexity of the paper-cut pattern.

(3) Yang-style cutting involves cutting away the background, leaving solid shapes and structural outlines.

(4) All types of serrated patterns can be used freely without limitation in one work.

(5) Circular patterns can be used alone, such as to represent the eyes of characters or buttons on clothing.

(6) The production of the crescent pattern is very complicated.

(7) In multicolored paper-cut, all techniques use the same method of coloring.

(8) The patterns of window decoration paper-cut only include flowers, birds, and fish.

(9) Gift flower paper-cut is mainly used to decorate windows.

(10) Three-dimensional paper-cut achieves its three-dimensional effect through the stacking of multiple layers of paper.

4 **Match the following types of paper-cut with their corresponding descriptions.**

(1) Window decorations   A. Primarily used to decorate gifts

(2) Gift flowers   B. Designed specifically for decorating windows, adding a festive atmosphere

(3) Animal paper-cut   C. Featuring animals as the subject matter, symbolizing various meanings

(4) Figure paper-cut   D. Vividly representing the form and expression of characters

1 | "双喜"的剪法
Cutting Method of Double Happiness

双喜字的起源相传与北宋著名政治家、文学家王安石有关。据说，王安石在科举考试中高中状元，同时又娶得美貌的妻子，可谓喜上加喜。为了表达内心的喜悦，他在红纸上写下了两个并排的"喜"字，贴在了大门上。自此以后，双喜字便成了婚礼场合的必备元素，流传至今。

The origin of Double Happiness motif is said to be associated with Wang Anshi, a renowned statesman and literary figure of the Northern Song Dynasty. It is said that Wang Anshi achieved the top score in the imperial examinations and married a beautiful young woman, which was indeed a double blessing. To express his joy, he wrote two "happiness" characters side by side on red paper and posted it on his gate. Since then, it has become an essential element in wedding, passed down through the ages.

"双喜"剪纸不仅具有装饰作用，还蕴含着丰富的文化内涵和美好寓意。两个"喜"字并排而立，象征着夫妻恩爱、天长地久。同时，双喜也寓意着好事成双、喜上加喜，寄托着人们对美好生活的向往和祝福。

Double Happiness paper-cut not only serves a decorative purpose, but also carries rich cultural connotations and beautiful meanings. The two "happiness" characters standing side by side symbolize conjugal love and eternal companionship. At the same time, Double Happiness also signifies that "good things come in pairs" and "joy upon joy," embodying people's aspirations and blessings for a better life.

在剪纸技艺上，"双喜"剪纸也有着独特之处。剪纸艺人通过巧妙的构思和精湛的技艺，将双喜字与各种吉祥图案相结合，创造出丰富多样的"双喜"剪纸作品。这些作品不仅具有观赏价值，也是中华民族传统文化的生动体现。

In terms of paper-cut skills, Double Happiness paper-cut also has its unique features. Paper-cut artists create a wide variety of Double Happiness works by combining this motif with various auspicious patterns through ingenious ideas and exquisite techniques. These works not only have ornamental value, but they are also vivid manifestations of traditional Chinese culture.

扫描二维码获取"双喜"剪制方法与教学视频
Scan the QR-code to get the methods and teaching video of cutting Double Happiness

所需材料：一张正方形红纸；一把剪刀；一支铅笔。

Material needed: a square piece of red paper, a pair of scissors, and a pencil.

Exercises

1 **Answer the following questions.**

(1) Describe the cultural significance of Double Happiness paper-cut.

(2) How is Double Happiness paper-cut used in weddings?

(3) What can you see from the five Chinese characters? Could you describe them?

福　禄　寿　喜　财
fú　　lù　　shòu　　xǐ　　cái

2 **Choose the best answer to each of the following questions.**

(1) The Double Happiness motif in Chinese paper-cut is often used to symbolize
_____.

    A. sadness   B. loneliness

    C. doubled joy   D. sorrow

(2) The origin of Double Happiness can be traced back to the era of _____.

    A. Tang Dynasty   B. Song Dynasty

    C. Ming Dynasty   D. Qing Dynasty

3 **Decide whether each of the following statements is true (T) or false (F).**

(1) Double Happiness paper-cut is only used in weddings in China.

(2) It is said that Wang Anshi wrote two "happiness" characters side by side to celebrate his success in the imperial examinations and his marriage.

(3) The origin of Double Happiness paper-cut dates back to the Northern Song Dynasty.

(4) Double Happiness paper-cut only has a decorative function without any cultural meanings.

(5) The two "happiness" characters in Double Happiness paper-cut symbolize good luck in business.

2 | "福"字的剪法
Cutting Method of Chinese Character "Fu"

在中文里，"福"字意为"幸福"或"祝福"，经常出现在春节期间的装饰元素中。剪纸中的"福"字常以各种风格出现，从简单到复杂不等。"福"字剪纸之所以受欢迎，在于它能够将美学与吉祥寓意相结合，既能增强节日氛围，又承载着人们对幸福和繁荣生活的美好愿望。

The character "Fu" means "happiness" or "blessing" in Chinese, and it is often used as a decorative element during the Spring Festival. The "Fu" character in paper-cut often appears in various styles, ranging from simple to complex. The popularity of "Fu" paper-cut lies in its ability to combine aesthetics with auspicious meanings. It not only enhances the festive atmosphere, but also serves as a carrier of people's wishes for a happy and prosperous life.

扫描二维码获取"福"字
剪制方法与教学视频
**Scan the QR-code to get
the methods and teaching
video of cutting Chinese
character "Fu"**

所需材料：一张正方形红纸；一把剪刀；一支铅笔。

Material needed: a square piece of red paper, a pair of scissors, and a pencil.

Exercises

1 **Answer the following questions.**

(1) Describe the significance of "Fu" paper-cut in Chinese culture.

(2) How does the upside-down "Fu" differ from the upright one in meaning?

2 **Choose the best answer to each of the following questions.**

(1) The character "Fu" in Chinese represents _____.

A. sadness   B. anger   C. happiness   D. fear

(2) During which festival is "Fu" paper-cut often displayed?

A. Mid-Autumn Festival.   B. Spring Festival.

C. Dragon Boat Festival.   D. Double Ninth Festival.

❸ **Decide whether each of the following statements is true (T) or false (F).**

(1) "Fu" paper-cut dates back to the Han Dynasty.

(2) The upside-down "Fu" is a symbol of bad luck.

❹ **Match the following terms with their corresponding descriptions.**

(1) "Fu" paper-cut

(2) Upside-down "Fu"

(3) Spring Festival

(4) Han Dynasty

A. A traditional Chinese festival celebrated in January or February

B. A paper-cut art form featuring the character "Fu"

C. The era when paper-cut is believed to have originated

D. A variation of "Fu" paper-cut that symbolizes the arrival of happiness

3 | 灯笼的剪法
Cutting Method of Lantern

灯笼剪纸是中国传统剪纸艺术中的一种重要形式，拥有悠久的历史。灯笼，作为中国传统文化的象征之一，代表着喜庆、吉祥和团圆。在古代，灯笼常用于节日庆典和婚礼等喜庆的场合，能为庆典增添浓厚的氛围。灯笼剪纸可以作为装饰来庆祝春节等传统节日，也常常作为礼品赠送亲友，寓意着祝福和好运。

Lantern paper-cut is an essential form of traditional Chinese papercutting, boasting a long and illustrious history. The lantern, as one of the symbols of traditional Chinese culture, represents jubilation, auspiciousness, and reunion. In ancient times, lanterns were often used on festive occasions and weddings, adding a festive atmosphere to the celebrations. Lantern paper-cut is often used as decoration to celebrate traditional festivals like the Spring Festival and is often given as a gift to relatives and friends, symbolizing blessings and good luck.

扫描二维码获取灯笼
剪制方法与教学视频
**Scan the QR-code to
get the methods and
teaching video of cutting
lantern**

所需材料： 一张正方形红纸；一把剪刀；一支铅笔。

Material needed: a square piece of red paper, a pair of scissors, and a pencil.

Exercises

1 **Answer the following questions.**

(1) Briefly describe the historical background and significance of lantern paper-cut in Chinese culture.

(2) On what occasions is lantern paper-cut commonly used, and what are its symbolic meanings?

(3) What aspects should artists pay attention to during the creation process of lantern paper-cut?

2 **Choose the best answer to each of the following questions.**

(1) Which of the following is not a tool used for lantern paper-cut?

A. Scissors.   B. Pencil.

C. Blades.   D. Engraving knife.

(2) What does the lantern primarily represent in traditional Chinese culture?

A. Sadness and separation.   B. Celebration and reunion.

C. Fear and anxiety.   D. Loneliness and silence.

3 **Decide whether each of the following statements is true (T) or false (F).**

(1) Lantern paper-cut is an integral part of Western art.

(2) Lantern paper-cut is commonly used to celebrate the Spring Festival, expressing people's wishes for family harmony and social stability.

(3) Lantern paper-cut is exclusively created using scissors and does not involve other tools.

4 **Match the following terms with their corresponding descriptions.**

(1) Brightness and hope

(2) Celebration and reunion

(3) Good fortune and blessings

A. Lantern paper-cut is often used at weddings and other joyous occasions.

B. Lantern paper-cut, when given as a gift, conveys deep affection and well-wishes to recipients.

C. The lantern, as a symbol of light, embodies people's aspirations for a better future.

4 | "春"字团花的剪法
Cutting Method of Circular Floral Paper-Cut with Chinese Character "Chun"

"春"字团花剪纸是中国传统文化中一项独特的手工艺，它将书法艺术与剪纸技艺巧妙融合，作品既具文字美感，又能烘托节日氛围。在这一艺术形式中，艺术家们以剪刀为笔，红纸为墨，精心勾勒出"春"字与周围繁复花卉的轮廓，通过剪、刻等手法，展现精细入微的图案和层次分明的立体感。"春"字团花不仅展现了春天的生机与活力，还寄托了人们对新年的美好祝愿和对幸福生活的向往。

Circular floral paper-cut with Chinese character "Chun" is a unique handicraft in traditional Chinese culture, which ingeniously combines calligraphy with papercutting techniques to create artistic works that embody both the beauty of characters and the festive atmosphere. In this art form, artists use scissors as brushes and red paper as ink, meticulously outlining the contours of the character "Chun" (spring) and the surrounding intricate floral patterns. Through cutting, engraving, and other techniques, they reveal delicate patterns and a sense of three-dimensionality with distinct layers. Circular floral paper-cut with Chinese character "Chun" not only showcases the vitality and energy of spring but also embodies people's good wishes for the new year and aspirations for a happy life.

"春"字团花剪纸以其独特的艺术魅力和深厚的文化内涵而深受人们喜爱。它不仅是春节期间家家户户常见的装饰品，也是中国传统文化的重要组成部分，承载着中华民族对美好生活的追求和向往。

Circular floral paper-cut with Chinese character "Chun" is deeply loved for its unique artistic charm and profound cultural connotation. It is not only a common decoration during the Spring Festival but also an essential part of traditional Chinese culture, carrying the Chinese nation's pursuit and yearning for a better life.

所需材料：一张正方形红纸；一把剪刀；一支铅笔。

Material needed: a square piece of red paper, a pair of scissors, and a pencil.

扫描二维码获取"春"字团花剪制方法与教学视频
Scan the QR-code to get the methods and teaching video of cutting circular floral paper-cut with Chinese character "Chun"

Exercises

1   **Answer the following questions.**

(1) How does circular floral paper-cut with Chinese character "Chun" embody the Chinese nation's pursuit and yearning for a better life?

(2) What are the main techniques used in creating circular floral paper-cut with Chinese character "Chun"?

(3) Why is the color red so significant in circular floral paper-cut with Chinese character "Chun"?

2   **Choose the best answer to each of the following questions.**

(1) Which of the following is NOT the characteristic of circular floral paper-cut with Chinese character "Chun"?

A. It combines calligraphy with paper-cut techniques.

B. It is used exclusively as a decoration for weddings.

C. It showcases the vitality of spring.

D. It embodies people's good wishes for the new year.

(2) What do artists use as their "brushes" in cutting circular floral paper-cut with Chinese character "Chun"?

A. Scissors.   B. Paintbrushes.

C. Pens.   D. Chisels.

(3) What material is typically used for circular floral paper-cut with Chinese character "Chun"?

A. Blue paper.   B. Yellow paper.

C. Green paper.   D. Red paper.

3   **Decide whether each of the following statements is true (T) or false (F).**

(1) Circular floral paper-cut with Chinese character "Chun" only involves simple cutting techniques without any engraving.

(2) Circular floral paper-cut with Chinese character "Chun" is a widely practiced art form in traditional Chinese culture.

(3) The character "Chun" means autumn in Chinese.

4 **Match the following terms with their corresponding descriptions.**

(1) Scissors

(2) Red paper

(3) Chun (春)

(4) Floral patterns

A. The material commonly used for creating the artworks

B. The central character featured in the artwork, representing spring

C. The tool used as a "brush" to create intricate patterns

D. Symbolic of prosperity and good luck in Chinese culture

Chapter 3

京剧
Peking Opera

　　京剧，在世界范围内被视为"中国戏剧"，是中国的国粹。京剧诞生于清乾隆年间，它继承了徽剧、汉剧、昆曲、秦腔等众多剧种的艺术特点，逐渐形成了一套完整的表演方法。京剧融合了音乐、演唱、哑剧、舞蹈、杂技和武术，表现形式生动多样。经过众多艺术家长期的舞台实践，京剧逐渐形成了技术性较强的程式化规范和严格的训练体系。京剧的表现手法虚实结合，在很大程度上摆脱了舞台表演的时间和空间限制。2006年，京剧被列入第一批国家级非物质文化遗产名录；2010年，京剧被列入联合国教科文组织《人类非物质文化遗产代表作名录》。

　　Peking Opera, known worldwide as the "national opera of China," is considered quintessence of Chinese culture. Originating in the reign of Emperor Qianlong in the Qing Dynasty, it has inherited the artistic characteristics of many opera forms such as Anhui Opera, Han Opera, Kunqu, and Shaanxi Opera. Gradually, it has developed a relatively complete set of performance techniques and methods. Peking Opera integrates music, singing, mime, dance, acrobatics, and martial arts, making its form of expression vivid and colorful. Through long-term stage practices by numerous artists, it has established a technically strong set of standardized conventions and rigorous training system. Its performance techniques combine the real and the virtual, allowing it to largely overcome the limitations of time and space in stage performances. In 2006, Peking Opera was included in the first batch of the National Intangible Cultural Heritage List. In 2010, it was inscribed on the UNESCO Representative List of the Intangible Cultural Heritage of Humanity.

京剧的起源
Origin of Peking Opera

元末明初，经过改良的昆山腔逐渐发展为昆曲。至清朝初期，昆曲因乐曲优雅、语言精妙、表演细腻，受到了清朝贵族的追捧和青睐。当时，北京梨园盛行昆曲和京腔，平民所喜爱的风格各异的地方戏曲被贵族阶层所摒弃。

At the end of the Yuan Dynasty and the beginning of the Ming Dynasty, the improved Kunshan Tune gradually evolved into Kunqu Opera. By the early Qing Dynasty, Kunqu Opera, with its elegant music, exquisite language, and delicate performances, was highly sought after and favored by the aristocrats of the Qing Dynasty. At that time, Beijing's opera circles were dominated by Kunqu Opera and Jingqiang Opera, while various styles of local operas beloved by the common people were shunned by the aristocratic class.

至乾隆时期，各种地方戏曲以为皇帝和太后祝寿为名，纷纷进京献艺。乾隆四十四年（1779 年），秦腔艺人魏长生入京，名动京师。至此，北京的剧坛出现了昆曲、京腔、秦腔等艺术形式相互竞争的局面。

During the Emperor Qianlong period, various local operas came to Beijing to perform in celebration of the emperor and empress dowager's longevity. In the 44th year of the Qianlong era (1779), the Shaanxi Opera performer Wei Changsheng arrived in Beijing, causing a sensation in the capital city. Since then, the Peking Opera circle has seen a competitive artistic landscape among Kunqu, Jingqiang, and Shaanxi Opera.

乾隆五十五年（1790 年），皇帝八十大寿，三庆徽班进京祝寿。此后，由安徽商人投资的戏班接踵而至，演出诸腔杂陈。徽班演出在北京观众群体中大受欢迎，逐渐称雄剧坛。至道光年间（1821 年—1850 年），京剧最终形成以二黄调（徽班腔调）和西皮腔（西秦腔调）为主的腔调特色。一时间，许多著名演员崭露头角。

In the 55th year of the Qianlong Emperor's reign (1790), Sanqing Hui Opera Troupe was summoned to Beijing to offer their congratulations to celebrate the emperor's eightieth birthday. Following this event, troupes funded by Anhui merchants flocked to the capital, presenting a diverse array of performances. The Hui troupe's shows were warmly welcomed by Beijing audience, gradually becoming dominant in the theater scene. By the Daoguang period (1821–1850), Peking Opera finally took shape with the Erhuang Tune (the Hui troupe's melody) and the Xipi Tune (the Western Qin melody) as its main vocal characteristics. During this time, many renowned actors emerged.

　　在京剧的形成过程中，四大徽班进京起到了极大的推动作用。徽班，是以安徽籍（主要为安庆地区）艺人作为主体，同时演唱多种曲调的戏曲班社。徽班最早多活动于安徽、江西、江苏、浙江。乾隆五十五年，为给皇帝祝寿，朝廷从扬州征调了以著名戏曲艺人高朗亭为台柱的三庆班入京，这也成为徽班进京的开始。此后，四喜班、启秀班、霓翠班、和春班、春台班也相继进入京城。

In the formation process of Peking Opera, the entry of the four major Anhui Opera Troupes into Beijing played a significant role. The Hui troupes were primarily composed of artists from Anhui Province (mainly Anqing area) and were known for performing a variety of musical tunes in their theatrical performances. Initially, these troupes were most active in the provinces of Anhui, Jiangxi, Jiangsu, and Zhejiang. In the 55th year of the Qianlong Emperor's reign, to celebrate the emperor's birthday, the famous opera troupe from Yangzhou, led by the renowned performer Gao Langting, known as the mainstay of Sanqing Troupe, was summoned to the capital, marking the beginning of the Hui troupes' arrival in Beijing. Following their success, other troupes such as the Sixi Troupe, Qixiu Troupe, Nicui Troupe, Hechun Troupe, and Chuntai Troupe also made their way to Beijing.

　　在演出过程中，这六个徽班逐步合并为三庆、四喜、春台、和春四大徽班。当时，地方戏曲争奇斗艳，京腔、秦腔等地方剧种在北京已广受欢迎。徽班在原来兼唱多种戏腔的基础上加入京腔、秦腔的唱腔，又吸收了秦腔在剧目、声腔、表演方面的精华。同时，为了适应北京观众的需求，四大徽班充分发挥各班演员的特长，逐渐形成了各自独特的艺术风格。

During the performance process, these six Anhui Opera Troupes gradually merged into four major Anhui Opera Troupes: Sanqing, Sixi, Chuntai, and Hechun. At that time, some local operas were competing with one other for their popularity while Jingqiang Opera and Shaanxi Opera had already been popular in Beijing for a while. The Anhui Opera Troupes added the tunes of Jingqiang and Shaanxi Opera on the basis of their multiple opera tunes, and also absorbed the essence of Shaanxi Opera in terms of repertoire, tunes, and performances. At the same time, in order to meet the needs of Beijing audiences and give full play to the specialties of actors from each troupe, four major Anhui Opera Troupes gradually formed their own unique artistic styles.

四大徽班中，三庆班以连演整本大戏的"轴子"见长，四喜班以演唱昆曲戏的"曲子"著称，和春班以擅演武戏的"把子"取胜，春台班以"童伶"出色。四徽班各见所长，极大丰富了徽班的表演特色和技艺。他们的演出得到了观众的广泛认可，并为当时戏曲市场的繁荣作出了很大贡献。嘉庆、道光年间，湖北地区的汉调（又称楚调）艺人入京，加入徽班演出，徽班艺人又兼习汉调。

Among the four major Anhui Opera Troupes, the Sanqing Troupe excelled in performing full-length plays known as Zhouzi, the Sixi Troupe was renowned for singing Kunqu Operas known as Quzi, the Hechun Troupe won recognition for their martial arts plays known as Bazi, and the Chuntai Troupe was distinguished by their talented child actors known as Tongling. Each of these troupes highlighted their unique strengths, greatly enriching the performance characteristics and skills of the Anhui Opera Troupes. Their shows were widely accepted by audiences and significantly contributed to the prosperity of the opera market at the time. During the Jiaqing and Daoguang periods, artists performing the Han Tune (also known as the Chu Tune) from the Hubei region came to Beijing to join the Anhui Opera Troupes performances, and the Anhui Opera Troupes artists also learned and incorporated the Han Tune into their repertoire.

徽班进京，是京剧形成的决定性事件。四大徽班对京剧的形成有以下四方面的影响。

The entry of Anhui Opera Troupes into Beijing is a decisive event in the formation of Peking Opera. The four major Anhui Opera Troupes had the following four aspects of influence on the formation of Peking Opera.

首先，徽班的表演融合了各种声腔，为京剧乐曲的丰富奠定了基础。其中，西皮高亢激越，二黄深沉稳重，极大地增强了音乐的表现力，使之能够展现不同的情绪及人物性格。

Firstly, the performances of Anhui Opera Troupes integrated various tunes and laid the foundation for the rich music of Peking Opera. Among them, Xipi tunes are high-pitched and impassioned, while Erhuang tunes are deep and steady, which greatly enhanced the expressiveness of music and enabled it to show different emotions and character traits.

其次，徽班入京后，依据北京观众的需求对徽剧剧目进行了大量改编，使情节更符合北京地区观众的观赏习惯，对人物的刻画也更加细腻。同时，徽班艺人广纳昆曲、秦腔等剧种的优秀剧目，扩充了京剧剧目种类，其题材涵盖历史故事、神话传说、民间生活等。

Secondly, after entering Beijing, Anhui Opera Troupes made extensive adaptations on the basis of Anhui Opera repertoires to cater to the tastes of Beijing audiences. This resulted in plots that were more tuned for the local viewers and more delicate character portrayals. At the same time, Anhui Opera artists also selected excellent repertoires from Kunqu Opera and Shaanxi Opera, increasing the types of Peking Opera repertoires and covering themes such as historical stories, myths and legends, and folk life.

再次，徽班进京汇聚了更多优秀的演员，使得不同地区演员的表演风格与技巧相互融合，提高了京剧表演的整体水平。

Thirdly, the entry of Anhui Opera Troupes into Beijing brought together more outstanding actors, enabling the performance styles and skills of actors from different regions to blend with each other, improving the overall level of Peking Opera performances.

最后，徽班进京也为京剧人才培养奠定了基础。大量优秀的戏曲艺人聚集在一起，通过师徒传承使这门艺术得以延续。徽班的表演还吸引了大量不同阶层的观众，并在对戏曲的创新中不断扩大观众群体，广泛的观众基础为京剧的繁荣发展提供了必要条件。

Lastly, the entry of Anhui Opera Troupes into Beijing laid the foundation for the cultivation of Peking Opera performers. A large number of outstanding traditional opera artists gathered together, and through master-apprentice inheritance, the continuation of this art was ensured. Besides, the performances of Anhui Opera Troupes attracted a large number of audiences from different social strata. The audience group was continuously expanded in the innovation of traditional opera. The extensive audience base provides necessary conditions for the prosperous development of Peking Opera.

总之，包容并蓄的徽班将汉调、二黄、西皮、昆曲、秦腔相融合，为各腔调向京剧演变提供了平台。因此，四大徽班进京也被视为京剧诞生的前奏，在京剧发展史上具有重要意义。

In conclusion, the inclusiveness of Anhui Opera Troupes paced the way to integrate Han Opera, Erhuang, Xipi, Kunqu Opera, and Shaanxi Opera, providing a platform for the evolution of various tunes into Peking Opera. Therefore, the entry of the four major Anhui Opera Troupes into Beijing is also regarded as the prelude to the birth of Peking Opera and has important significance in the history of Peking Opera's development.

Exercises

1 Form a group and discuss the following questions.

(1) Do you have any experience of watching a performance of Peking Opera? What is it like?

(2) Why do you think Peking Opera is becoming more and more popular among young people?

2 Choose the best answer to each of the following questions.

(1) Before the emergence of Peking Opera, the educated elite had a preference for _____.

A. Shannxi Opera   B. Anhui Opera

C. Yue Opera   D. Kunqu Opera

(2) What is the significance of the four major Anhui Opera Troupes in the history of Peking Opera?

A. They were the first to perform Peking Opera abroad.

B. They marked the beginning of Peking Opera's popularity.

C. They are considered the founders of modern Peking Opera.

D. Their arrival in Beijing is seen as the prelude to the birth of Peking Opera.

Section 2

京剧的繁荣及主要流派
Prosperity and Main Schools of Peking Opera

经历了漫长的初始发展过程，京剧进入了繁荣期。清道光年间，京剧在北京的戏曲舞台上已经占据了主导地位，逐渐从一个地方剧种发展为全国性的剧种。京剧之所以能成为中国的国粹，离不开一代又一代老艺术家们的传承与创新，他们使京剧艺术始终保持活力和吸引力。20世纪初，京剧走出国门，让世界看到了中国艺术之美，促进了中外文化交流。

After a long initial development process, Peking Opera entered a prosperous period. During the Daoguang period of the Qing Dynasty, Peking Opera had already occupied a dominant position on the opera stage in Beijing. Gradually, it developed from a local opera genre into a national one. The reason why Peking Opera has been able to become the quintessence of China is inseparable from the inheritance and innovation of generations of artists, who have been keeping Peking Opera art always full of vitality and attractiveness. In the early 20th century, Peking Opera also went abroad, showing the beauty of Chinese art to the world and promoting cultural exchanges between China and foreign countries.

清朝同治、光绪年间活跃在舞台上的十三位著名京剧、昆曲艺术家，极大地促进了京剧的发展和繁荣。晚清画师沈蓉圃曾将这十三位艺术家绘入一幅工笔画中，此画名为《同光十三绝》。画中的十三位艺术家分别是老生程长庚、卢胜奎、张胜奎、杨月楼，小生徐小香，武生谭鑫培；青衣梅巧玲、时小福、余紫云，老旦郝兰田，昆旦朱莲芬；京丑刘赶三，昆丑杨鸣玉。

During the reigns of Emperor Tongzhi and Emperor Guangxu in the Qing Dynasty, thirteen famous Peking Opera and Kunqu Opera artists who were active on the stage greatly promoted the development and prosperity of Peking Opera. Shen Rongpu, a painter in the late Qing Dynasty, once painted these thirteen artists in a fine brushwork painting, which was named *Thirteen Outstanding Opera Artists of the Tongzhi and Guangxu Periods*. They include the Laosheng (elder male) performers Cheng Changgeng, Lu Shengkui, Zhang Shengkui, and Yang Yuelou; the Xiaosheng (young male) performer Xu Xiaoxiang; the Wusheng (martial male) performer Tan Xinpei; the Qingyi (dignified female) performers Mei Qiaoling, Shi Xiaofu, and Yu Ziyun; the Laodan (elderly female) performer Hao Liantian; the Kundan (Kunqu female) performer Zhu Lianfen; the Jingchou (Beijing clown) performer Liu Gansan; and the Kunchou (Kunqu clown) performer Yang Mingyu.

《同光十三绝》，（清）沈蓉圃
Thirteen Outstanding Opera Artists of the Tongzhi and Guangxu Periods, painted by Shen Rongpu in the Qing Dynasty

画中的人物惟妙惟肖、栩栩如生，形态自然、各具表情。此画为研究早期京剧的服饰、扮相和各行角色的艺术特征留下了极为珍贵的形象资料。

The figures in the painting are so exquisitely depicted that they are not only vivid and lifelike but also possess natural postures and diverse expressions. This painting has left extremely valuable visual materials for the study of the costumes, makeup, and artistic characteristics of various roles in early Peking Opera.

对于这幅画中十三位京剧和昆曲艺术家能否代表当时京剧的最高水平，学界目前仍有争议，但这些艺术家对京剧艺术的贡献毋庸置疑。他们都因其独特的技艺和对京剧发展所作的贡献而闻名，其艺术遗产至今仍然影响着京剧这种艺术形式。

In academic circles, there is still controversy over whether these thirteen Peking Opera and Kunqu artists depicted in the painting can represent the highest level of Peking Opera performance at that time. However, the contributions these artists made to the art of Peking Opera are beyond no doubt. They are all renowned for their unique skills and contributions to the development of Peking Opera. Their artistic legacies still influence the art form of Peking Opera to this day.

在京剧发展进程中，对独特表演艺术的追求和传承催生了"自成流派"这一特殊现象。简单来说，流派就是京剧表演者运用表演技巧，在其塑造的一系列人物形象中，所体现出来的独特的、区别于其他演员的艺术特色和鲜明的表演风格。每一个流派都有一位在表演艺术方面独树一帜并取得很高成就的宗师，一些年轻表演者学习、模仿其表演技法，于是这种具有特色的表演便逐渐拥有相当数量的门徒和追随者，自此得以广泛传播，在京剧这一大的艺术形式中衍生出众多派系。

In the process of the development of Peking Opera, the pursuit and inheritance of unique performing arts have led to the emergence of a special phenomenon—the formation of independent schools. In simple terms, a school is the unique artistic characteristics and distinct performing styles that Peking Opera performers demonstrate in a series of characters they create by using performing skills and which distinguish them from other actors. Each school has a master who is unique in performing arts and has achieved high accomplishments. Some young performers learn and imitate their performance techniques. Thus, this distinctive style of performance gradually gains a considerable number of disciples and followers. From then on, it is promoted and has derived many schools within the major art form of Peking Opera.

京剧流派的特征通常涉及舞台表演艺术中的唱、念、做、打等方面，不过往往突出体现在唱腔艺术上。不同流派通常也有一些能集中体现其特色的代表性剧目。基于"模仿与学习"的流派传承并非盲目"死记硬背"。比如，程砚秋就要求他的学生充分发挥自身长处，在一定条件下坚决反对死记硬背式的学习。

The characteristics of Peking Opera schools usually involve a series of aspects such as singing, speaking, acting, and fighting in stage performing arts, but they are often prominently reflected in the art of singing. Different schools usually also have some representative repertoires that can centrally reflect the characteristics of their school. The inheritance of schools based on "imitation and learning" is not blind rote learning. For example, Cheng Yanqiu required his students to give full play to their own strengths and firmly opposed rote learning under certain conditions.

从京剧二百余年的发展历史可以看出，一个特定历史时期京剧艺术高峰的出现，总是伴随着京剧艺术流派的蓬勃发展。一个历史时期的京剧代表人物，大多都是京剧流派的创始人。在不同的发展阶段，各流派也呈现出不同的特点。下文将介绍 20 世纪 20 年代的几个主要艺术流派：梅派、程派、尚派和荀派。

From the history of Peking Opera's development over the past two hundred years, it can be seen that the peaks of Peking Opera art in a certain historical period always coincide with the vigorous development of Peking Opera art schools. The representative figures of Peking Opera in a historical period are mostly the founders of the schools. At different development stages, schools have shown different characteristics. The following will introduce several major art schools of the 1920s: the Mei School, the Cheng School, the Shang School, and the Xun School.

梅派为旦角流派，创始人为京剧表演艺术家梅兰芳。梅派艺术博大精深，颇具魅力，在唱、念、做、舞、音乐、服装和剧目方面都有创新和发展。梅派将唱、念、做、舞有机融合，表演强调中和平衡，不主张过分突出某一部分的特点。这种思想体现了中国哲学和美学"中正平和"的思想，追求分寸、恰到好处，反对夸张、过火的表演。

The Mei School is a Dan role school, founded by the Peking Opera performing artist Mei Lanfang. The Mei School's art is profound and charming, with innovations and developments in singing, speaking, acting, dancing, music, costumes, and repertoire. The Mei School integrates singing, speaking, acting, and dancing in a harmonious way, emphasizing moderation and balance, rather than highlighting any single aspect of the performance. This philosophy reflects the neutrality and harmony in the Chinese philosophy and aesthetics, pursuing restraint and appropriateness, and opposing exaggerated or overdone performances.

梅派创始人梅兰芳，是京剧"四大名旦"之首。在中国人心目中，提起京剧，就绕不开"梅兰芳"三个字。他不仅是京剧艺术的传承者，也是这门国粹艺术的革新者。

他在艺术上的造诣极高，同时在人格与人品上也令人称道。梅兰芳独特的艺术风格，最终也成就了以他名字命名的流派。

Mei Lanfang, the founder of the Mei School, is considered the foremost among the "Four Great Dan Actors" of Peking Opera. In the minds of the Chinese people, the art of Peking Opera is inseparable from the name "Mei Lanfang." He was not only a successor of Peking Opera art but also an innovator of this quintessential art form. His artistic achievements were unparalleled, and his character and moral integrity were equally admirable. The unique artistic style of Mei Lanfang ultimately led to the establishment of the school named after him.

梅兰芳（1894—1961），
京剧表演艺术家
**Mei Lanfang (1894–1961), a master
of Peking Opera performance**

梅兰芳是一位精通京剧和昆曲的表演大师。梅派艺术特点的形成，除了得益于梅兰芳在京剧方面的积累和体悟，还得益于他对昆曲艺术的研习。梅兰芳也是京剧艺术的改革家和实践家。他善于将他人艺术之长融于自己的表演，全方位秉承创新、借鉴、改革的原则。在唱腔方面，梅兰芳一改青衣唱腔细高之弊，他的演唱舒展醇厚、刚柔并济、变化丰富，可以通过演唱恰当地表达人物情感。在表演方面，梅兰芳强调人物感情变化，改变了传统青衣重唱轻做的做法，将身段、手法、步法、眼神及面部表情融为一体，处处显得自然顺畅。梅兰芳还借鉴昆曲，重视剧目的舞蹈表演，对丰富旦行艺术作出了重大贡献。

Mei Lanfang was a performing master proficient in both Peking Opera and Kunqu Opera. The formation of the artistic characteristics of the Mei School is not only due to his accumulation and understanding of Peking Opera, but also benefits from his study of Kunqu Opera. Mei Lanfang was also a reformer and practitioner of Peking Opera art. He was good at integrating the strengths of others' arts into his own performances. In all aspects, he adhered to the principles of innovation, reference, and reform. In terms of singing, Mei Lanfang changed the drawback of the high-pitched and thin singing of the Qingyi role. His singing was smooth, mellow, combining hardness and softness, and rich in changes. He could appropriately express the emotions of characters through singing. In terms of performance, he emphasized the emotional changes of characters and changed the traditional practice of the Qingyi role that emphasized singing over acting. He integrated body postures, gestures, footwork, eye expressions, and facial expressions, making everything appear natural and smooth. Mei Lanfang also drew on Kunqu Opera and attached importance to the dance performances in the plays, making significant contributions to enriching the art of the Dan role.

除了表演本身，梅兰芳在传统剧目的整理加工方面同样建树突出。他编演新剧、再创老戏，融合昆曲技法，探索时装戏，具有极强的创新意识。他的加工使得旧剧目焕发新光彩，如《宇宙锋》《贵妃醉酒》。他还创编了众多脍炙人口的新剧目，如《霸王别姬》《穆桂英挂帅》。其中《霸王别姬》为梅派著名代表作，剧中的唱腔、剑舞等精彩片段常演常新，历久不衰。

In addition to his performances themselves, Mei Lanfang made outstanding contributions in the collation and processing of traditional plays. He compiled and performed new plays, recreated old ones, integrated Kunqu Opera techniques, and explored modern plays, showing an extremely strong sense of innovation. His processing made old plays shine with new brilliance, such as *Cosmic Blade* and *Drunken Beauty*. He also created many popular new plays, such as *Farewell My Concubine* and *Mu Guiying Takes Command*. Among them, *Farewell My Concubine* is the famous representative work of the Mei School. The wonderful segments such as the singing and sword dance in the play are often performed with new interpretations and remain popular over times.

除了艺术上的成就，梅兰芳"蓄须拒演"的事迹也是中国抗日战争时期的一段佳话。1937 年"七七事变"后，抗日战争全面爆发，不久上海沦陷。当时在上海生活和演出的梅兰芳，在国内外均享有盛誉。梅兰芳是旦角演员，表演时面部妆容须非常精致，不能有胡须。他意识到自己可能会被日本人强迫演出，于是蓄须明志，以此表明自己坚决不为日军演出的决心。长期不演出使得梅兰芳陷入窘迫，只好卖房子维持生活。直到抗战胜利后，梅兰芳才剃掉胡须，重登舞台继续表演。他拒演的行为，得到了中国民众的敬佩和支持；他的民族气节，激励了无数中国人，为中国文化界树立了榜样。

In addition to his artistic achievements, Mei Lanfang's story of "growing a beard and refusing to perform" is also a much-told tale during the War of Resistance against Japanese Aggression. After the "July 7th Incident" in 1937, the War of Resistance Against Japan fully broke out, and soon Shanghai fell to the Japanese forces. Mei Lanfang, who was living and performing in Shanghai at that time, enjoyed high reputations both at home and abroad. Mei was a Dan actor. When performing, he needed to have a very delicate facial makeup and cannot have a beard. When he realized that he might be forced to perform by the Japanese, he grew a beard to show his determination not to perform for the Japanese army. Due to the long-term absence of performances, Mei fell into financial distress and had to sell his house to make a living. It was not until after the victory of the War that Mei Lanfang shaved off his beard and returned to the stage to continue performing. His act of refusing to perform won the admiration and support of Chinese people. His national integrity inspired countless Chinese people and set an example for the Chinese cultural circle.

　　梅兰芳的艺术成就是中国京剧艺术史上的一座丰碑，其作品在今天仍然是中国人民的精神财富。他高尚的民族气节和精神品质，永远值得后人敬仰和缅怀。

　　Mei Lanfang's artistic achievements are a monument in the history of Peking Opera art in China. His works are still the spiritual wealth of the Chinese people today. His noble national integrity and spiritual qualities will always be worthy of the admiration and remembrance of future generations.

　　程派为旦角流派，创始人为程砚秋。程砚秋勇于创新，扬长避短，根据自己的嗓音条件，创造了新颖别致的唱腔，这种唱腔艺术于 20 世纪 20 年代后期发展为独特的流派。

　　The Cheng School is a genre for Dan roles, founded by Cheng Yanqiu. Cheng Yanqiu was brave in innovation and made the best use of his own advantages and bypassed the disadvantages. According to his own vocal conditions, he created a novel and unique music for voices. In the late 1920s, this kind of vocal art developed into a distinctive school.

程砚秋（1904—1958），
京剧表演艺术家
Cheng Yanqiu (1904–1958), a master of Peking Opera performance

　　程派艺术的精髓在声乐方面尤为突出。鉴于其嗓音高音不足但清醇、沉厚的特点，程砚秋创造出一种婉转幽咽、若断若续、细若游丝般的唱腔，能将剧中人物的哀伤幽怨之情淋漓尽致地表现出来，极具感染力。程砚秋的念白沉稳有力、节奏分明，能充分展现人物的内心情感。在舞台表演方面，程派亦有独到之处。程砚秋功底扎实，手、眼、身、步均可根据自身条件加以雕琢。程砚秋虽然身材高大，但走起来仪态优美、庄重。表演时，程砚秋善于运用眉眼，其"挑眉"的表情能将悲剧女性的情感展现出来，独具魅力。

　　The essence of Cheng School art was particularly prominent in the aspect of vocal music. Given that his voice was not high-pitched enough but was mellow, clear, and deep,

Cheng Yanqiu created a kind of singing style that was gentle and lingering, intermittently delicate like a gossamer. This style could vividly and incisively express the sad and resentful emotions of the characters in the play, and was extremely infectious. Cheng Yanqiu's recitation was steady and powerful, with a distinct rhythm, fully expressing the inner emotions of the characters. In terms of stage performance, the Cheng School also had its own unique features. Cheng Yanqiu had a solid foundation in performance skills, and he could polish his hand gestures, eye expressions, body movements, and steps according to his own conditions. Although he was tall, Cheng Yanqiu walked gracefully and with dignity. When performing, he was good at using his eyes and eyebrows. His expression of "raising the eyebrows" could show the emotions of tragic female characters, which was uniquely charming.

程砚秋是京剧艺术的革新家，他在继承各家精华的基础上，进行卓有成效的创新。他擅长从京剧的其他行当，甚至其他剧种、曲种及民间音乐中汲取养料，将其融入京剧音乐中。如在《锁麟囊》《英台抗婚》中，程砚秋吸收了多种地方戏曲甚至西欧歌曲中的音调。编创成为程派精品剧目的还包括《文姬归汉》《六月雪》《红拂传》等。

Cheng Yanqiu was a reformer of Peking Opera art. Building upon the essence inherited from various sources, he made effective innovations. He was adept at drawing inspiration from other roles in Peking Opera, and even from other types of operas, tunes, and folk music, and integrated these elements into Peking Opera music. In works such as *The Locking Bag* and *Ying Tai's Resistance to Marriage*，he absorbed melodies from various regional operas and even Western European songs. Works like *Cai Wenji's Return to Han*，*Snow in June*, and *The Legend of Hong Funü* were also created and refined into fine pieces of the Cheng School.

程砚秋为京剧的繁荣和发展同样作出了巨大贡献。与梅兰芳的低调稳健不同，程砚秋主张京剧在遵循规则和传统的同时要适应现代社会。中华人民共和国成立后，程砚秋致力于对戏曲遗产进行调查、挖掘和收集，为中国京剧表演理论化提供了资料。

Cheng Yanqiu also made great contributions to the prosperity and development of Peking Opera. Different from Mei Lanfang's low-key and steady approach, he advocated that Peking Opera should adapt to modern society while adhering to rules and traditions. After the founding of the People's Republic of China, he was committed to investigating, excavating and collecting opera heritage, providing materials for theorizing Chinese Peking Opera performance.

程砚秋自学苦读，具有深厚的文化艺术修养。在长期的演出实践中，他从理论上对京剧的诸多根本性问题进行了探索，并通过教学、演讲和著书立说等方式将这些内容公之于众。他积极投身于戏曲人才培养实践，彰显出戏曲教育家的风范。

Cheng Yanqiu studied hard on his own and had profound cultural and artistic accomplishments. In his long-term performing practice, he theoretically explored many fundamental issues of Peking Opera and made them public through teaching, giving speeches, and writing books. He actively practiced in cultivating opera talents, demonstrating the spirit of an opera educator.

抗日战争时期，程砚秋同样拒绝为日本人演出，与梅兰芳先生的"蓄须明志"南北辉映。

During the War of Resistance Against Japan, Cheng Yanqiu also refused to perform for the Japanese. His act, together with Mei Lanfang's decision to grow a beard as a sign of his determination not to perform for the enemy, shone brightly in the north and south of China, setting an inspiring example.

程砚秋不仅取得了极高的个人艺术成就，还在戏曲改革、戏曲教育、文化交流及个人品德等方面对后世产生了极大影响，堪称一代京剧大师。

Cheng Yanqiu not only has extremely high personal artistic achievements, but also has been extremely influential on later generations in aspects such as opera reform, opera education, cultural exchanges, and personal morality. He is a real master in Peking Opera.

尚派也是旦角流派，创始人为京剧表演艺术家尚小云。尚派在保留京剧中旦角原有元素的基础上，在表演形式、场景、服装方面融入了其他元素，内容上更加丰富。尚派根据自身文武兼修、各行皆工的特长，创编了很多传统剧目。在服装上，尚派根据意大利清朝宫廷画家郎世宁的香妃半身戏装像，改进了传统的女靠，并应用到《梁红玉》的角色中，使人物形象更加鲜明。在表演方面，尚派融入了民族戏曲载歌载舞的表演方法。为丰富旦角的表演形式，尚派在旦角表演中加入武生元素。这些都体现了尚派京剧的包容性和较强的可塑性。

尚小云（1900—1976），
京剧表演艺术家
Shang Xiaoyun (1900–1976), a master of Peking Opera performance

The Shang School is also a Dan school in Peking Opera, founded by Shang Xiaoyun, a Peking Opera performing artist. The Shang School retains the original elements of the Dan role in Peking Opera, and integrates other elements in terms of performing forms, scenes, and costumes on this basis, making itself richer in content. Based on its own specialties of being proficient in both civil and martial arts and being skilled in all aspects, the Shang School has recreated many traditional repertoires. In terms of costumes, according to the half-length military portrait of Fragrant Concubine by Giuseppe Castiglione, an Italian court painter of the Qing Dynasty, the traditional female military costume has been improved and applied to the role in *Liang Hongyu*, making the character image more vivid. In terms of performance method, the singing and dancing features in other operas is integrated. In order to enrich the performance forms of the Dan role, elements of martial male roles are added to the Dan's performance. All these reflect the inclusiveness of the Shang School of Peking Opera and show its strong plasticity.

尚派创始人尚小云音域独特，高亢清亮，气力充沛，情绪饱满，念白爽朗直率、情感丰富，表演身段幅度大，有节奏感，夸张却不失美感。尚小云戏路宽广，以青衣和刀马旦见长，编演了很多尚派独有的剧目。尚派的代表作有《福寿镜》《昭君出塞》《战金山》等。

The founder of the Shang School, Shang Xiaoyun, had a unique vocal range, which was high-pitched, clear, full of strength and emotions. His speaking was straightforward and hearty, rich in emotions. The performance movements were large in amplitude, rhythmic, exaggerated yet aesthetically pleasing. Shang Xiaoyun could portray a wide range of character types, specializing in both Qingyi (dignified female role) and Daomadan (warrior female role), and he created many unique plays for the Shang School. Representative works of the Shang School include *The Mirror of Blessing and Longevity*, *The Beauty Zhaojun Leaves for the Frontier*, and *The Battle of Golden Mountain*, among others.

尚小云本人素以热诚重义著称。他广交四海宾朋，为兴办班社，不惜倾其所有。他极为重视戏剧寓教于乐之功能，执着于戏曲教育之大业。为推动京剧艺术的发展，尚小云可谓殚精竭虑、鞠躬尽瘁，全力培养后备人才。其崇高的敬业精神，着实令人敬佩。

Shang himself was known for his warm-heartedness, loyalty, and righteousness. He made friends widely from all over the world. In order to establish an opera troupe, he was willing to give up all he had. He attached great importance to the function of drama in educating through entertainment and was dedicated to the great cause of opera education. For the development of Peking Opera art, he spared no effort and was wholeheartedly committed to cultivating reserve talents. His lofty professional dedication is truly awe-inspiring.

荀派也是旦角流派，其创始人为荀慧生。荀慧生也致力于京剧艺术革新的探索。他汲取了河北梆子旦角艺术之长，融京剧青衣、花旦、闺门旦、刀马旦的表演于一炉，兼收小生、武生等行当的技艺，形成了独树一帜的艺术表演特色。

The Xun School is also a school of the Dan role, founded by Xun Huisheng. Xun Huisheng was also committed to exploring innovations in the art of Peking Opera. He absorbed the strengths of the Dan role art of Hebei Bangzi, integrated the performances of Peking Opera's Qingyi (dignified female role), Huadan (vivacious female role), Guimendan (noble female role), and Daomadan (martial female role) into one, and also incorporated the skills of other roles such as Xiaosheng (young male) and Wusheng (martial male), thereby forming a unique characteristic in artistic performance.

荀派京剧擅长塑造天真活泼、热情奔放的年轻女子形象。荀派特有的"生活化"表演风格，不但丰富了古典戏曲的表现手法，还推动了古典戏曲向现代戏曲的转变，对研究中国戏曲发展史具有特殊意义。其代表作品包括《红娘》《杜十娘》《荆钗记》等。

荀慧生（1900—1968），
京剧表演艺术家
Xun Huisheng (1900–1968), a master
of Peking Opera performance

荀慧生塑造的人物都个性鲜明，比如直言快语的红娘、性格刚烈的尤三姐、淳朴善良的李凤姐等。荀派之所以具有旺盛的生命力，正是因为艺术表现上的生活化及人物塑造上的鲜活化。

The Xun School of Peking Opera excels at creating the images of innocent, lively, and passionate young girls. The unique "life-like" performance style of the Xun School not only enriches the expressive techniques of classical opera but also propels the transition from classical to modern opera. It holds special significance for the study of the history of Chinese opera development. Representative works include *The Matchmaker*, *The Story of Du Shiniang*, and *The Story of the Thorn Hairpin*. The figures created by Xun Huisheng all have distinct personalities, such as the outspoken Red Maid, the strong-willed You Sanjie, and the simple and kind Li Fengjie. The reason why the Xun School has a strong vitality is precisely because it brings art to life and enlivens the characters.

梅派、程派、尚派、荀派的创始人被合称为京剧"四大名旦"。他们不仅在艺术上取得了卓越成就，也极大地推动了京剧艺术的发展，使旦角在京剧中的地位得到了空

前提高。他们的艺术成就和精神风貌，至今仍然激励着一代又一代京剧演员。

The founders of the Mei School, Cheng School, Shang School, and Xun School are jointly known as the "Four Great Dan Masters" of Peking Opera. They not only achieved outstanding artistic accomplishments but also greatly advanced the development of Peking Opera, elevating the status of the Dan roles within the art form to an unprecedented level. Their artistic achievements and spiritual demeanor continue to inspire generations of Peking Opera performers to this day.

自 1852 年广东粤剧团在旧金山开始商演起，中国戏曲传播已走过 170 余年的历史。其中，京剧作为中国戏曲的代表，也在这百余年中努力走向国际舞台。很多京剧表演艺术家也对京剧的海外传播作出了突出贡献。

Since 1852, when a Cantonese opera troupe from Guangdong began performing commercially in San Francisco, the dissemination of Chinese opera has a history of more than 170 years. Throughout more than one century's spreading its influence, Peking Opera, as a representative of Chinese opera, has made its effort to step onto the international stage. Many Peking Opera performing artists have also made outstanding contributions to the overseas dissemination of Peking Opera.

梅兰芳于 1919 年、1924 年和 1956 年先后三次东渡日本演出，每次出访都受到日本各界的热烈欢迎，日本媒体也对梅兰芳的几次公演大加赞赏。由于中国和日本同处汉文化圈，京剧演出在日本的接受度很高。

In 1919, 1924 and 1956, Mei Lanfang went to Japan three times to perform Peking Opera. Each visit was warmly welcomed by all sectors of Japanese society. Japanese media also highly praised Mei Lanfang's several public performances. Since China and Japan are both in the Chinese cultural sphere, the performances in Japan had a high degree of acceptance.

梅兰芳的欧美巡演在国际文化交流方面有着更大的意义。1930 年，受美国大使邀请，梅兰芳前往美国，开启了为期 72 天的轰动演出。在美国，梅兰芳受到各界人士的欢迎和高度赞扬，并结识了许多美国知名艺术家。美国波莫纳学院和南加利福尼亚大学均授予梅兰芳名誉文学博士学位。1935 年，应苏联对外文化协会邀请，梅兰芳在莫斯科和列宁格勒（今圣彼得堡）两地演出。苏联艺术家对梅兰芳的表演艺术甚为推崇，认为梅兰芳的表演为他们提供了有益的借鉴和启示。

Mei Lanfang's European and American tour had a greater significance in international cultural exchange. Invited by the American ambassador in 1930, Mei Lanfang traveled to the United States and launched a 72-day sensational performance. In the US, Mei Lanfang was welcomed and highly praised by people from all walks of life and met many well-known American artists. Both Pomona College and the University of Southern California awarded him an honorary Doctor of Literature degree. In 1935, at the invitation of the All-Union Society for Cultural Relations with Foreign Countries, he performed in Moscow and Leningrad (now St. Petersburg). Soviet artists highly praised his performing arts, believing that they provided them with beneficial references and inspirations.

梅兰芳的演出增进了各国人民对中国古典戏曲的了解，为京剧赢得了国际声誉；同时，这些海外经历也为他的艺术创新提供了灵感。他将西方的表演艺术、审美观念融入京剧，对京剧的表演形式、服装、化妆、舞台设计等方面进行创新和改革，丰富了京剧的艺术表现力。

Mei Lanfang's performances enhanced the understanding of Chinese classical opera among people from various countries and earned international acclaim for Peking Opera. At the same time, his overseas experiences provided inspiration for artistic innovation. He integrated Western performing arts and aesthetic concepts into Peking Opera, innovating and reforming aspects such as performance forms, costumes, makeup, and stage design, thereby enriching the artistic expressiveness of Peking Opera.

1932 年，程砚秋至欧洲进行考察。他游历了欧洲多个国家，参观了当地的著名剧院，仔细观摩西方的戏剧演出，深入了解西方戏剧的表演形式、舞台布景、灯光设计等方面的特点和技术。他还积极参与当地的艺术座谈等交流活动，与欧洲的戏剧界人士、艺术家进行深入沟通和交流，分享彼此对于戏剧艺术的理解和看法，探讨中西方戏剧的差异和共通之处。

In 1932, Cheng Yanqiu went to Europe for a study tour. He traveled to many European countries, visited the renowned local theatres, and carefully observed the Western drama performances, gaining in-depth insights into the characteristics and techniques of Western drama in terms of performance forms, stage settings, and lighting designs. He also actively participated in local art symposiums and other exchange activities, engaging in in-depth communication and exchanges with European theatre figures and artists, sharing their understandings and views on the art of drama, and exploring the differences and similarities between Chinese and Western drama.

在欧洲考察期间，程砚秋受到西方戏剧"非写实"特征的影响。在其公开发表的文章中，程砚秋多次提及"写意""非写实"等理念，这些理念也被视为戏曲演出的准则。程砚秋还探索了西方戏剧的优势，吸收了许多西方的舞台元素（如舞台设备、布景、灯光、戏院设施等）去增加传统戏曲的表现力。

During the study tour in Europe, Cheng Yanqiu was influenced by the "non-realistic" characteristics of Western drama. In his published articles, Cheng mentioned concepts such as "Xieyi" (freehand) and "non-realistic" many times, and these concepts have also been regarded as the criteria for opera performances. Moreover, he also explored the advantages of Western drama and absorbed many Western stage elements such as stage equipment, scenery, lighting, and theater facilities to enhance the expressiveness of traditional Chinese opera.

程砚秋在中西方戏剧交流中所收获的心得，均在他旅欧归来所著的《程砚秋赴欧考察戏曲音乐报告书》中进行了非常详细的阐述。这一戏曲改良方案内容全面、极具跨文化视野，可以说是中国古典戏曲研究的重要著作，对中西方戏剧的交流互鉴产生了深远影响。

All the insights that Cheng obtained through the exchanges between Chinese and Western operas were elaborated in great detail in his *Report on Cheng Yanqiu's Study of Opera Music in Europe* after his return from the trip. This opera improvement plan is very comprehensive and has a remarkable cross-cultural perspective. It can be regarded as an important work in the study of Chinese classical operas and has exerted a profound impact on the mutual learning and exchange between Chinese and Western operas.

在京剧逾两百年的发展史中，这门艺术从未停滞不前或墨守成规。京剧艺术家们从地方戏曲甚至国外戏剧艺术中汲取养分，极大地增强了这门艺术本身的艺术表现力和魅力，成就其国粹的地位。京剧的流派之多、剧目之丰，不仅体现了这门艺术的成熟与繁荣，也映照了艺术家们在不同历史时期对观众需求的深刻洞察和不断创新的精神。这些京剧艺术家的爱国情操、创新精神、钻研精神为京剧增添了无限光彩，而他们也成为后辈的楷模。传统艺术如同在时间的枝头不断绽放的花朵，以独特的姿态诉说着文明的传承与创新。

Throughout its over-two-hundred-year development history, the art of Peking Opera has never remained stagnant or adhered rigidly to established conventions. Peking Opera artists have drawn nourishment from local operas and even foreign dramatic arts, which has significantly enhanced the artistic expressiveness and charm of this art form itself, thus establishing its status as a quintessence of Chinese culture. The numerous schools and abundant repertoires of Peking Opera not only demonstrate the maturity and prosperity of this art but also reflect the artists' profound insights into the needs of the audience and their continuous innovative spirit in different historical periods. The patriotic sentiment, innovative spirit, and studious attitude of these Peking Opera artists have added infinite luster to this quintessential art of Peking Opera and have also served as role models for the younger generations. Traditional arts are like flowers that continuously bloom on the branches of time, speaking of the inheritance and innovation of civilization in a unique manner.

Exercises

1 **Discuss the following questions with your group members.**

(1) Discuss the relationship between the innovation of Peking Opera artists like Mei Lanfang and Cheng Yanqiu and the preservation of traditional Peking Opera elements. How can we strike a balance between innovation and tradition in the development of traditional art forms like Peking Opera?

(2) Discuss the far-reaching and long-term impacts of Peking Opera masters such as Mei Lanfang, Cheng Yanqiu, Shang Xiaoyun, and Xun Huisheng on the development and evolution of Peking Opera and traditional Chinese culture.

2 **Choose the best answer to each of the following questions.**

(1) In the process of Peking Opera's development, the formation of schools mainly reflects _____.

A. the imitation of foreign drama

B. the pursuit of unique performing arts and inheritance

C. the random combination of different performing styles

D. the decline of traditional Peking Opera

(2) Which of the following is NOT a contribution of Mei Lanfang to Peking Opera?

A. He integrated Kunqu Opera techniques into Peking Opera performances.

B. He reformed the Qingyi role's singing style to be more mellow and varied.

C. He sticked to traditional singing styles without innovation.

D. He processed and created many classic plays.

(3) Which of the following is an important factor in the prosperity of Peking Opera?

A. Adhering strictly to traditional performing styles without any change.

B. Ignoring the influence of local operas.

C. The innovation and inheritance of generations of artists.

D. Lack of communication with foreign dramatic arts.

Section 3

京剧角色分类及京剧脸谱
Classification of Roles and Facial Makeup of Peking Opera

京剧与其他很多剧种一样，主要分为四个行当，分别是生、旦、净、丑。行当指戏曲演员根据所演不同的角色类型及其表演艺术上的特点划分的角色类别。每种角色在服装、化妆、动作和唱腔上都有鲜明的特点。

Like many other forms of Chinese opera, Peking Opera is primarily divided into four main Hangdang: Sheng (male roles), Dan (female roles), Jing (painted face roles, typically for male characters with distinctive makeup), and Chou (clown roles, often for comic or villainous characters with a distinctive facial marking). The term "Hangdang" refers to the classification of roles in traditional Chinese opera, based on the types of characters portrayed and the unique characteristics of their performance art. Each role type has distinct features in terms of costume, makeup, movement, and vocal style.

生，泛指剧中男主角。随着表演艺术的提高与细化，生行逐渐分化，清初时已经形成了不同支系。按照人物的年龄、身份、性格特征和表演特点，生大致可分为老生、小生、武生、娃娃生等。

The term "Sheng" generally refers to the male protagonist in a drama. As the art of performance has improved and become more refined, the category of Sheng has gradually differentiated, and by the early Qing Dynasty, different subcategories had already been established. Typically, Sheng can be broadly divided into Laosheng, Xiaosheng, Wusheng, and Wawasheng based on the character's age, status, personality traits, and performance characteristics.

老生主要扮演中年以上、性格正直刚毅的正面人物，因多戴髯口，故又称须生、胡子生。老生角色重唱功、用真声，念韵白，动作造型庄重端方。京剧《斩马谡》里的诸葛亮、《将相和》里的蔺相如均为老生角色。老生中还分出一行叫作红生，主要扮演三国戏中的关羽和宋朝开国皇帝赵匡胤，因勾画红脸，故称红生。红生是戏曲舞台上独特的造型。

Laosheng in Peking Opera primarily portrays middle-aged and older characters with upright and resolute personalities. Often wearing a beard, they are also known as Xusheng or "bearded roles." Laosheng roles emphasize singing with the true voice, reciting in a rhythmic manner, and performing movements that are solemn and dignified. Characters such as Zhuge Liang in *Beheading of Ma Su* and Lin Xiangru in *The Harmony of Civil and Military* are examples of Laosheng roles. Within the Laosheng category, there is a special type known as Hongsheng, which mainly depicts historical figures like Guan Yu from the Three Kingdoms stories and Zhao Kuangyin, the founding emperor of the Song Dynasty. These characters are referred to as Hongsheng due to their red facial makeup, symbolizing their loyalty and bravery. Hongsheng is a distinctive presence on the opera stage, known for its vivid and symbolic appearance.

《斩马谡》中的诸葛亮
Zhuge Liang in *Beheading Ma Su*

《华容道》中的关羽
Guan Yu in *Huarong Trail Encounter*

与老生相对，小生扮演青年男性。小生在不同剧种中的表演各具特色，装扮不戴胡子，动作造型儒雅倜傥，如经典传统剧目《白蛇传》中的许仙。

In contrast to Laosheng, Xiaosheng represents young male characters. Xiaosheng performances vary in style across different opera genres, with the characters typically not wearing a beard and exhibiting elegant and debonair movements. Xu Xian from the classic traditional play *The Legend of the White Snake* is a typical figure of Xiaosheng.

武生扮演擅长武艺的人物角色，分长靠武生和短打武生两类。长靠武生扮演大将，以扎大靠、穿厚底靴而得名，重腰腿工和武打，表现人物的大将风度和英武气概，如京

《白蛇传》中的许仙
Xu Xian in *The Legend of the White Snake*

剧《长坂坡》里的赵云就是长靠武生。短打武生穿抱衣抱裤和薄底靴，动作轻捷矫健，跌扑翻打勇猛炽烈，代表角色有《十字坡》中的武松、《三岔口》中的任堂惠。

《十字坡》中的武松
Wu Song in *Crossroads Ridge*

Wusheng portrays characters who are adept in martial arts, divided into two types: Changkao Wusheng and Duanda Wusheng. Changkao Wusheng, playing the roles of generals, is named for wearing elaborate armor and thick-soled boots. They focus on mid-air acrobatics and combat, showcasing the character's grand general demeanor and heroic valor. For instance, Zhao Yun in the Peking Opera *The Changban Slope* is an example of Changkao Wusheng. Duanda Wusheng, on the other hand, wears tight-fitting clothing and thin-soled boots, characterized by close combat, agile and robust movements, and fierce and passionate fighting skills. Representative roles include Wu Song in *Crossroads Ridge* and Ren Tanghui in *San Cha Kou*.

娃娃生专门扮演儿童角色，头上戴孩儿发，身上穿儿童服装。京剧《三娘教子》中的薛倚哥、《汾河湾》中的薛丁山均为娃娃生角色。

Wawasheng is a role type specifically for portraying children, characterized by wearing childlike hairdos and children's costumes. In Peking Opera, roles such as Xue Yige in *San Niang Teaching Her Son* and Xue Dingshan in *At Fenhe Bay* are performed by Wawasheng actors.

旦行扮演的是不同年龄、不同身份及不同性格的女性角色。旦角大致分为正旦、花旦、闺门旦、武旦、老旦、彩旦几种类型行当。这里主要介绍正旦、花旦、武旦和老旦。

《三娘教子》中的薛倚哥
Xue Yige in *San Niang Teaching Her Son*

Dan represents female roles, and actors in this category portray a wide range of female characters of different ages and personalities. Dan roles are further divided into subtypes such as Zhengdan, Huadan, Guimendan, Wudan, Laodan, and Caidan. Zhengdan, Huadan, Wudan, and Laodan are mainly introduced here.

　　正旦，因常穿青素褶子，故又称青衣，主要扮演举止端庄的青年或中年女性，多为正剧或者悲剧人物。正旦造型娴静端庄，多用韵白，唱、念、做诸功兼重。典型的正旦角色有《白蛇传》中的白素贞。

Zhengdan is also known as Qingyi, often dressed in plain blue garments. Zhengdan primarily portrays dignified young or middle-aged female characters, often in serious or tragic roles. The Zhengdan character is depicted as gentle and dignified, with a strong emphasis on singing, recitation, and acting skills. Typical Zhengdan roles include Bai Suzhen in *The Legend of the White Snake*.

《白蛇传》中的白素贞
Bai Suzhen in *The Legend of the White Snake*

　　花旦，与正旦相对，扮演性格活泼开朗或泼辣豪爽的青年女性，常带有喜剧色彩。花旦大多着短褂、短裤、短袄、短裙，造型妩媚妍丽、娇憨活泼，语言更接近于日常生活，唱腔秀丽灵巧，动作比较灵敏。经典京剧剧目《红娘》中的红娘就是花旦。

Huadan, in contrast to Zhengdan, portrays young female characters who are lively, cheerful, or even bold and unrestrained, often with a touch of comedy. Huadan characters typically wear short jackets, short pants, short coats, and short skirts, and are characterized by their charming, beautiful, cute and lively appearances. Their language is closer to daily life, singing styles are delicate and dexterous, and movements are agile and full of vitality. The matchmaker in the classic Peking Opera play *Hong Niang* is an example of Huadan.

《红娘》中的红娘
The matchmaker in *Hong Niang*

老旦是扮演老年妇女角色的行当，重唱功，如京剧《穆桂英挂帅》中的佘太君。

Laodan is the role type that portrays elderly women characters, focusing on singing skills. She Taijun in the Peking Opera *Mu Guiying Takes Command* is a typical figure of Laodan.

《穆桂英挂帅》中的佘太君
She Taijun in *Mu Guiying Takes Command*

武旦是一些精通武艺的女性角色，塑造的是女英雄、女侠客、女将军之类的人物（如《红鬃烈马》中的代战公主）。武旦行内还可分两类：一类为穿长靠、插靠旗的女将，即长靠武旦或刀马旦；另一类为穿战衣战裙、短打装扮、无官职的勇武女侠，即短打武旦。刀马旦重身段功架，强调角色的优雅和仪态，经常描绘骑马或持武器的女性；短打武旦重跌扑翻打，身手矫健骁勇，展示角色在行动中的敏捷和勇敢。这些角色经常涉及复杂的打斗场面和武术表演。这两种武旦角色在京剧中都是不可或缺的，为描绘各种戏剧性叙事中强大且有能力的女性角色增添了深度。

Wudan in Peking Opera are female roles proficient in martial arts, portraying heroines, female swordsmen, female generals, and other characters (e.g. Princess Daizhan in *The Fiery-maned Ferocious Horse*). Within the category of female warriors in Peking Opera, there are two types: one is the female general who wears long armor and flags, also known as Changkao Wudan or Dao Ma Dan (a female role skilled in both martial arts and horsemanship); the other is Duanda Wudan, namely valiant female swordsman who wears battle clothes and battle skirts,

《红鬃烈马》中的代战公主
Princess Daizhan in *The Fiery-maned Ferocious Horse*

dressed in a short combat outfit, and has no official position. Dao Ma Dan focuses on the postures and gestures, emphasizing the elegance and demeanor of the characters. It often depicts women riding horses or holding weapons. The second type of female warrior focuses on acrobatic fighting skills such as falling, lunging, somersaulting, and fighting. They are agile and valiant, demonstrating the agility and bravery of the characters during actions. These roles often involve complex fighting scenes and martial arts performances. Both types of female warrior roles are indispensable in Peking Opera, adding depth to the portrayal of powerful and capable female characters in various dramatic narratives.

净指的是京剧中的花脸，以面部化妆勾勒脸谱为突出标志。常扮演英勇有力、性格豪迈粗犷的角色。净角唱腔音色洪亮宽阔，动作大开大阖、顿挫鲜明。净行还细分为正净、副净、武净三大类。比如包公就是正净，以唱功为主。副净一般是一出戏的次要角色或奸佞角色，比如曹操、董卓等。武净侧重武打戏。

Jing, known as the "painted face" in Peking Opera, is distinguished by its facial makeup that outlines the facial patterns. These roles often depict characters who are valiant and strong, with bold and rugged personalities. The vocal timbre of Jing roles is loud and resonant, and their movements are grand, with distinct pauses. The category of Jing is further divided into three main types: Zhengjing (main painted face), Fujing (secondary painted face), and Wujing (martial painted face). For instance, the well-known character Bao Gong is a Zheng Jing, focusing primarily on singing. Fujing often plays minor roles or villainous characters in a play, such as Cao Cao and Dong Zhuo. Wujing specializes in martial combat scenes.

《铡美案》中的包公
Bao Gong in *The Case of Executing Chen Shimei*

《群英会》中的曹操
Cao Cao in *Gathering of Heroes*

丑角面部化妆时用白粉在鼻梁眼窝间勾画脸谱，俗称小花脸。丑角的表演一般不重唱功，而是以念白的口齿清楚、清脆流利为主，多用日常语言，表现上层人物时才用韵律化的念白。丑角用幽默诙谐的对话和肢体语言来吸引观众，是对表演中严肃元素的一种平衡。丑角可以表现幽默、机智的正面人物形象，也可以表现灵魂丑恶、道德败坏的反面人物。

The Chou role, characterized by the application of white makeup with patterns drawn between the nose bridge and the eye sockets, is commonly referred to as the "little painted face." The performance of Chou roles typically does not emphasize singing skills. Instead, it focuses on clear and crisp recitation, often using daily language. Only when portraying upper-class characters will it use rhythmical spoken lines. Chou roles engage the audience with humorous and witty dialogue and body language, serving as a balance to the serious elements in the performance. They can portray humorous and witty positive characters, as well as negative characters with evil souls and corrupt morals.

根据扮演人物的身份、性格和技术特点，丑角还可以分为文丑和武丑。文丑有扮演帝王身边侍从或权臣等的袍带丑、扮演儒生书吏的方巾丑、扮演花花公子的褶子丑、扮演下层百姓的茶衣丑和扮演男性老年角色的老丑等。武丑讲究吐字清晰真切，语调清脆，动作敏捷，注重翻、跳、跌、扑的武功，扮演机智幽默、武艺高超的人物。

Chou roles are divided into two main types based on the characters' status, personality, and technical skills: Wenchou (civilian clown) and Wuchou (martial clown). Wenchou encompasses various subtypes, such as Paodaichou, portraying attendants or powerful officials around emperors in regal robes; Fangjinchou, depicting scholars or clerks with square headcloths; Zhezichou, characterizing dandies or playboys; and Chayichou or Laochou, representing commoners or elderly men. Wu Chou, in contrast, is known for clear and distinct pronunciation, a crisp intonation, and agile movements. They focus on acrobatic martial arts skills, including tumbling, jumping, falling, and tackling, often portraying characters who are witty, humorous and highly proficient in martial arts.

丑角的脸谱
An example of the facial makeup of Chou role

脸谱的起源与古时参加狩猎或者祭祀的舞者们所戴的面具有关，色彩浓烈丰富、五官突出。后来这种装饰的色彩和纹样被用于戏曲，逐渐发展为程式化的脸谱。京剧脸谱是一种独特的造型手法，演员根据剧作中的人物性格、身份、社会地位等，用中国传统色彩在面部进行夸张的描绘，以展现人物形象、突出角色特征。

The origin of facial makeup, or Lianpu, is related to the masks worn by dancers in ancient times who participated in hunting or sacrificial rituals. These masks were characterized by their intense, rich colors, and exaggerated facial features. Later, these decorative colors and patterns were adopted in traditional opera, gradually evolving into the stylized facial makeup. In Peking Opera, the facial makeup is an exaggerated depiction on the actor's face using traditional Chinese colors, based on the character's personality, identity, and social status in the drama. This is a unique makeup styling technique to present the character's image and highlight the role's characteristics.

京剧脸谱一般指净角的花脸。花脸脸谱的面部主要选用赤、白、黑、黄、青、金、银等色，辅之以其他颜色衬托主色调。京剧脸谱具有强烈的视觉冲击力和张力，能使人眼前一亮，产生夺人眼球的舞台效果。复杂的面部化妆是一种符号语言，可以帮助观众快速识别和理解每个角色的本质。

Peking Opera facial makeup generally refers to the painted faces of the Jing roles. The facial makeup primarily uses colors such as red, white, black, yellow, green, gold, and silver, supplemented by other colors to set off the main hue. The facial makeup in Peking Opera has a strong visual impact and tension, which can catch people's eyes and create a striking stage effect. The intricate facial makeup serves as a symbolic language, helping the audience quickly identify and understand the essence of each character.

在中国传统文化中，红色是吉祥之色。在很多节庆中，中国人都会使用红色作为装饰。在京剧中，红色还有"正义"的寓意。忠义、耿直的义士的脸谱多为红色，比较典型的有《三国演义》里的关羽、《杨家将》里的孟良。

In traditional Chinese culture, the color red is considered auspicious and is widely used in many celebrations as a decorative element. In Peking Opera, red also symbolizes justice. Characters known for their loyalty, righteousness, and uprightness often have facial makeup predominantly in red. Some typical examples include Guan Yu from *Romance of Three Kingdoms* and Meng Liang from *The Generals of the Yang Family*.

黑色在脸谱文化中象征性格严谨、刚强、勇敢、刚正不阿、铁面无私。经典剧目《秦香莲》中的包拯、《桃园结义》中的张飞均是黑色脸谱的代表角色。

In the culture of facial makeup, the color black symbolizes a character with a strict, strong, brave, and upright personality—someone who is impartial and incorruptible. Classic characters such as Bao Zheng from the play *Qin Xianglian* and Zhang Fei from *The Oath of the Peach Garden* are representatives of the black facial makeup.

在京剧中，白色赋予人物喜怒无常、阴森的情感特质。曹操是白色脸谱的代表角色。大面积的白色加上细长弯曲的黑色纹路，表现了曹操心思复杂、善于心计的枭雄形象。

In Peking Opera, the color white is given to characters who are characterized by capricious emotions and a sinister aura. Cao Cao is a quintessential character represented with a white facial makeup.The broad application of white, complemented by thin, curved black lines, reflects his intricate mind and cunning nature, embodying the image of a shrewd and formidable leader.

紫色妆容通常表现聪明和成熟的人物特点。这种颜色可以用于年长的政治家或聪明的学者这样的角色，暗示复杂性和反思性。

Characters with purple facial makeup typically represent individuals who are intelligent and mature. This color can be used for roles such as elderly statesmen or wise scholars, often suggesting complexity and a reflective nature.

拥有黄色或金色面部妆容的人物通常与强大和雄心勃勃联系在一起。这种颜色可用于皇帝或高级官员等角色。

Characters with yellow or gold facial makeup are typically associated with powerful and ambitious individuals. This color can be used for roles such as emperors or high-ranking officials.

蓝色或绿色妆容通常表现凶狠、冲动和好斗的人物性格，常用于军事指挥官和战士。

Blue or green facial makeup typically exhibit fierce, impulsive, and combative personalities, commonly used for military commanders and warriors.

Exercises

1 **Answer the following questions.**

(1) What are the four major roles in Peking Opera?

(2) What subcategories can Sheng be divided into in Peking Opera? And what are their respective characteristics?

(3) How does the Chou role contribute to the overall narrative and emotional balance of the performance in Peking Opera?

2 **Choose the best answer to each of the following questions.**

(1) Which of the following group of words could best describe Laosheng roles in Peking Opera?

A. Positive, righteous, scholarly.

B. With martial skills, positive, brave.

C. Graceful, young, male.

D. Red-faced.

(2) If the following character is to play in a Peking Opera, which of them does not belong to the Dan role?

A. Cinderella.

B. Mulan.

C. Hera.

D. Archelaus.

(3) Which of the following facial makeups represents the role of Cao Cao in *Romance of the Three Kingdoms*?

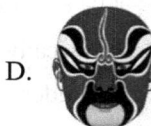

A.

B.

C.

D.

(4) Red facial makeup in Peking Opera usually represents _____.

    A. treachery   B. bravery

    C. cowardice   D. craftiness

(5) Black facial makeup in Peking Opera is often associated with_____.

    A. kindness   B. loyalty

    C. deceitfulness   D. weakness

Section 4

京剧脸谱的绘制技法
Painting Techniques of Facial Makeup in Peking Opera

    绘制京剧脸谱时必须要了解所绘人物的性格、身份和背景，因为脸谱的色彩、图案与这些因素紧密相连，如红脸的关羽代表忠义，白脸的曹操表示奸诈。熟悉各种脸谱谱式也很重要，比如整脸是整个脸膛以一种颜色为主再勾画五官，三块瓦脸用黑色突出眉、眼、鼻窝等部位，十字门脸是从脑门至鼻梁有通天立柱纹与左右眼窝黑纹相连呈"十"字，等等，不同谱式体现不同的人物性格特点。

When painting Peking Opera facial makeup, it's necessary to understand the personality, identity and background of the character being depicted. This is crucial because the colors and patterns of the facial makeup are closely related to these factors. For example, Guan Yu with a red face represents loyalty and righteousness, while Cao Cao with a white face symbolizes treachery. Meanwhile, one should also be familiar with various patterns of the facial makeup. For instance, the "whole face" pattern mainly features one color covering the whole face with the facial features outlined; the "three-tile face" pattern uses black to highlight parts such as eyebrows, eyes, and nasal fossae; the "cross-door face" has a vertical line running from the forehead to the bridge of the nose, which connects with the black lines at the left and right eye sockets, forming a shape like the Chinese character " 十 ," etc. Different patterns reflect different personality traits of the characters.

绘制工具材料的选择也有讲究，颜料可以用京剧脸谱专用油彩颜料，色彩浓郁、持久且覆盖性好；画笔要准备不同大小的毛笔，勾线用小毛笔，填色用稍大些的羊毫、兼毫毛笔。初学者也可以用国画颜料或水彩笔进行绘制。

The selection of painting tools and materials also requires attention. As for pigments, special oil paints for Peking Opera facial makeup can be used, which have rich colors, good durability, and excellent covering ability. Different sizes of writing brushes should be prepared. Small writing brushes are used for outlining, while slightly larger goat-hair or combination hair brushes are used for filling in colors. Beginners can also use traditional Chinese painting pigments or watercolor pens instead.

开始绘制时，绘画者应先用铅笔或炭笔在纸上轻轻画出脸谱面部大致轮廓，包括脸型和五官位置，要保证左右对称，之后沿着铅笔的痕迹清晰地勾画出轮廓；接着根据人物性格选取合适的底色进行涂抹，如忠诚勇敢的角色用红色、正直刚毅的角色用黑色等，涂抹的时候要均匀、平整，让底色完全覆盖脸谱表面；然后在底色上依据人物特点绘制有象征意义的图案和线条，如代表身份地位的龙纹、虎纹，表现性格的云纹、波纹等，绘制时要注意线条的粗细、疏密、曲直变化；再用毛笔和颜料对图案进行晕染，让色彩过渡自然，增强立体感和层次感；最后对眼睛、眉毛、嘴等关键部位精细勾勒，突出五官的神态和表情，勾勒的线条要刚劲有力、流畅自然。完成绘制后要整体检查一遍，确保没有遗漏的地方，并保证脸谱线条清晰、颜色均匀。如果有不满意的地方，比如颜色不够饱满或者线条有瑕疵，就用相应的颜料、画笔进行修补完善。

When starting to paint, one should first use a pencil or charcoal pencil to gently sketch the approximate outline of the facial makeup on the paper, including the shape of the face and the positions of the facial features. Make sure that the left and right sides are symmetrical. After that, clearly draw the outline along the marks left by the pencil. Then, choose an appropriate base color according to the character's personality and apply it. For example, red is often used for loyal and brave characters, while black is used for upright and resolute ones. When applying the color, it should be even and smooth so that the base color can completely cover the surface of the facial makeup. Next, draw symbolic patterns and lines on the base color according to the characteristics of the character. For example, dragon patterns and tiger patterns represent status and position, and cloud patterns and ripple patterns reflect personality traits. Pay attention to the changes in the thickness, density, and curvature of the lines when drawing. After that, use a writing brush and pigments to blend the colors of the patterns so that the color transition is natural and the three-dimensional and layered sense is enhanced. Finally, carefully outline the key parts like eyes, eyebrows, and mouth to highlight the expressions of the facial features. The lines outlined should be vigorous, forceful, smooth, and natural. After the painting is completed, check it as a whole to ensure there is no omission, and make sure the lines are clear and the colors are even. If there are any unsatisfactory parts, such as insufficiently saturated colors or flawed lines, use corresponding pigments and brushes to repair and improve them.

1 绘制关公京剧脸谱
Painting Facial Makeup of Guan Gong in Peking Opera

关羽，又称关公，是中国东汉末年蜀国名将。在中国传统文化中，关羽是忠诚、正义和勇敢等美德的代表，备受尊崇和敬仰。在中国古典小说《三国演义》中，关羽因看不惯有权势之人的欺凌而杀了霸凌之人，逃至涿县，遇到了同样胸怀正义和宏大志向的刘备和张飞，三人意气相投，遂在桃园结为异姓兄弟。这就是著名的"桃园三结义"。三人都担忧国家命运，立誓拯救苍生，最终一起成就了一番事业，建立三国中的蜀国。这段故事成为中国传统文化的经典，在各类戏曲中广为传唱。

Guan Yu, also known as Guan Gong (Lord Guan), was a famous general of the Kingdom of Shu in the late Eastern Han Dynasty of China. In traditional Chinese culture, Guan Yu is a representative of virtues such as loyalty, justice, and bravery, and is highly respected and venerated. In the Chinese classic novel *Romance of the Three Kingdoms*, Guan Yu couldn't bear to see the bullying by the powerful, and killed the bully. He then fled to Zhuo County, where he met Liu Bei and Zhang Fei who also harbored a sense of justice and lofty aspirations. The three of them hit it off immediately and thus became sworn brothers in a peach orchard. This is the very famous story of "The Sworn Brotherhood in the Peach Orchard." The three of them were concerned about the fate of the country and swore to save the common people. Eventually, they achieved great undertakings together and established the Kingdom of Shu among the Three Kingdoms. This story has become a classic in traditional Chinese culture and is widely sung in various traditional operas.

在《三国演义》故事中，关羽对刘备忠心耿耿，无论面临何种艰难险阻，也从未动摇过。在与曹操军队的交战中，刘备军队战败，关羽为了保护刘备的两位夫人，暂时归降曹操。当时，曹操十分欣赏关羽的武艺和忠义，一心想要将他收于麾下，不仅以礼相待，还提出了非常丰厚的条件挽留关羽。然而，当关羽得知刘备在袁绍处，毅然决定离开曹操去寻找刘备。一路上，关羽勇闯五关，斩杀六将，面对重重阻碍也毫不退缩，只为回到刘备身边。这样的忠诚和坚定，使关羽这一角色深受人们喜爱。这个故事也是"身在曹营心在汉""过关斩将"等成语的来源。

In the story of *Romance of the Three Kingdoms*, Guan Yu was always loyal to Liu Bei and never wavered no matter what difficulties and obstacles he faced. During the battle between Liu Bei and Cao Cao, Liu Bei's army was defeated. In order to protect Liu's two wives, Guan Yu temporarily surrendered to Cao Cao. At that time, Cao Cao greatly admired Guan Yu's martial arts skills and loyalty, and was eager to recruit him into his camp. During the time of staying in Cao's camp, Cao Cao not only treated him with courtesy but also offered very generous conditions to persuade Guan Yu to stay in his army. However, when Guan Yu learned that Liu Bei was with Yuan Shao, he resolutely decided to leave Cao Cao and set out to find Liu Bei. Along the way, Guan Yu bravely broke through five passes and slew six generals. Facing numerous obstacles, he never flinched, and there was only one belief in his heart—to return to Liu Bei's side. Such loyalty and determination have made the character of Guan Yu a favorite. This story is also the origin of the Chinese idioms such as "身在曹营心在汉" (having his heart in Liu's army while physically staying in Cao's camp) and "过关斩将" (breaking through passes and slaying generals).

《过五关》是京剧红生戏的传统剧目，取材于《三国演义》第二十七回。京剧中关羽的忠义故事非常感人。故事中，关羽不顾重重困难，离开曹操，终于与刘备团聚。作为对曹操先前善意的回报，当关羽和曹操再次在战场上相遇时，关羽选择不杀曹操。

The Farewell to Cao Cao and Slaying of Generals is a traditional play of the Hongsheng role in Peking Opera, which is based on the 27th chapter of *Romance of the Three Kingdoms*.

The story of Guan Yu's loyalty and righteousness in Peking Opera is really touching. In the story, Guan Yu left Cao Cao despite numerous difficulties and finally reunited with Liu Bei. As a return for Cao Cao's previous kindness, when Guan Yu and Cao Cao met again on the battlefield, Guan Yu chose not to kill Cao Cao.

虽然在《三国演义》小说和相关戏剧中，关羽的故事有虚构的部分，但是关羽这个人物的精神内涵符合中国传统文化的内核——勇敢、忠义。关羽既是一位杰出的历史人物，又是许多中国人的世俗信仰。他的形象和精神跨越了时空，在传统文化和现代文化中都散发着独特的魅力，激励着人们追求正义、勇敢和诚信。

Although some parts of Guan Yu's stories in the novel *Romance of the Three Kingdoms* and related operas are fictional, the spiritual connotation of this figure aligns with the core of the traditional Chinese culture—courage, loyalty, and righteousness. Guan Yu is not only an outstanding historical figure but also a secular belief for many Chinese people. His image and spirit have transcended time and space, exuding a unique charm in both traditional and modern cultures, inspiring people to pursue justice, bravery, and integrity.

扫描二维码获取关公京剧脸谱绘制方法与教学视频
Scan the QR-code to get the methods and teaching video of painting facial makeup of Guan Gong in Peking Opera

所需材料：一支铅笔；一块橡皮；红色、黑色和肉色水彩笔。

Material needed: a pencil; an eraser; red, black, and flesh-tone watercolor pens.

2 绘制包公京剧脸谱
Painting Facial Makeup of Bao Gong in Peking Opera

包拯，又称包公，是北宋时期一位颇受赞誉的官员，在中国被视为正义的化身。在漫长的历史中，他的传奇故事出现在各种文学和戏剧作品中。

Bao Zheng, also known as Bao Gong, was a well-praised official of the Northern Song Dynasty, who is respected as a symbol of justice in China. Throughout the long history, his legendary stories have appeared in a variety of literary and dramatic works.

包公的典型形象是黑脸，额头上有一个白色的月牙形胎记。关于包公的故事大多围绕他与权贵的斗争，这些权贵甚至包括皇亲国戚。皇帝赐予他三副铡刀，用来处决罪犯：狗头铡用于犯罪的平民，虎头铡用于官员，龙头铡用于皇亲国戚。

Bao Gong's typical image is a black face with a white crescent-shaped birthmark on his forehead. Most of the stories about him are about his determination to fight against those higher-ranked officials, even the relatives of the emperor. He had also been given three huge choppers by the emperor to execute criminals: one decorated with a dog's head for commoners, one with a tiger's head for government officials and one with a dragon's head for imperial kinsfolk.

传统京剧剧目《铡美案》讲述的就是包公审理的一桩著名案件。陈世美本是个穷苦书生，家有妻子秦湘莲和两个孩子。秦湘莲一直全力支持他参加科举考试。然而，陈世美高中状元并得到皇帝赏识后，隐瞒了自己已有妻儿的事实，娶了公主为妻。为了不让谎言被戳穿，陈世美竟派杀手去杀害自己的家人，以保住驸马的荣华富贵。包公得知秦香莲的冤情后，不顾公主的阻挠，严厉惩处了陈世美，用龙头铡将其斩首。

One of his most famous cases is performed in the traditional Peking Opera *The Case of Executing Chen Shimei*. Chen Shimei was originally a poor scholar who had a wife named Qin Xianglian and two kids. His wife had been fully supporting him while he was to participate in the Imperial Examination. However, after he got the first place in the examination and was recognized by the Emperor, he married one of the princesses by hiding the fact that he had a wife and children back at home. To cover up the truth, Chen then sent assassinators to kill his family so that he could continue to enjoy the glory and wealth that the royal marriage brought him. When Bao Gong got to know Qin's grievance, he severely punished Chen and executed him with the dragon-head chopper despite the princess's objection.

包公的故事不仅为中国人所津津乐道，还流传到了日本、韩国、新加坡等国。包公不仅是一个历史人物，更承载着中国民间文化中对公正、正义的追求。

扫描二维码获取包公京剧脸谱绘制方法与教学视频
Scan the QR-code to get the methods and teaching video of painting facial makeup of Bao Gong in Peking Opera

The stories of Bao Gong are not only widely beloved by Chinese people, but also have spread to many countries such as Japan, Republic of Korea, and Singapore. He is not only a historical figure but also carries the pursuit of fairness and justice in Chinese folk culture.

所需材料：一支铅笔；一块橡皮；红色、黑色和肉色水彩笔。
Material needed: a pencil; an eraser; red, black, and flesh-tone watercolor pens.

Exercises

1 **Answer the following questions.**

(1) What can the red face of Guan Gong reveal about his character?

(2) What does the black face and moon-shaped mark of Bao Gong imply about his character?

(3) What kind of core cultural values of China are manifested in the Chinese people's love for Guan Gong and Bao Gong?

Practice painting the face.

Choose one of the two facial makeup patterns and practice drawing it.

3 | 绘制孙悟空京剧脸谱
Painting Facial Makeup of Sun Wukong in Peking Opera

孙悟空，又称美猴王，是中国神话和文学中最具标志性的角色之一。他集智慧与勇气于一身，以敢于挑战权威的叛逆精神闻名于世，更因其护送唐僧西天取经、历尽艰辛的传奇故事，成为深受人们喜爱的神话英雄。

Sun Wukong, also known as the Monkey King, is one of the most iconic figures in Chinese mythology and literature. Blending wisdom and courage, he is renowned for his rebellious spirit that dares to challenge authority. His legendary journey, on which he escorted Tang Monk on a pilgrimage to the West to obtain Buddhist sutras despite numerous hardships, has made him a beloved mythological hero cherished by people.

小说《西游记》生动刻画了孙悟空的成长历程。一开始，孙悟空肆意追求无拘无束的绝对自由，但在护送唐僧取经的过程中历经重重磨难后，孙悟空开始对自由有了新的认识。他逐渐褪去顽劣本性，对唐僧生发出真挚的师徒之情，无论是被误解还是受责罚，都始终不离不弃，恪守护法之责，最终在取得真经后受封"斗战胜佛"。

The novel *Journey to the West* vividly portrays Sun Wukong's journey of growth. Initially, Sun Wukong recklessly pursued absolute freedom without constraint. However, after going through numerous hardships during the process of escorting Tang Monk to obtain Buddhist sutras, Sun Wukong began to have a new understanding of freedom. Gradually shedding his mischievous nature, he developed a sincere master-disciple bond with Tang Monk. Whether facing misunderstandings or punishments, he always stayed by Tang Monk's side and earnestly fulfilled his duty as a guardian. Eventually, he was granted the title "Victorious Fighting Buddha" after they obtained the sacred sutras.

孙悟空这一经典形象深刻体现了中华民族的核心价值观。他所体现的忠诚担当、智慧勇气与正义精神，持续引导人们坚守正道、勇于创新。

The classic image of Sun Wukong profoundly embodies the core values of the Chinese nation. The loyalty, responsibility, wisdom, courage, and righteousness he represents continue to inspire people to uphold moral principles and embrace innovation.

在京剧中，孙悟空的脸谱通常以金色为主，象征着他的神性和强大。鲜明的线条和大胆的色彩反映了他勇猛和坚毅的性格。他脸上猴子般的特征也强调了他的敏捷和机智。

Sun Wukong's facial makeup in Peking Opera typically features a golden color, symbolizing his divine and powerful nature. The sharp lines and bold colors reflect his fierce and determined character. The monkey-like features on his face also emphasize his agility and quick-wittedness.

扫描二维码获取孙悟空
京剧脸谱绘制方法与
教学视频
Scan the QR-code to get the methods and teaching video of painting facial makeup of Sun Wukong in Peking Opera

所需材料：一支铅笔；一块橡皮；红色、黑色和肉色水彩笔。

Material needed: a pencil; an eraser; red, black, and flesh-tone watercolor pens.

Exercises

1 **Answer the following questions.**

(1) Where did you first get to know about Sun Wukong?

(2) Is there any figure in your culture or other cultures that is similar to Sun Wukong? Please provide an example.

(3) Watch an excerpt of *Journey to the West*, and imitate the face and action of Sun Wukong.

2 **Practice painting the face.**

Paint the facial makeup of Sun Wukong by following the above steps.

Chapter 4

串珠手工艺品
Beaded Handicrafts

　　串珠工艺可以上溯到遥远的旧石器时代。当时的人们巧妙地利用穿孔的兽骨与贝壳等物，以绳子串联，打造出别具一格的串珠饰品。时光流转，来到现代社会，串珠工艺愈发多样，花式层出不穷，展现了无穷的创意与魅力。

　　Beading craftsmanship dates back to the Paleolithic Age. People in those primitive times skillfully employed pierced animal bones and shells and other natural materials, threading them together with rope to create unique and alluring beaded ornaments. As the time slips by and progresses into the modern era, the craft of beading transformed into a vibrant and diverse art form, with a never-ending array of patterns and designs coming to the fore, each exhibiting boundless innovation and allure.

Section 1

串珠发展概况
An Overview of the Development of Beading

　　串珠作为一种古老的艺术形式，其历史可以追溯至原始社会时期。早在旧石器时代，人们就开始将兽骨、贝壳、动物牙齿、骨管、石头等材料进行打制、研磨和钻孔，而后用绳子或皮条将其串联起来，制成最初的串珠装饰品，佩戴在脖颈、手腕处，或悬挂在衣服上。北京周口店山顶洞人遗址是中国出土装饰品最早的一处遗址，所出土的串珠装饰品不仅展示了先人的审美观念和创造力，还反映了当时的手工艺水平，特别是那些以鹿类和小型食肉类的犬齿穿孔制成的装饰品，更是展现了古人在资源利用方面的智慧和创意。

Beading, an ancient art form, can be traced back to the primitive society. As early as the Paleolithic Age, people began to shape, grind, and drill materials such as animal bones, shells, animal teeth, bone tubes, and stones, and then strung them together with ropes or leather strips to make the earliest beaded decorations, which were worn around the neck, wrist or hung on clothes. The Upper Cave Man Site in Zhoukoudian, Beijing, is the earliest archaeological site where decorations were excavated in China. The unearthed beaded decorations not only reveal the aesthetic concepts and creativity of our ancestors, but also reflect the handicraft level of that time. In particular, the decorations made by piercing the canine teeth of deer and small carnivores demonstrate the wisdom and creativity of ancient people in harnessing natural materials.

商代和西周时期流行佩玉。这一时期出土的佩饰以玉佩饰和玉组佩为主。匠人们巧妙地将各种材质的珠子与玉制品串联与组合，制作成造型繁复的玉组佩或串饰。西周时期的文物六璜联珠串饰，现藏于山西博物院，出土时位于墓主人胸部。该串饰由绿色料珠、红色玛瑙珠串联 6 件玉璜，玉璜上均刻有龙纹。该串饰制作工艺精湛，造型精美，是目前保存下来的西周玉器中的精品。

Wearing jade was very popular during the Shang Dynasty and the Western Zhou Dynasty. The unearthed cultural relics in this period were mainly jade pendants and jade group pendants. Craftsmen ingeniously strung and combined beads of various materials with jade products to create jade group pendants or string ornaments with complicated shapes. For example, the six jade pendant and bead string ornament is a cultural relic of the Western

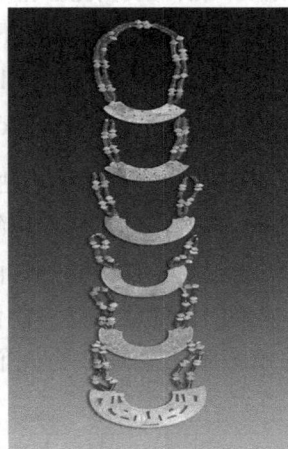

（西周）六璜联珠串饰，山西博物院藏
Six jade pendant and bead string ornament of the Western Zhou Dynasty, housed in the Shanxi Museum

Zhou Dynasty and is currently housed in the Shanxi Museum. When unearthed, it was located on the chest of the tomb owner. This string ornament comprises green material beads and red agate beads stringing together six jade Huang, all engraved with dragon patterns. Its superb craftsmanship and exquisite design make it a masterpiece among the existing jade objects of the Western Zhou Dynasty.

春秋战国时期，随着铁器的广泛应用及工具制造技术的改进，社会生产力得到了显著提升。玉石等硬质材料的切割、雕琢、打磨等工艺取得了质的飞跃。串珠的材质范畴得以拓展，不再局限于传统的玉石、玛瑙、琉璃等材料，水晶、绿松石、青金石等材料也纷纷出现。同时，金属冶炼技术的进步使金、银等贵金属被广泛应用于串珠及配件的制作中，使得串饰不仅具有装饰功能，更成为彰显佩戴者身份、地位与品位的重要标志。

During the Spring and Autumn period and the Warring States period, with the wide application of ironware and the improvement of tool manufacturing technology, social productivity was significantly enhanced. Craftsmanship in cutting, carving, and polishing hard materials such as jade achieved a qualitative leap. The material range of beaded items was expanded. Besides traditional materials like jade, agate, and colored glaze, more types of materials such as crystal, turquoise, and lapis lazuli began to be used to make beads. Meanwhile, advancements in metal smelting technology facilitated the extensive use of precious metals like gold and silver in the production of beaded items and accessories, making the ornaments not only have decorative functions but also become important symbols to showcase the wearer's status and taste.

蜻蜓眼玻璃珠作为春秋战国时期珠子制作的杰出代表，深受当时王公贵族的青睐。有学者认为，蜻蜓眼玻璃珠即传说中的"随侯珠"，与和氏璧齐名，并称"随和之宝"。曾侯乙墓和徐家岭楚墓出土的蜻蜓眼玻璃珠，为人们提供了宝贵的实物资料。

Dragonfly eye glass beads, as an outstanding representative of bead making during the Spring and Autumn period and the Warring States period, were deeply favored by the noblemen and royalty at that time. Some scholars believe that the dragonfly eye glass beads are the legendary "Suihou Beads," which were as famous as He Shi Jade Disk and jointly known as the Treasures of Sui and He. The dragonfly eye glass beads unearthed from the tomb of Marquis Yi of Zeng and the Chu tomb at Xujialing have provided us with valuable physical materials.

曾侯乙墓出土的战国蜻蜓眼玻璃珠，
湖北省博物馆藏
Dragonfly eye glass bead in the Warring States period, excavated from the Tomb of Marquis Yi of Zeng, kept in Hubei Provincial Museum

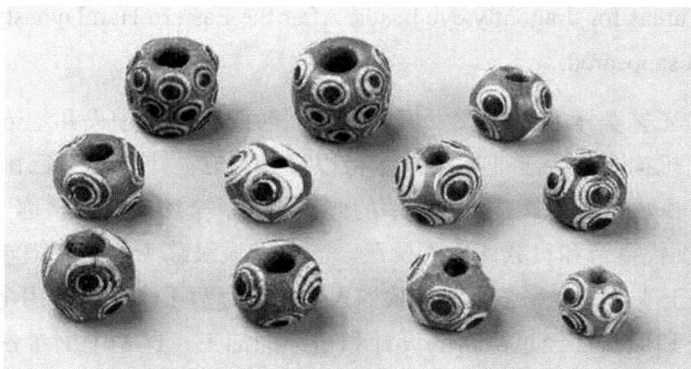

河南省南阳市淅川县徐家岭楚墓出土的战国早期蜻蜓眼玻璃珠
Dragonfly eye glass beads in the early Warring States period, excavated from Chu tombs at Xu Jialing in Xichuan County, Nanyang City, Henan Province

蜻蜓眼玻璃珠是古代一种类似于蜻蜓复眼造型、以眼睛图案作为装饰的圆形玻璃珠，也常称为蜻蜓眼珠、眼式珠或复合眼珠。蜻蜓眼玻璃珠最早可能源于公元前 3000 年的古埃及，并逐渐在北非、西亚、南欧等地中海沿岸地区流行，多制成串珠或坠子，用作辟邪的护身符。除圆形外，它还有橄榄形、扁方形、扁鼓形等多种形状。

Dragonfly eye glass beads in ancient times were round glass beads similar to the compound eyes of dragonflies which were often called dragonfly eye beads, eye pattern beads or compound eye beads. They may originate in ancient Egypt around 3000 BCE and gradually became popular in regions along the Mediterranean such as North Africa, West Asia, and South Europe. They were threaded into a string of beads or pendants to be used as amulets to ward off evil spirits. Apart from the round dragonfly eye glass beads, there are also olive-shaped, flat square-shaped, and flat drum-shaped ones.

春秋晚期，蜻蜓眼玻璃珠传入中国，并一直流行至两汉时期。中国古代工匠融入东方审美，制造出一系列本土蜻蜓眼玻璃珠。蜻蜓眼玻璃珠作为装饰品常镶嵌于剑、带钩、铜镜以及青铜器等器物上，并被赋予一定的等级及礼制含义。战国时期，楚地及其周边地区成为蜻蜓眼玻璃珠最为流行的地区。东汉以后，蜻蜓眼玻璃珠渐趋绝迹。

During the late Spring and Autumn period, dragonfly eye glass beads were introduced to China and remained popular until the Han Dynasty. Ancient Chinese craftsmen integrated eastern aesthetics and produced a series of indigenous dragonfly eye glass beads. As ornaments, dragonfly eye glass beads were often inlaid on objects such as swords, belt hooks, bronze mirrors, and bronze vessels, and were endowed with certain hierarchical and ritual meanings. During the Warring States period, the Chu region and its surrounding areas became the most popular areas for dragonfly eye beads. After the Eastern Han Dynasty, dragonfly eye beads gradually disappeared.

　　秦汉时期，工艺美术获得极大发展。尤其在西汉时期，中央和地方为了管理手工业设立了专门的机构，使手工业生产技术得以显著提升。串珠工艺已由单纯的配饰逐渐拓展至服饰等领域，金缕玉衣即为其中的典型代表。金缕玉衣，又称"玉衣""玉匣"或"玉柙"，是汉代皇帝和贵族死后的殓服。河北满城汉墓（西汉中山靖王刘胜之墓）出土的两套金缕玉衣，保存完整，其形状如人体，各由两千多块玉片用金丝编缀而成，每块玉片的大小和形状都经过严密的设计和精细的加工。这是中国考古发掘中出土年代最早、最完整的玉衣。

In the Qin and Han dynasties, arts and crafts made great progress. Especially in the Western Han Dynasty, the central and local governments set up special institutions to manage the handicraft industry, which greatly improved the production technology. The beading craft gradually expanded from simple accessories to fields such as clothing and the jade suit sewn with gold thread was a typical representative. Jade suit sewn with gold thread, also known as "jade clothes" "jade coffin" or "jade coffin case," was the burial suit for emperors and aristocrats after death in the Han Dynasty. Two sets of jade suits unearthed from the Han Tombs in Mancheng, Hebei Province, are well-preserved. They are shaped like human bodies, each consisting of more than 2,000 jade pieces strung together with gold wire. The size and shape of each jade piece were meticulously designed and finely processed. This is the earliest and most complete jade suit unearthed in the archaeological excavations in China.

（西汉）刘胜金缕玉衣，河北博物院藏
Liu Sheng's jade suit sewn with gold thread in the Western Han Dynasty, kept in Hebei Museum

在汉朝时期，佛教由印度传入中国，至隋唐时期臻于鼎盛。佛教徒用以念诵计数的串珠被称为佛珠，亦称数珠或念珠。一般而言，佛珠由 108 颗珠子穿成一串，也有 14 颗、18 颗、21 颗、27 颗、36 颗、42 颗、54 颗或 1080 颗穿成一串的。一串念珠中珠子的数量具有象征意义，并与佛经中的教义紧密相连。佛珠的材质丰富多样，通常用香木车成小圆粒并贯穿成串，也有用玛瑙、玉石、陶瓷等制成的。佛珠既可用于计数，又可用作装饰，颗数较少的念珠可套在手腕上，颗数较多的念珠可挂于颈间。

During the Han Dynasty, Buddhism was introduced to China from India and reached its peak during the Sui and Tang dynasties. The beads strung together for Buddhists to record the number of chanting sutras are called Buddhist beads, also known as counting beads or prayer beads. A strand of Buddhist beads usually consists of 108 beads. There are also strands composed of 14, 18, 21, 27, 36, 42, 54 or 1,080 beads. The number of beads in a strand of prayer beads carries symbolic meaning and is closely associated with the doctrines in Buddhist sutras. Buddhist beads are made of a wide variety of materials. Small round beads are often carved from fragrant wood and strung together. Serving both as counting tools and decorative ornaments, Buddhist beads can also be made of agate, jade, ceramics, and other materials. Shorter strand with fewer beads can be worn around the wrist, while longer strand with more beads can be hung around the neck.

唐代经济繁荣、文化多元，对外交流频繁。这一时期，华美的璎珞出现并逐渐流行。璎珞亦作"缨络"，是由串珠玉制成的颈饰。佛教传入中国后，璎珞这一装饰元素广泛出现在壁画、石雕和泥塑等佛教艺术作品中，比如甘肃敦煌莫高窟的唐代壁画中就有佩戴璎珞的唐代舞伎形象。此后，随着贵族妇女的纷纷仿效，璎珞逐渐成为日常生活中的饰品。

The Tang Dynasty witnessed prosperous economy, diverse culture, and frequent foreign exchanges. During this era, the magnificent Yingluo appeared and gradually gained popularity. Yingluo was a type of neck adornment made of strung pearls and jades. After Buddhism was introduced to China, Yingluo could frequently be spotted in the Buddhist artworks such as murals, stone carvings, and clay sculptures. For instance, images of dancers who wore Yingluo could be found in the Tang Dynasty murals of the Mogao Caves in Dunhuang, Gansu Province. Later on, Yingluo was emulated by noble women and gradually transformed into an accessory in daily life.

通常而言，璎珞的形制为以金或银打造的项圈，其下部垂挂各类珠宝，中间装饰有金、玉锁片。唐代颇为流行的七宝璎珞颈饰，一般由金、银、玛瑙、琉璃、砗磲、

115

珍珠和玫瑰这七种珠宝串缀而成。七宝璎珞也泛指用各种珍宝制作而成的璎珞。

Generally speaking, the form of Yingluo is a collar crafted from gold or silver, with diverse jewels dangling from the lower part and gold and jade lock pieces adorning in the middle. The seven treasures Yingluo neck ornaments, which were highly popular in the Tang Dynasty, were typically strung together seven types of jewels, namely gold, silver, agate, glazed ware, giant clam, pearl, and rose. It also generally referred to those made with various treasures.

在隋唐时期，女性于不同场合佩戴的璎珞，常常呈现为装饰颈、胸的多层项链，或者是款式考究的单层项链。其中，最具代表性的当属 1957 年在陕西西安出土的隋代李静训墓中的嵌珍珠宝石项链。它由 28 个镶有小珍珠的金质球形链珠组成，项链上端正中的扣钮上镶嵌着刻有鹿纹的深蓝色珠饰，项链下端居中是一个大圆金饰，上面镶嵌着一块鸡血石，鸡血石四周镶有 24 颗小珍珠，鸡血石左右两侧各有方形和圆形金饰，上面镶嵌着蓝色珠饰。鸡血石下挂着一个水滴形金饰，上面镶嵌着一块长达 3.1 厘米、极为罕见的青金石。这条项链鲜艳夺目，堪称举世无双的艺术精品。

（隋）嵌珍珠宝石项链，中国国家博物馆藏
Pearl and gemstone-inlaid necklace of the Sui Dynasty, kept in National Museum of China

During the Sui and Tang dynasties, the Yingluo worn by women on various occasions often presented as multi-layered necklaces or single-layered ones with exquisite styles to adorn the neck and the chest. Among them, the most representative one was the pearl and gemstone-inlaid necklace from the tomb of Li Jingxun of the Sui Dynasty which was unearthed in Xi'an, Shaanxi Province in 1957. It consisted of 28 gold spherical chain beads inlaid with small pearls. The button at the midpoint of the upper end of the necklace was inlaid with a dark blue bead decoration engraved with a deer pattern. At the middle of the lower end of the necklace was a large round gold decoration, on which a piece of bloodstone was inlaid. The bloodstone was surrounded by 24 small pearls. On both sides of the bloodstone were square and circular gold ornaments embedded with blue beads. Underneath the bloodstone hung a water-drop-shaped gold decoration, on which a very rare lapis lazuli of up to 3.1 centimeters was inlaid. This necklace is radiant and dazzling, and can be considered a unique artistic masterpiece.

另外，2002 年于陕西省西安市南郊米氏墓出土的唐代水晶项链也极具代表性。此水晶项链距今已有 1300 多年的历史。整串水晶项链由 92 颗水晶珠、3 颗蓝色玻璃珠、4 枚金扣、2 颗紫水晶吊坠及 2 颗绿松石吊坠组成，晶莹剔透，雍容华贵。

Additionally, the crystal necklace of the Tang Dynasty unearthed from the tomb of the Mi family in the southern suburbs of Xi'an, Shaanxi Province in 2002 was also highly representative. It has a history of over 1,300 years. The entire crystal necklace consists of 92 crystal beads, three blue glass beads, four gold clasps, two amethyst pendants, and two turquoise pendants. It is limpid and elegant.

（唐）水晶项链，西安市文物保护考古研究院藏
Crystal necklace of the Tang Dynasty, kept in Xi'an Institute of Cultural Relics Protection and Archaeology

在宋、元、明时期，项链的样式愈发丰富，制作工艺亦更为精湛。清代在制定服饰典章时借鉴历代朝服佩玉礼制，将佛教的念珠定为穿着礼服时的佩戴饰物，称之为朝珠。一副朝珠由 108 颗圆珠串缀而成，大体由珠身、佛头、纪念、背云、大小坠角组成。佛头是朝珠中的 4 颗大珠，将朝珠四等分，又称为"分珠"。在朝珠两侧有 3 个珠串，每串 10 颗小珠，称作"纪念"，一边为两串，一边为一串。使用时男女有别，男用两串在左，女用两串在右，不能戴错。朝珠用圆珠串缀，挂于颈项，垂于胸前。按照清制，皇帝、后妃、文官五品、武官四品以上皆佩戴朝珠。皇帝戴东珠，皇太后及皇后须挂一盘东珠和两盘珊瑚珠，其他王公大臣不准用东珠，其余质料不限，玛瑙、翡翠、琥珀、珊瑚、碧玺等均可用。

During the Song, Yuan and Ming dynasties, the styles of necklaces became increasingly diverse and the manufacturing techniques also became more exquisite. When the Qing Dynasty established its dress code, the imperial court drew on the ritual system of jade ornaments worn with ceremonial costumes in previous dynasties and designated Buddhist beads as accessories to match ceremonial costumes, which were called court beads. A set of court beads are made up of 108 round beads strung together and generally consist of bead bodies, Fotou ("Buddha heads"), Jinian, Beiyun (back pendant), and large and small pendant corners. Fotou are four large beads which divide a strand of court beads into four equal parts, and they are also known as dividing beads. On each side of the strand of court beads, there are three bead strings, each with ten small beads, known as Jinian. There are two strings on one side and one string on the other side. When worn, there is a distinction between men and women. For men, the two strings are on the left; and for women, the two strings are on the right. It is important to wear them correctly. A strand of court beads, made of round beads, was worn around the neck with the beads hanging down in front of the chest. According to the regulations of the Qing Dynasty, the emperor, empress, concubines, civil officials of the fifth rank and above, and military officials of the fourth rank and above were all required to wear court beads. The emperor wore Dongzhu (pearls from Northeast China), while the empress dowager and the empress were required to wear one strand of Dongzhu and two strands of coral beads. Other nobles and officials were forbidden from using Dongzhu, but they could use beads which were made of other materials, such as agate, jadeite, amber, coral, tourmaline, etc.

　　一副朝珠中的 108 颗珠子代表着一年中的 12 个月、24 个节气和 72 候。皇帝会在不同的场合佩戴不同质地的朝珠，如祭地时佩戴琥珀或蜜蜡朝珠，祭日时佩戴红珊瑚朝珠，祭月时佩戴绿松石朝珠，祭天时佩戴青金石朝珠。故宫博物院收藏的青金石朝珠，周长 150 厘米，由 108 颗青金石珠穿成。此朝珠有 4 颗大珊瑚珠，将朝珠四等分，上端的珊瑚珠称为"佛头塔"，用黄丝带与碧玺背云相接，下有碧玺坠角。在"佛头塔"下方两侧以珊瑚珠组成纪念三串，坠角分别嵌红、蓝宝石。

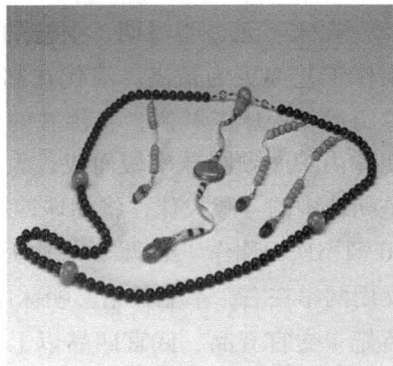

（清）青金石朝珠，故宫博物院藏
Lapis lazuli court beads in the Qing Dynasty, kept in the Palace Museum

The 108 beads of a set of court beads represent twelve months, twenty-four solar terms, and seventy-two climatic terms of a year. Emperors wore court beads of different materials on different occasions. They wore amber or beeswax court beads when sacrificing to the Earth, red coral ones when sacrificing to the Sun, turquoise ones when sacrificing to the Moon, and lapis lazuli ones when sacrificing to the Heaven. The lapis lazuli court beads kept in the Palace Museum has a circumference of 150 centimeters and is strung with 108 lapis lazuli beads and 4 large coral beads. These 4 coral beads divide the court beads into four equal parts. The large coral bead on the top is known as "Buddha head pagoda," which is connected to the tourmaline Beiyun with a yellow silk ribbon and has a tourmaline pendant at the bottom. Three strings of Jinian are strung on both sides below the Buddha head pagoda with ruby and sapphire pendants at the bottom.

十八子手串是由佛教念珠演化而成的一种饰物，可以佩戴于衣服上、挽在手腕上或在闲暇时把玩。它由 18 颗珠子组成，故而得名。其材质一般为翡翠、珍珠、碧玺、蜜蜡、珊瑚、伽楠木等。

The eighteen-bead bracelet is a kind of ornament evolved from Buddhist beads, which can be worn on clothes, wound around the wrist, or played with in leisure time. It consists of 18 beads and thus gets its name. Its materials are generally jade, pearls, tourmaline, beeswax, coral, agarwood, and so on.

故宫博物院藏有多件十八子手串，其中清朝碧玺珠翠手串最具代表性。该手串周长 30 厘米，由 18 颗粉色碧玺珠穿成，间有翠质结珠两个，即佛头。其中一个佛头下面接一个佛塔，系丝线及一个珊瑚杵，下连翡翠盘长背云，上下各系一颗珍珠。再下面是两个果实形深绿色翡翠坠角，坠角上有两颗小珍珠。该手串颜色柔和清澈，设计精美，工艺精湛。

The Palace Museum houses many eighteen-bead bracelets, among which the tourmaline, jade, and emerald bracelet in the Qing Dynasty is the most representative. The bracelet is 30 centimeters in circumference and is made of 18 pink tourmaline beads. There are two emerald beads in between, namely "Buddha heads." Under one of the Buddha heads is a "Buddha pagoda," tied with silk thread and a coral pestle, followed by an emerald Panchang-shaped pendant, with a pearl attached to the top and bottom respectively. Further below are two fruit-shaped dark green jade pendants, with two small pearls on the pendants. Its color is soft and clear, with exquisite design and superb craftsmanship.

（清）碧玺珠翠手串，故宫博物院藏
Tourmaline, jade, and emerald bracelet in the Qing Dynasty, kept in the Palace Museum

天珠，是一种蚀花或染色的玉髓珠，常用来制作串饰。考古发掘与研究表明，最早的天珠可追溯至公元前 2200 年左右的美索不达米亚。中国春秋时期，天珠已传至新疆、关中及豫西南一带，两汉时期传至湖南、云南和西藏阿里等地区。2013 至 2015 年，新疆吉尔赞喀勒墓地出土一件圆板状天珠和六件圆柱状天珠，年代距今约 2600 至 2400 年。

Dzi beads, the etched or dyed chalcedony beads, are often used to make string ornaments. Archaeological excavations and research show that the earliest Dzi beads can be traced back to around 2200 BCE in Mesopotamia. During the Spring and Autumn period in China, Dzi beads had spread to Xinjiang, the Guanzhong area, and the southwestern part of Henan. During the Han Dynasty, they spread to Hunan, Yunnan, and Ali in Xizang. From 2013 to 2015, one round plate-shaped and six cylindrical Dzi beads were unearthed from the Jirzankale Tomb in Xinjiang, dating back 2,600–2,400 years ago.

圆板状天珠，新疆吉尔赞喀勒墓地出土
Round plate-shaped Dzi beads, unearthed from the Jirzankale Tomb in Xinjiang

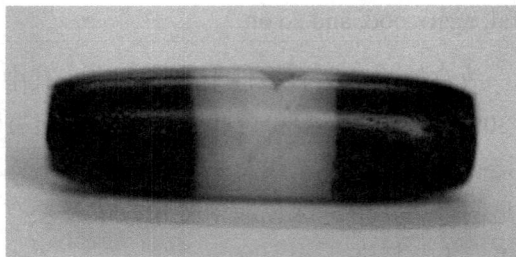

圆柱状天珠，新疆吉尔赞喀勒墓地出土
Cylindrical Dzi beads, unearthed from the Jirzankale Tomb in Xinjiang

　　天珠在藏文中有明亮、闪光之意，是西藏和喜马拉雅山地带颇受欢迎的一种珠饰。天珠多为圆柱状，或接近橄榄形，表面布满黑白相间的图案。天珠在藏文化、藏药及喜马拉雅地区宗教文化中具有重要地位。天珠上的图案往往具有对称性，有眼形、圆形、方形、双波纹形等，而且不同的图案具有不同的象征意义。

　　Dzi beads, which mean brightness or shining in Tibetan, are a highly popular type of bead ornament in Xizang and the Himalayan region. They are mostly cylindrical or nearly olive-shaped, with black and white interlaced patterns covering the surface. Dzi bead has an important position in Tibetan culture, Tibetan medicine and the religious culture of the Himalayan region. The patterns on Dzi beads are often symmetrical, which are eye-shaped, round, square, double-ripple-shaped, among others, but different patterns also carry distinct symbolic meanings.

　　串珠从古老文明演进至现代社会，不单具有装饰的作用，更承载着深厚的文化内涵。串珠在传承中逐渐大众化和时尚化。在大街小巷，常能见到人们佩戴着各种材质和风格的串珠手链、项链，用以展现个性和时尚。各类充满创意的串珠 DIY（自己动手制作）店铺纷纷兴起，人们可以尽情发挥创意，制作出五花八门的串珠手工艺品。现如今，科技的快速发展使得串珠的制作工具更为先进，材料更为优质，工艺愈发多样。串珠越来越受到人们的喜爱，并在传承与创新中继续向前发展。

From ancient civilizations to modern society, beads have evolved far beyond mere decoration; they also carry profound cultural significance. Over time, beads have gradually become more popular and fashionable. On streets and alleys, people can often be seen wearing beaded bracelets and necklaces made of various materials and in diverse styles to express individuality and fashion. A variety of creative bead-threading DIY (Do It Yourself) shops have sprung up, enabling people to unleash their creativity and craft a wide array of beaded handicrafts. Nowadays, rapid technological advancements have made beading tools more advanced, materials of higher quality, and techniques more diversified. Bead-threading is growing in popularity and continues to move forward in the inheritance and innovation.

Exercises

1 **Answer the following questions.**

(1) Beading has been practiced for centuries in many countries. What do you think are the main reasons why beading remains popular today?

(2) How does beading art contribute to cultural preservation and transmission?

(3) Some beaded items possess their symbolic meaning. Could you provide an example to illustrate?

2 **Choose the best answer to each of the following questions.**

(1) Which of the following material was NOT commonly used in ancient beadwork?

A. Shell beads.   B. Plastic beads.

C. Stone beads.   D. Bone beads.

(2) What kind of beads is regarded by some scholars as the legendary "Suihou Beads" and were as famous as He Shi Jade Disk and were jointly known as the Treasures of Sui and He?

A. Rosary beads.   B. Dzi beads.

C. Court beads.   D. Dragonfly eye glass beads.

(3) Which of the following statements is true as far as court beads are concerned?

A. Common people from all social classes could wear court beads.

B. Court beads were made of only one type of material.

C. Men and women wore court beads in different ways.

D. Court beads were worn by all officials regardless of their ranks.

(4) What kind of court beads would be chosen when the emperor in the Qing Dynasty offered sacrifice to the Heaven?

    A. Lapis lazuli court beads.   B. Amber or beeswax court beads.

    C. Red coral court beads.   D. Turquoise court beads.

(5) How many beads are there typically in a set of court beads, and what symbolic meanings do these beads carry?

    A. A set of court beads has 108 beads, representing 12 months, 24 solar terms, and 72 climatic terms of a year.

    B. A set of court beads has 18 beads, representing the 18 kinds of weapons to ward off demons and monsters.

    C. A set of court beads has 27 beads, representing the 27 days of the lunar month.

    D. A set of court beads has 36 beads, representing the 36 celestial beings in Buddhism.

Section 2

串珠基本技法
Basic Beading Techniques

编制串珠手工艺品时，所选用的珠子材质涵盖塑料、玻璃、陶瓷、木质、天然水晶、人工合成水晶、珍珠、仿珍珠、玉石、仿玉石以及金银等贵金属。在选择串珠工艺品的珠子材质时，需要综合考虑作品的风格、用途、预算以及个人喜好等因素，以创作出令人满意的作品。

When making beaded handicrafts, the bead materials chosen include plastic, glass, ceramics, wood, natural crystal, synthetic crystal, pearls, imitation pearls, jade, faux jade, precious metals like gold and silver, etc. When selecting the bead materials for beaded handicrafts, factors like the style, purpose, budget of the beadwork, and personal preferences should be taken into consideration in order to produce satisfactory works.

当前市场中最受欢迎的串珠材质当属亚克力珠子。亚克力珠子俗称有机玻璃珠子，因其重量轻、不易破裂、光泽度好、成本较低而在串珠工艺品的制作中得到广泛应用。珠子的尺寸大小各异，直径从 1 毫米到 30 毫米不等。

Acrylic beads, commonly known as polymethyl methacrylate (PMMA) beads, are the most popular beading material in the current market. They are widely used when threading beaded handicrafts because of their light weight, resistance to breakage, good glossiness, and low cost. The beads come in diverse sizes, with diameters ranging from 1mm to 30mm.

制作串珠手工艺品通常采用无弹力渔线，它透明、不易断、牢固结实。渔线的粗细需根据珠子大小来选择，珠子越小，所选渔线越细。一般情况下，选择直径为 0.2 毫米到 0.5 毫米之间的渔线即可。如果是编大型的花瓶、纸巾盒等所用珠子较大的装饰品，则需选择直径为 0.6 毫米的粗渔线。

Non-elastic fishing line is usually adopted for weaving beaded handicrafts. It is transparent, not prone to breaking, and firm as well as strong. The thickness of the fishing line needs to be selected based on the size of the beads. The smaller the beads are, the thinner the selected fishing line will be. Generally, a fishing line with a diameter ranging from 0.2mm to 0.5mm is appropriate. If weaving large items such as vases or tissue boxes where larger beads are used, a thick fishing line with a diameter of 0.6mm should be chosen.

在串珠的整个过程中，需分清左右线。双手拿一段渔线，位于左手边的渔线为左线，位于右手边的渔线为右线。在接近左线线尾约 2 厘米处折一下做标识，以区分左线和右线。在制作过程中，要始终保持左线在左手边，右线在右手边。

Throughout the entire process of threading beaded handicraft, it is essential to distinguish between the left and right lines. Take a section of fishing line with both hands. The fishing line which is on the left hand side is called the left line, the fishing line which is on the right hand side is the right line. Mark the left line by folding it about 2cm from the end of the left line. Remember to keep the left line always on the left hand side and right line on the right hand side in the whole threading procedure.

对于串珠爱好者而言，学会基本的渔线串珠技法十分重要。渔线串珠技法是串珠艺术的基础。熟练掌握诸如单穿法、对穿法、回穿打结法、接线等技巧，能够为后续创作出精美的串珠作品奠定坚实基础。

For enthusiasts of beading art, it is of great significance to learn basic skills of threading beads with fishing line, which is the basis of beading art. Through proficiently mastering skills like single threading method, opposite threading method, back threading and knotting method, and adding fishing line, a solid foundation can be established for the subsequent creation of exquisite beadworks.

单穿法也称加珠法，是指用渔线直接穿珠子，直至所需的长度。它是最简单、最基本的串珠方法，一般用于加珠。穿珠时，珠孔的大小应与线的粗细相吻合。若线太细，则穿的珠子不够稳定；若线太粗，则穿线不顺畅。

The single threading method, also known as the bead adding method, refers to directly threading beads with the fishing line until the desired length is achieved. It is the simplest and the most basic method of threading beads, and is typically employed for adding beads. While threading beads, it is crucial to ensure that the size of the bead holes aligns with the thickness of the line. If the line is too thin, the threaded beads will lack stability. If the line is too thick, threading will not proceed smoothly.

对穿法就是将渔线分别从左右相反的两个方向穿过一颗珠子。具体而言，左线是从左往右从珠孔的右侧穿出，右线则是从右往左从珠孔的左侧穿出。

Opposite threading method is that the fishing line goes through a bead from opposite directions on the left and right respectively. To be specific, the left line goes through the bead hole from left to right and emerges at the right side of the bead, while the right line goes through the bead hole from right to left and emerges at the left side of the bead.

回穿打结法分为右线回穿打结法和左线回穿打结法，简称为右线回线和左线回线。右线回穿打结法就是右线尾部从右往左穿过右手边的最后一颗珠子，穿过去之后形成一个线圈，左线从下往上套进圈中，拉紧左线和右线，使线圈缩小，形成一个结，再用力将结拉进珠子里，这样结就被隐藏在珠子中，完成了右线回穿打结，也就是右线回线。左线回穿打结法就是左线尾部从左往右穿过左手边的最后一颗珠子，穿过去之后形成一个线圈，右线从下往上套进圈中，拉紧左、右线，使线圈缩小，形成一个结，再用力将结拉进珠子里，将结隐藏在珠子中，完成了左线回穿打结，也就是左线回线。

The back threading and knotting method can be divided into the right-thread back threading and knotting method and the left-thread back threading and knotting method, which are simply known as the right-thread back line and the left-thread back line respectively. For the right-thread back threading and knotting method, the tail of the right thread goes through the last bead on the right hand side from right to left to form a loop. Then, the left thread is inserted into the loop from the bottom up. Tighten the right and left threads to make the loop shrink and form a knot. Subsequently, pull the knot forcefully into the bead. Thus, the knot is concealed within the bead, completing the right-thread back threading and knotting, that is, the right-thread back line. As for the left-thread back threading and knotting method, the tail of the left thread passes through the last bead on the left hand side from left to right to form a loop. Next, the right thread is threaded into the loop from the bottom up. Tighten the right and left threads to make the loop shrink and form a knot. Finally, pull the knot forcefully into the bead. In this way, the knot is hidden in the bead, completing the left-thread back threading and knotting, that is, the left-thread back line.

倘若渔线即将耗尽，而所编的串珠工艺品仍未完工，此时则需进行接线操作。先将一根新渔线穿过快用完渔线所在的珠子，接着将快用完的渔线穿过所在珠圈的珠子，然后右线回穿打结加以固定，最后用剪刀剪掉线头。如此一来，渔线便接好了。

When the fishing line is on the verge of running out and the beaded handicraft being crafted is still unfinished, an adding line procedure is requisite. First of all, thread a new fishing line through the bead where the almost used-up fishing line lies. Next, make the nearly used-up fishing line pass through the beads within the bead circle and then complete the right-thread back threading and knotting for firmness. Finally, use scissors to cut off the thread end. As a result, the fishing line is successfully added.

1 │ 串珠葫芦
Beaded Calabash

葫芦是一种藤本植物，在中国各地均有栽培，且因品种不同而形态各异。葫芦在中国有着悠久的种植历史，河姆渡遗址出土的葫芦籽经考古鉴定已有 7000 多年历史。葫芦鲜嫩时可做蔬菜食用，长老晒干后，是盛水、酒等物的理想盛器。

The calabash, a vine plant, is cultivated throughout China and exhibits diverse shapes due to its numerous varieties. The Calabash has a long history of cultivation in China, with calabash seeds excavated from the Hemudu ruins dating back to more than 7,000 years ago, as confirmed by archaeological evidence. When fresh and tender, the calabash can be eaten as vegetable, and when mature and dried, it is an ideal container for water, wine, and other things.

葫芦在中国文化中也具有重要地位。在古代，医生常用葫芦来盛放药物，而人们对于葫芦里具体装的是什么药往往不清楚，因此产生了一句汉语俗语："我不知道他葫芦里头卖的是什么药。"这句俗语后来用来比喻不知道别人到底打的什么主意。另外，葫芦还是中国民间传说中八仙之一铁拐李的法器。

The calabash also holds an important position in Chinese culture. In ancient China, doctors often used calabashes to hold medicine, but common people were unclear about specific medicine in the calabashes. Therefore, there is the saying, "I don't know what medicine he has in his calabashes," meaning I'm wondering what he has up his sleeve. This saying is later used metaphorically to describe not knowing what someone else is planning or intending. In addition, calabash is the magic weapon possessed by Tieguai Li who is one of the Eight Immortals in Chinese folklores.

在汉语发音中，"葫芦"与"福禄"谐音，象征长寿健康、吉祥平安，有美好的寓意，因此葫芦饰品也一直深受中国人民喜爱。

In Chinese pronunciation, the calabash (Hulu) is homophonic to Fulu, which is the symbol of longevity and health, and good luck and peace, carrying positive connotations. Therefore, the calabash ornaments have long been cherished by the Chinese people.

所需材料：198 颗直径为 8 毫米的红色亚克力地球珠；4 米直径为 0.5 毫米的渔线；卷尺；剪刀。

Materials needed: 198 red acrylic globe-like beads with a diameter of 8mm, 4-meter fishing line with a diameter of 0.5mm, a tape measure, and a pair of scissors.

制作串珠葫芦共需 4 米渔线，但渔线太长不便于制作，因此可先取 2 米渔线进行制作，待渔线将用完之际再加剩下的 2 米渔线。

4-meter fishing line is needed to thread the beaded calabash. Since it is not easy to handle a very long string, we start to use 2-meter fishing line to thread the beads. Once the fishing line is used up, another 2-meter fishing line can be added to continue threading the beads.

扫描二维码获取串珠
葫芦制作方法与
教学视频
Scan the QR-code to get the methods and teaching video of threading beaded calabash

开始制作前，先将 2 米渔线对折，位于左手边的渔线为左线，位于右手边的渔线为右线。在接近左线线尾约 2 厘米处折一下做标识，以区分左线和右线。在制作串珠葫芦的过程中，注意区分左线和右线，左线始终保持在左手边，右线始终保持在右手边。因为制作时右线消耗得比较快，因此右线比左线留长约 30 厘米。

Before you start, fold the 2-meter fishing line in half. The fishing line which is on the left hand side is called the left line, and the fishing line which is on the right hand side is called the right line. Mark the left line by folding it about 2cm from the end of the left line. When threading the beaded calabash, it's very important to distinguish the left line from the right line. Remember to keep the left line always on the left hand side and right line on the right hand side in the whole making procedure. Because the right line is consumed faster, please keep the right line about 30cm longer than the left line.

Exercises

1 **Answer the following questions.**

(1) Can you sum up the functions of the calabash?

(2) Have you watched the animation cartoon *Calabash Brothers*? Can you tell the story in this animated TV series?

(3) There are lots of deities in Chinese folklores and mythologies. Can you tell the story about them?

Search for the relevant materials and match the Eight Immortals in Chinese folklore with their magic weapons.

(1) Han Zhongli   A. calabash

(2) He Xiangu   B. bamboo percussion instrument

(3) Lan Caihe   C. sword

(4) Tieguai Li   D. round fan

(5) Han Xiangzi   E. jade tablet

(6) Cao Guojiu   F. flower basket

(7) Zhang Guolao   G. lotus

(8) Lü Dongbin   H. vertical bamboo flute

2 | 串珠金鱼
| Beaded Goldfish

金鱼，亦称"金鲫鱼"，系野生鲫鱼经过突变以及长期人工家化选育而成的观赏鱼类。金鱼原产于中国，被称为中国的"国鱼"。在 12 世纪时的南宋，已有金鱼家化的遗传研究。现如今，世界各国的金鱼均由中国直接或间接引种。在 16 世纪的明朝，金鱼由中国传入日本，17 至 18 世纪传入欧洲，在 19 世纪传入美国。

Goldfish, also known as golden crucian carp, is a type of ornamental fish which was originally cultivated from wild crucian carp through mutation, long-term artificial domestication and selective breeding. With its origin in China, goldfish is known as the "national fish" of China. The genetic research of goldfish's domestication had already begun in the 12th century in the Southern Song Dynasty. Nowadays, goldfish all over the world have been introduced directly or indirectly from China. Goldfish were introduced from China to Japan in the 16th century during the Ming Dynasty and reached Europe between the 17th and 18th centuries. By the 19th century, they were introduced into the United States.

金鱼颜色多样，有红、橙、紫、蓝、古铜、墨、银白、五花、透明等。金鱼形态各异、品种繁多，有红狮头、红虎头、龙睛、鹤顶红、一斛珠、朝天眼、红白顶红、短尾琉金、红珍珠、蓝尾蝶等。金鱼的命名蕴涵着浓厚的中国传统文化元素，人们不仅以狮子、老虎、龙、鹤等瑞兽祥禽来命名金鱼，还采用了"一斛珠"等诗词歌赋中的名称。在中国文化中，金鱼象征着活力、吉祥，有年年有余、金玉满堂的寓意，这与中国文化中追求家庭和睦、社会稳定的观念密切相关。"鱼"与"余"或"玉"谐音，"金鱼"与"金玉"谐音。成语"金玉满堂"，极言财富之多，亦形容学识丰富。

The color of goldfish is diversified, ranging from red, orange, purple, blue, copper-colored, ink color, silver, multicolored, transparent, and so on. Goldfish come in many shapes and varieties, such as Red Lionhead, Red Tigerhead, Dragon Eye, Redcap Oranda, Yihuzhu, Chaotianyan (with eyes facing upwards), Red and White Oranda, Shorttail Ryukin, Red Pearlscale, Blue Butterfly's Tail, and so on. Having revealed traditional Chinese culture, the goldfish varieties are named after auspicious creatures such as lion, tiger, dragon, and crane, and also after certain literature terms of poem, Ci, song, and prose poem such as "Yihuzhu." In Chinese culture, goldfish symbolizes vitality and auspiciousness, meaning having a surplus year after year and filling the hall with gold and jade, which is closely related to the idea of the Chinese people in pursuing family harmony and social stability. "鱼" (fish) is homophonic of "余" (surplus) or "玉" (jade). "金鱼" (goldfish) is homophonic of "金玉" (gold and jade). The idiom "金玉满堂" is used to mean an abundance of wealth, and it is also used in the praise of talented person.

人们从饲养金鱼中能得到文化和精神上的享受。作为美的使者，金鱼已然成为中国人日常生活中喜闻乐见的艺术题材，也寄托了人们对美好生活的向往和追求。金鱼图案常出现在服装、瓷器、邮票、玻璃制品、风筝、剪纸等物品上，串珠金鱼也是非常受欢迎的装饰品。

People obtain cultural and spiritual enjoyment from keeping goldfish. Serving as ambassadors of beauty, goldfish have become popular subject matter of various forms of art in Chinese people's daily life. Goldfish also shows the people's aspirations and pursuit for a better life. Goldfish pattern often appears on clothing, porcelain, stamp, glasswork, kite, paper-cut, and so on, and beaded goldfish are also very popular decorations.

扫描二维码获取串珠金鱼制作方法与教学视频
Scan the QR-code to get the methods and teaching video of threading beaded goldfish

所需材料： 24 颗直径为 8 毫米的黄色亚克力地球珠；21 颗直径为 6 毫米的透明地球珠；1 颗直径为 8 毫米的红色亚克力地球珠；2 颗直径为 12 毫米的黑色塑料圆珠；3 个塑料鱼尾；1 米直径为 0.5 毫米的渔线；卷尺；剪刀。

Materials needed: 24 yellow acrylic globe-like beads with a diameter of 8mm, 21 transparent acrylic globe-like beads with a diameter of 6mm, one red acrylic globe-like bead with a diameter of 8mm, two black plastic round beads with a diameter of 12mm, three plastic fish tails, 1-meter fishing line with a diameter of 0.5mm, a tape measure, and a pair of scissors.

开始制作前先将 1 米渔线对折，位于左手边的渔线为左线，位于右手边的渔线为右线。在接近左线线尾约 2 厘米处折一下做标识，以区分左线和右线。在制作串珠金鱼的过程中，注意区分左线和右线，左线始终保持在左手边，右线始终保持在右手边。因为制作时左线消耗得比较快，因此左线比右线多留约 20 厘米。

Before you start, fold the 1-meter fishing line in half. The fishing line which is on the left hand side is called left line, and the fishing line which is on the right hand side is called right line. Mark the left line by folding it about 2cm from the end of the left line. When threading the beaded goldfish, it's very important to distinguish the left line from the right line. Remember to keep the left line always on the left hand side and right line on the right hand side. Because the left line is consumed faster, please keep the left line about 20cm longer than the right line.

Exercises

1 **Answer the following questions.**

    (1) Do you have the experience of keeping goldfish as a pet?

    (2) Have you discovered why goldfish make great pets?

2 **Judge whether each of the following statements on goldfish is true (T) or false (F).**

    (1) The genetic research of goldfish's domestication had already begun in China in the Southern Song Dynasty.

    (2) Goldfish is a type of ornamental fish which was originally cultivated from Mandarin fish.

    (3) Goldfish was introduced from China to Japan in the 18th century during the Qing Dynasty.

    (4) Some goldfish varieties are named after auspicious creatures such as lion, tiger, dragon, and crane.

    (5) Goldfish symbolizes vitality, longevity, health, and auspiciousness.

3 | 串珠生肖狗
Beaded Zodiac Dog

在中国传统文化中，狗是"忠诚"和"义气"的象征。狗的叫声与"旺"的发音类似，也有吉祥的寓意。狗还是十二生肖中的一员。十二生肖也称作十二属相，是中国特有的一种民俗现象。中国的十二生肖以十二年为一轮回，每个农历年对应一个生肖。十二生肖分别是十二种动物，它们是鼠、牛、虎、兔、龙、蛇、马、羊、猴、鸡、狗、猪。

Dog is the symbol of loyalty and righteousness in traditional Chinese culture. The dog's barking sounds similar to the pronunciation of "旺" (Wang) in Chinese, which implies good luck. The dog is also one of the 12 zodiac animals. Shi'er Shengxiao or Shi'er Shuxiang (12 zodiac animals) is a kind of Chinese folk custom. The Chinese zodiac goes through a 12-year cycle of animals—the rat, ox, tiger, rabbit, dragon, snake, horse, sheep, monkey, rooster, dog, and pig—with the animal changing every lunar year.

十二生肖对中国传统文化产生了重大而深远的影响，它们是年画、雕塑、饰品等民间艺术表现的重要内容。十二生肖有各自的寓意，在中国民俗艺术中，生肖狗被视为守门镇宅、保平安的象征。

The 12 zodiac animals have had a significant and far-reaching impact on traditional Chinese culture, and they are important subject matters expressed in folk arts such as Spring Festival pictures, sculptures, and ornaments. The 12 zodiac animals have their own symbolic meanings. The zodiac dog in Chinese folk art is regarded as the symbol of guardian of the house and peace-keeper.

所需材料： 83 颗直径为 8 毫米的黄色亚克力地球珠；35 颗直径为 8 毫米的红色亚克力地球珠；2 颗直径为 8 毫米的塑料黑色圆珠；1.9 米直径为 0.5 毫米的渔线；4 段 35 厘米直径为 0.5 毫米的渔线；卷尺；剪刀。

Materials needed: 83 yellow acrylic globe-like beads with a diameter of 8mm, 35 red acrylic globe-like beads with a diameter of 8mm, two black plastic round beads with a diameter of 8mm, 1.9-meter fishing line with a diameter of 0.5mm, four 0.35-meter fishing lines with a diameter of 0.5mm, a tape measure, and a pair of scissors.

扫描二维码获取串珠生肖狗
制作方法与教学视频
Scan the QR-code to get the methods and teaching video of threading beaded zodiac dog

制作串珠生肖狗共需 3.3 米渔线，其中用 1.9 米渔线串小狗的身体，4 段 35 厘米的渔线分别串小狗的四条腿。

3.3-meter fishing line is needed to thread the beaded zodiac dog. Among which, 1.9-meter fishing line is used to thread the puppy's body, four 35cm fishing lines are used to thread the puppy's four legs respectively.

开始制作前先将 1.9 米渔线对折，位于左手边的渔线为左线，位于右手边的渔线为右线。在接近左线线尾约 1 厘米处折一下做标识，以区分左线和右线。在制作串珠生肖狗的过程中，注意区分左线和右线，左线始终保持在左手边，右线始终保持在右手边。保持左线比右线长约 20 厘米。

Fold the 1.9-meter fishing line in half before starting the threading procedure. The fishing line which is on the left hand side is called left line, the fishing line which is on the right hand side is called right line. Mark the left line by folding it about 1cm from the end of the left line. When making the beaded zodiac dog, it's very important to distinguish the left line from the right line. Remember to keep the left line always on the left hand side and right line on the right hand side. Keep the left line about 20cm longer than the right line.

Exercises

1 Answer the following questions.

(1) What kind of tasks can dog perform for human beings?

(2) Why do many people treat the dog as one of their family members?

(3) Have you heard any story about dogs' loyalty to their masters?

(4) What is the symbolic meaning of dogs in your culture?

2 Search for the relevant materials and match the twelve zodiac animals with the 12 Earthly Branches.

(1) dragon		A. Zi
(2) snake		B. Chou
(3) monkey		C. Yin
(4) ox		D. Mao
(5) horse		E. Chen
(6) tiger		F. Si
(7) rooster		G. Wu
(8) pig		H. Wei
(9) rat		I. Shen
(10) rabbit		J. You
(11) dog		K. Xu
(12) sheep		L. Hai

3 **Choose the best answer to each of the following questions.**

(1) A girl was born in 2025, what is her animal sign?

A. Dragon.　　　　　　　　　B. Snake.

C. Horse.　　　　　　　　　　D. Dog.

(2) The year of the dragon began in 2024. For the following years ahead, which year will be the year of the dog?

A. 2027.　　　　　　　　　　B. 2028.

C. 2029.　　　　　　　　　　D. 2030.

(3) What's your Chinese animal sign?

A. rat　　　　B. ox　　　　C. tiger　　　　D. rabbit

E. dragon　　F. snake　　G. horse　　　H. sheep

I. monkey　　J. rooster　　K. dog　　　　L. pig

Chapter 5

⊏⊐⊏⊐⊏⊐⊏⊐⊏⊐⊏⊐⊏⊐⊏⊐

中国饮食文化
Chinese Food Culture

中国地域辽阔、人口众多，饮食文化源远流长、博大精深，与悠久历史相互交融，呈现出丰富多样的特点。中国菜肴不仅是味觉的享受，更承载着深刻的文化内涵，生动地折射出中国传统文化的精髓、价值观念及地域多样性。

China boasts a vast territory and a large population. Its food culture, with a long history that runs deep and wide, has intertwined with its time-honored past, thus demonstrating rich and diverse features. Chinese cuisine is far more than a means to satiate one's hunger; rather, it represents a cultural experience laden with profound significance, vividly reflecting the essence, values, and regional diversity of traditional Chinese culture.

Section 1

中国饮食文化概述
An Overview of Chinese Food Culture

中国人民自古以来极为重视饮食，"民以食为天"的观念深入人心。中华民族创造的饮食文化辉煌灿烂、独具特色。中国饮食文化源远流长，起源于远古先民早期的用火熟食，它先后经历了新石器时代的萌芽孕育阶段、夏商周时期的初步成型阶段、秦汉至唐宋的蓬勃发展阶段，于明清时期趋于成熟并定型，而后步入近现代的繁荣创新阶段。

Since ancient times, Chinese people has attached great importance to diet, and the concept that "food is the first necessity of the people" has been deeply rooted in people's hearts. The food culture created by Chinese people is magnificent, splendid, and unique. The

Chinese food culture has a long history. It originated from the practice of cooking food with fire by the ancestors in ancient times. Subsequently, it went through the embryonic stage in the Neolithic Age, the initial formation stage in the Xia, Shang and Zhou dynasties, the vigorous development stage from the Qin and Han dynasties to the Tang and Song dynasties, reached maturity and took shape in the Ming and Qing dynasties, and then entered the prosperous and innovative period in modern and contemporary times.

在各个历史时期，中国饮食烹饪无论是在物质层面还是精神层面，均呈现出鲜明的特色，尤其体现在炊餐器具、食物原料、烹饪技法、饮食品种、饮食著述、饮食思想等方面。中国饮食文化也展现出兼容并包的博大胸怀。它在不断吸收和借鉴其他文化元素、保持包容创新的同时，也对世界饮食文化，尤其是周边国家的饮食烹饪产生了深远影响。

In each historical period, Chinese cuisine has demonstrated distinct characteristics both in the material and spiritual aspects, particularly in aspects such as cooking and dining utensils, food ingredients, cooking techniques, food varieties, dietary writings, and dietary thoughts. Moreover, Chinese food culture demonstrates a broad and inclusive trait. While constantly absorbing and drawing on the elements of other cultures and maintaining an inclusive and innovative attitude, it has also exerted a profound influence on the world's food culture, especially on the cuisine of neighboring countries.

中国菜肴是中国文化的重要组成部分。由于资源、气候、地理、历史、烹饪技术和生活方式等因素的影响，中国菜肴有多种多样的烹饪风格。在清初，最著名和最有影响力的烹饪风格当属传统的"中国四大菜系"——川菜、鲁菜、粤菜和苏菜，它们分别代表着中国的西、北、南、东四方菜系。后来，闽菜、浙菜、湘菜和徽菜四大新地方菜系分化形成，与原来的四大菜系共同构成"中国八大菜系"。这些菜系凭借各式各样的烹饪方法而各具特色、各有所长。

Chinese cuisine is an important part of Chinese culture. There have been a multitude of cooking styles in China due to factors such as resources, climate, geography, history, cooking techniques, and lifestyle. In the early Qing Dynasty, the best known and most influential cooking styles were the traditional "four major schools of Chinese cuisine"—Sichuan, Shandong, Guangdong, and Jiangsu cuisines, which represent cuisines of western, northern, southern, and eastern China respectively. Later, four new schools of Chinese cuisine, namely, Fujian, Zhejiang, Hunan, and Anhui cuisines, were differentiated and formed. Along with the original four major cuisines, they made up the "eight major schools of the Chinese cuisine." These cuisines are distinguished by a variety of cooking methods, each with its own strengths.

鲁菜又称山东菜，起源于山东省。作为中国历史最悠久的菜系之一，它以咸鲜的口味以及精湛细腻的烹饪技艺而闻名。鲁菜的烹饪方法多样，尤以爆炒、烤、煮、炸等为特色，讲究调味适中，原汁原味。鲁菜的许多菜品都使用海鲜和肉类食材进行烹制，这反映出该地区丰富的自然资源。鲁菜口味浓郁且富有营养价值，堪称中国北方菜系的代表，深受全国食客的喜爱。代表性名菜包括糖醋鲤鱼、葱烧海参等。

Shandong cuisine, also known as Lu cuisine, originated in Shandong Province. As one of the most time-honored Chinese cuisines, it is famous for its savory and fresh flavors as well as its exquisite and delicate cooking techniques. Shandong cuisine features a wide variety of cooking methods, particularly stir-frying, roasting, boiling, and deep-frying, with a focus on balanced seasoning and the original flavors of the ingredients. Many dishes of Shandong cuisine are cooked with seafood and meat ingredients, reflecting the region's abundant natural resources. Shandong cuisine, with its rich flavors and high nutritional value, is truly a representative of northern Chinese cuisines and is deeply loved by diners across the country. Signature dishes include Sweet and Sour Carp and Braised Sea Cucumber with Scallions.

四川素有"天府之国"的美誉，也是美食的天堂。川菜口味浓郁，以辛辣味为特点，大量使用大蒜、辣椒以及独特的花椒。2010 年，联合国教科文组织宣布四川省省会成都为"美食之都"，这也是对川菜精湛烹饪技艺的认可。川菜的烹饪方法包括炒、蒸、炖、烤，而快炒则是川菜中最常用的烹饪方式之一。川菜有众多著名的菜品，包括宫保鸡丁、麻婆豆腐、水煮鱼等。

Sichuan, known as the Land of Abundance, is also a paradise for food lovers. Sichuan cuisine is rich in flavor and characterized by its pungency and spiciness, making extensive use of garlic, chili peppers, and unique Sichuan peppercorns. In 2010, UNESCO designated Chengdu, the capital of Sichuan Province, as a City of Gastronomy, which is a recognition of the exquisite cooking techniques of Sichuan cuisine. The cooking methods of Sichuan cuisine include stir-frying, steaming, stewing, and roasting, with quick stir-frying being one of the most commonly used cooking methods. There are a great number of well-known Sichuan dishes, such as Gong Bao Chicken, Mapo Tofu, Sliced Fish in Hot Chili Oil, and so on.

以淮扬菜为代表的江苏菜（亦称"苏菜"）非常精致，菜品色彩丰富且富有艺术性。苏菜由苏州、扬州、南京、镇江四市的地方美食发展而来，在长江中下游地区颇受欢迎。苏菜厨师注重在菜肴中突出各类食材本身独特的自然风味。为了体现其宫廷菜的渊源，苏菜的烹饪方法极为精细且讲究。常用的烹饪方法有炖、焖、煨、煮等，大多数方法都能保留食材的原汁原味，并且保持食材清爽、新鲜与温和的口感。江苏名菜有文思豆腐、糖醋鳜鱼和扬州炒饭等。

Jiangsu cuisine or Su cuisine, represented by Huaiyang cuisine, is very refined and presented colorfully and artistically. Developed from the local food of four cities—Suzhou, Yangzhou, Nanjing, and Zhenjiang, Jiangsu cuisine enjoys great popularity in the middle and lower reaches of the Yangtze River. The chefs of Jiangsu cuisine emphasize bringing out the distinct natural flavors of various ingredients in their dishes. Reflecting its imperial origin, Jiangsu cuisine uses very elaborate and precise cooking methods. The commonly used methods include stewing, braising, simmering, and boiling, most of which can preserve the original flavors while maintain clarity, freshness, and mildness of the ingredients. Famous Jiangsu dishes include Wensi Tofu, Sweet and Sour Mandarin Fish, and Yangzhou Fried Rice.

粤菜起源于中国南部的广东省，以清淡、鲜美和注重原汁原味的烹饪风格而闻名。传统粤菜中香料的使用量很少，以避免压倒主要食材的味道。由于广东气候温和，物产丰富，粤菜在选材上非常讲究，多使用海鲜、禽类和新鲜蔬菜，力求体现食材的天然风味。粤菜烹饪方法多样，包括蒸、煮、炒等，其中以蒸最为常见，此外还包括煎、双蒸、炖和炸。粤菜中常使用的调味品有葱、糖、盐、酱油、米酒、玉米淀粉、醋、葱油等。传统粤菜有烧鹅、蒸鱼、鲜虾肠粉、云吞面等。粤菜还以种类繁多的汤品而闻名，比如海鲜汤、银耳汤、冬瓜汤等。此外，粤菜还讲究刀工和火候的控制，菜品往往清淡爽口，适合大众口味。

Guangdong cuisine originated in Guangdong Province in southern China. It is known for its light, fresh, and natural flavor, with a focus on preserving the original taste of the ingredients. In traditional Guangdong cuisine, spices are used in modest amounts to avoid overwhelming the flavor of primary ingredients. Due to the mild climate and abundant resources in Guangdong, ingredient selection in Guangdong cuisine is meticulous, using mostly seafood, poultry, and fresh vegetables, aiming to highlight the natural flavors of the food. The cooking methods are diverse, including steaming, boiling, and stir-frying, with steaming being the most common. Other methods include shallow frying, double steaming, braising, and deep-frying. Condiments commonly used in Guangdong cuisine include spring onions, sugar, salt, soy sauce, rice wine, corn flour, vinegar, scallion oil, and so on. Traditional Guangdong dishes include Roast Goose, Steamed Fish, Scalded Shrimp Rice Noodle Rolls, and Wonton Noodles. Guangdong cuisine is also famous for the great variety of soups such as Seafood Soup, White Fungus Soup, and Wax Gourd Soup. Additionally, Guangdong cuisine emphasizes knife skills and precise heat control, resulting in dishes that are light and refreshing, appealing to a wide range of tastes.

　　闽菜发源于福建省的 3 个沿海城市（厦门、福州、泉州），因高超的海鲜烹饪技艺而享有盛誉。闽菜以清淡、软嫩著称，尤其注重鲜味，食材包括鱼类、贝类、甲鱼、蘑菇和竹笋。鱼露和虾油是闽菜的常见调味品。闽菜最常用的烹饪方法包括炖、焖、蒸和煮，特色名菜包括佛跳墙、炸牡蛎、荔枝肉等。

　　Originated from three seaside cities (Xiamen, Fuzhou, and Quanzhou) of Fujian Province, Fujian cuisine enjoys a great reputation for its superb seafood-cooking techniques. Fujian cuisine is known for being light, soft, and tender, with particular emphasis on an umami taste. Fish, shellfish, turtles, mushrooms, and bamboo shoots are often used as ingredients. Fish sauce and shrimp oil are common condiments in Fujian cuisine. The most commonly employed cooking methods in Fujian cuisine include braising, stewing, steaming, and boiling. The most famous dishes in Fujian cuisine are Fo Tiao Qiang, Fried Oysters, Lychee Meat, and so on.

　　浙菜精致高雅，烹饪方法有很多，包括煎、炖和焖。浙菜口感鲜嫩、味道醇厚。杭帮菜是浙菜的代表，起源于浙江省杭州市。它以口味清淡鲜美和烹饪技艺精湛著称。杭帮菜强调食材的天然风味，烹调方式多为蒸、炖、煮等，以保留食材的新鲜和营养。杭帮菜有很多著名的菜肴，其中包括叫花鸡、西湖醋鱼、东坡肉和龙井虾仁。这些菜肴清淡却不失风味，深受国内外食客的喜爱。杭帮菜不仅是杭州文化不可或缺的一部分，也体现了江南烹饪传统的精髓。

　　Zhejiang cuisine is dainty and refined. Many cooking methods are employed in Zhejiang cuisine, including sautéing, stewing, and braising. It features fresh and tender textures, as well as rich and mellow flavors. Hangzhou cuisine, a representative of Zhejiang cuisine, originated in Hangzhou, Zhejiang Province. It is known for its light, fresh flavors and delicate cooking techniques. Hangzhou cuisine emphasizes the natural taste of ingredients, often using methods such as steaming, stewing, and boiling to preserve freshness and nutrition. Famous dishes include Beggar's Chicken, West Lake Vinegar Fish, Dongpo Pork, and Longjing Shrimp. These dishes are light yet flavorful, making Hangzhou cuisine popular among diners both domestically and internationally. Hangzhou cuisine is not only an integral part of Hangzhou's culture but also reflects the essence of Jiangnan's culinary traditions.

　　湘菜历史悠久，食材种类繁多，色泽浓郁，口味辛辣，且带有烟熏和腌制的风味。几乎所有中国菜的烹饪技法，如腌制、调味、烟熏、慢炖、蒸和油炸，都能在湘菜中见到。湘菜以其热辣的口味、鲜香的气味和浓重的色泽而闻名。常见的烹调方法有炖、炸、锅烧、焖、熏等。湘菜大量使用辣椒、葱和蒜，以"纯辣"著称，不似川菜"麻辣"的口感。最受欢迎的湘菜有啤酒鸭、干锅鸡、家常豆腐、毛氏红烧肉、珍珠丸子、剁椒鱼头、牛肉米粉、莲子羹等。

Hunan cuisine has a long history, with a great variety of ingredients. It has rich colors, spicy tastes, and smoked and pickled flavors. Almost all Chinese cooking techniques like pickling, spicing, smoking, simmering, steaming, and frying can be used in Hunan cuisine. Hunan cuisine is well known for its hot and spicy flavors, fresh aroma, and deep colors. Common cooking methods include stewing, frying, pot-roasting, braising, and smoking. Through the extensive use of chilli peppers, shallots, and garlic, Hunan cuisine is known for being "purely hot" rather than "spicy and numbing" as in Sichuan cuisine. The most popular Hunan dishes include Beer Duck, Dry-Wok Chicken, Homemade Tofu, Mao's Braised Pork, Pearly Meatballs, Fish Head Steamed with Chopped Chilli, Beef Rice Noodles, Sweet Lotus Seeds Soup, etc.

徽菜起源于安徽省徽州地区。徽菜以其香气浓郁、口味醇厚和独特的烹饪技艺而闻名，注重火候与刀工，常使用炖、煮、蒸等烹饪方法，强调菜肴色、香、味的统一。徽菜的代表性菜品包括红烧狮子头、臭豆腐、臭鳜鱼等。这些菜肴多采用当地新鲜食材，充分展现了徽州地区的自然风味。徽菜不仅在中国广受欢迎，还吸引了越来越多的国际食客，成为中国美食文化的重要组成部分。

Huizhou cuisine originated from the Huizhou region in Anhui Province. It is renowned for its rich aroma, mellow taste, and unique cooking techniques. Huizhou cuisine pays great attention to heat control and knife skills, often employing cooking methods such as stewing, boiling, and steaming, emphasizing the unity of the color, aroma, and taste of the dishes. The representative dishes of Huizhou cuisine include Braised Pork Meatballs in Brown Sauce, Stinky Tofu, Stinky Mandarin Fish, etc. These dishes mostly utilize fresh local ingredients, fully demonstrating the natural flavor of the Huizhou region. Huizhou cuisine is not only widely popular in China but also attracts an increasing number of international diners, becoming an important part of Chinese food culture.

中国的饮食哲学深深植根于以阴阳原理为代表的平衡观念之中。传统中医认为要通过均衡的营养来维持身体的和谐，这一理念也体现在菜肴的烹制过程中。一顿典型的中餐包括各种各样的菜肴——口味上讲究甜、酸、苦、辣、咸的平衡，口感也丰富多样。这种对平衡的讲究还延伸到了菜肴的视觉呈现上，鲜活的色彩以及富有艺术感的摆盘是用餐体验的重要方面。

Chinese food philosophy is deeply rooted in the concept of balance, represented by the principles of Yin and Yang. Traditional Chinese medicine believes in maintaining harmony in the body through balanced nutrition. This philosophy is also reflected in the preparation of dishes. A typical Chinese meal includes a variety of dishes—a balance of flavors such as sweet, sour, bitter, spicy, and salty, and the textures are also varied. This attention to balance extends to the visual presentation of dishes, where vibrant colors and artistic arrangements are essential aspects of the dining experience.

尽管中国饮食文化深深植根于传统之中,但它也并非一成不变。随着城市化、全球化的浪潮使各地区间的交流越来越密切,各地方菜系呈现相互融合的态势,并受到国际饮食元素的影响。融合菜系以及对传统菜肴的现代演绎在国际化大都市中越来越受欢迎。

While deeply rooted in tradition, Chinese food culture is not immune to change. With the waves of urbanization and globalization, the exchanges among different regions have become increasingly close, leading to a blending of regional cuisines and international influences. Fusion cuisine and modern interpretations of traditional dishes have become more and more popular in cosmopolitan cities.

此外,社交媒体的兴起对中国饮食文化在全球的推广发挥了重要作用。通过美食博主,专业厨师及美食爱好者们在社交媒体上的内容创作与分享,中国美食的魅力得以跨越地理边界,触达全球受众。这种多元化烹饪理念的交流也丰富了中国饮食文化的内涵。

In addition, the rise of social media has played a significant role in promoting Chinese food culture globally. Food bloggers, chefs, and enthusiasts share their love for Chinese cuisine, making it more accessible and appealing to a broader audience. This exchange of culinary ideas has also enriched the connotation of Chinese food culture.

Exercises

① **Finish the following tasks in groups.**

(1) Work in pairs, appreciate the following English quotes about food, and tell your partner what kind of food you like best.

A life without a feast is like a long road without a hotel.

— Democritus

There is no sincere love than the love of food.

— George Bernard Shaw

One cannot think well, love well, sleep well, if one has not dined well.

— Virginia Woolf

All happiness depends upon a leisurely breakfast.

— John Gunther

(2) What do you usually have for three meals a day?

(3) Which cuisine do you like best, why?

Match each of the dishes with the school of cuisine it belongs to.

(1) Scalded Shrimp   A. Shandong cuisine

(2) Li Hongzhang Hodgepodge   B. Sichuan cuisine

(3) Braised Sea Cucumber with Scallion   C. Jiangsu cuisine

(4) Fried Oysters   D. Guangdong cuisine

(5) Spicy Slices of Poached Pork   E. Fujian cuisine

(6) Dry-Wok Chicken   F. Zhejiang cuisine

(7) West Lake Fish in Vinegar Gravy   G. Hunan cuisine

(8) Sweet and Sour Mandarin Fish   H. Anhui cuisine

Complete the following table with the missing information.

School of cuisine	Materials	Cooking methods	Characteristics
Shandong			
Sichuan			
Jiangsu			
Guangdong			
Fujian			
Zhejiang			
Hunan			
Anhui			

中国节日特色美食
Chinese Festival Delicacies

中国是一个有着悠久历史和丰富文化庆典的国家，节日特色美食种类繁多，蕴含着深厚的文化象征意义。这些世代相传的节日佳肴在家庭团聚中扮演着核心角色，也为节日增添了独特的魅力。

China, a country steeped in long history and rich cultural celebrations, boasts a diverse tapestry of holiday specialties which carry deep symbolic significance. These festive delicacies, passed down through generations, play a central role in family gatherings and add a unique charm to festivals.

中国春节，也称作中国新年，是中国最隆重的节日。春节是辞旧迎新、阖家团圆的欢乐时刻。饺子是春节标志性的食物。饺子的形状类似中国古代的钱币，象征着财富和繁荣。春节也有吃年糕的习俗，以求来年步步高升、事事顺利。无论是饺子还是年糕都有着美好的寓意，表达了人们对于新一年的期待及美好的祝愿。

The Spring Festival, also called Chinese New Year, is the grandest festival for Chinese people. The Spring Festival is a time of joy, renewal, and family togetherness. Dumplings, or Jiaozi, are the iconic food of the Spring Festival, which symbolize wealth and prosperity, with their shape resembling ancient Chinese coins. There is also a custom of eating New Year cake (Nian'gao) during the Spring Festival. People have a bite of the New Year cake, hoping for progress and good luck in the coming year. Both Jiaozi and Nian'gao carry wonderful auspicious meaning, expressing everyone's expectations and good wishes for the new year.

农历正月十五是元宵节，是中国农历新年里的第一个月圆夜，象征春天的回归。元宵节可以看作是中国春节的最后一天，换句话说，元宵节是春节的一个重要组成部分，同时也为春节画上了句号。在这一天晚上，人们纷纷走上街头赏灯、猜灯谜、放焰火，尽享节日欢乐。元宵节吃元宵自宋代起已成为中国人的习俗。元宵在中国南方通常称为汤圆。元宵是一种用糯米粉做成的圆团形食品，其馅料有甜咸之分。元宵或汤圆在外形、名称上都表达了"团圆"之意，承载着诸事圆满、家庭和睦、幸福美满的美好期许。

The Lantern Festival is celebrated on the 15th day of the first month in the Chinese lunar calendar. It is the first full moon night in the Chinese lunar year, symbolizing the return of the spring. The Lantern Festival may be regarded as the last day of the Spring Festival. In other words, the Lantern Festival is an important part of the Spring Festival, which marks the end of Chinese New Year celebrations. On that night, people flock to the streets and enjoy themselves by watching lanterns, guessing lantern riddles, and setting off fireworks. Eating Yuanxiao (sweet dumplings) during the Lantern Festival has been a custom among Chinese people since the Song Dynasty. Yuanxiao is also called Tangyuan in different regions of southern China. It is a round-shaped food made of glutinous rice flour. The fillings can be either sweet or salty. The shape and name of both Yuanxiao and Tangyuan are similar to the meaning of "reunion," representing the Chinese people's aspiration for all aspects of life to be flawless, for families to be reunited in harmony, and for a state of happiness and contentment to prevail.

每年农历二月二日这一天被称作龙抬头或青龙节。传说有一年天下大旱，饿死了许多人。一条青龙不愿意看到百姓受灾挨饿，未经玉帝允许，偷偷给人间降雨。为了惩罚青龙，玉帝把青龙压在一座大山下，并颁下圣旨：除非金豆开花，否则青龙永远别想出来。然而，百姓们发现大豆和玉米粒都是金色的，而且炒的时候会爆开花。于是，人们在院子里用炒开花的大豆和玉米祭拜玉帝。玉帝不能违背诺言，下令在农历二月二日释放青龙。这一天就逐渐变成了人们用玉米花来庆祝玉帝释放青龙的节日。

The second day of the second lunar month each year is known as Dragon Head-Raising Day or the Qinglong (Green Dragon) Festival. Legend has it that one year, a severe drought struck the world, causing many people to starve to death. A green dragon, unwilling to see people suffer, secretly brought rain to the earth without obtaining the Jade Emperor's permission. To punish the dragon, the Jade Emperor trapped it under a huge mountain and decreed: the green dragon shall never be released unless golden beans blossom. However, the common people discovered that both soybeans and corn kernels were golden in color, and would burst open like flowers when fried. So, people offered these "blooming golden beans" in tribute to the Jade Emperor in their yards. Not to break his promise, the Jade Emperor ordered to release the dragon on the second day of the second lunar month. Gradually, this day became a festival, during which people celebrated the Jade Emperor's release of the green dragon by eating puffed corn kernels.

在这一天，人们会依照此日独特的龙元素将诸多食物冠以"龙"字，比如吃饺子被赋予"食龙耳"的雅称，春卷被称为"龙鳞"，面条被称为"龙须面"，馄饨被称为"龙牙"，爆米花被称为"龙子"。这些传统习俗也保留至今。

On this day, people bestow the title of "dragon" on many foods based on the unique dragon elements of this day. For example, eating dumplings is endued with the elegant name of "eating dragon ears," spring rolls are called "dragon scales," noodles are named "dragon beard noodles," wontons are referred to as "dragon teeth," and popcorn is known as "dragon seeds." These traditional customs have also been preserved to this day.

清明节，又称扫墓日，是中国重要的传统节日之一。它不仅是人们祭奠先祖的日子，也是民族身份认同的重要纽带。中国传统历法将一年划分为 24 个节气，清明是第 5 个节气，其时间处于每年公历 4 月 4 日至 4 月 6 日的区间内。清明过后，气温回升，降水增多，正是春耕、春播的大好时节，因此，清明节也与农事活动关系密切。清明节距今已有 2500 多年的历史，其传统习俗丰富多样。在中国南方，人们会在清明节吃青团。它是一种时令小吃，皮由糯米粉和绿色植物汁混合制成，填充豆沙、肉松或蛋黄等馅料。

Qingming Festival, also called the Tomb Sweeping Day, is one of the most important traditional Chinese festivals. It is not only a time for Chinese people to show respects to ancestors but also a tie for them to recognize their national identity. The traditional Chinese calendar divides a year into 24 solar terms and Qingming is the fifth solar term, which falls between April 4th and April 6th of the Gregorian calendar. After the festival, the temperature rises up and rainfall increases. It is the high time for spring plowing and sowing. The festival therefore has a close relationship with agriculture. Qingming Festival, accompanied by a rich variety of traditional customs, has a history of over 2,500 years. In South China, people are likely to eat Sweet Green Rice Balls during Qingming Festival. It is a seasonal snack made from a mixture of glutinous rice flour and green plant juice which is stuffed with red bean paste, meat floss or egg yolk.

端午节也是中国的传统节日，在农历五月初五（通常对应阳历的六月）。关于端午节的由来，说法甚多，其中最广为人知的是为了纪念楚国的爱国诗人、政治家屈原（公元前约 340 年—公元前 278 年）。端午节的重要习俗——赛龙舟和吃粽子，也与纪念屈原的传说相融合，共同构成了端午节丰富的文化内涵。粽子呈金字塔形，以糯米为主料，肉、坚果、豆类等食材都可作为馅料，外面用竹叶包裹。此外，喝雄黄酒、制作并佩戴香囊也是端午节传统习俗。

The Dragon Boat Festival is also a traditional Chinese festival that takes place on the fifth day of the fifth lunar month (usually in June according to the Gregorian calendar). There are many legends about its origin, the most popular of which is in commemoration of Qu Yuan (c.340–278BCE), a patriotic poet and statesman in the State of Chu. The important customs of the Dragon Boat Festival—dragon boat racing and eating Zongzi—are also integrated with the legend of honoring Qu Yuan, jointly forming the rich cultural connotation of the Dragon Boat Festival. Zongzi is pyramid-shaped, made of glutinous rice filled with a variety of ingredients such as meat, nuts, and beans, and wrapped in bamboo leaves. Besides, there are also different customs like drinking realgar wine and making and wearing sachets.

中秋节有 3000 多年的历史，可以追溯到商代时人们对月亮的崇拜。中秋节在中国文化中具有重要地位，有许多相关文学著作和民间传说。"中秋"一词最早出现在战国时期《周礼》一书中，但在该书中，"中秋"一词只与时间和季节有关。北宋时期，农历八月十五被官方确立为中秋节。对中国人来说，中秋节意味着阖家团圆，满月象征着繁荣与幸福。赏月和吃月饼是各地中秋节的传统习俗。月饼如同满月，象征着团圆。中秋节也是桂花盛开的时节，赏桂花、食用桂花制作的各种食品也是中秋节的习俗。从古至今，老百姓以月之圆喻人之团圆，将念乡思人之情、对丰收的感恩之意和对幸福的祈盼借各种庆祝方式表达出来，使中秋节成为丰富多彩、弥足珍贵的文化遗产。

Mid-Autumn Festival has a history of over 3,000 years, dating back to moon worship in the Shang Dynasty. It has an important place in Chinese culture, with many related literary works and folklore. The term "Mid-Autumn" first appeared in the book *Rites of Zhou*, written in the Warring States period. But the term was only related to time and seasons. In the Northern Song Dynasty, the 15th day of the 8th lunar month was officially established as the Mid-Autumn Festival. To the Chinese, Mid-Autumn Festival means family reunion. A full moon is a symbol of prosperity and happiness. Appreciating the moon and eating mooncakes are traditional customs of the day, as the round shape symbolizes unity in the Chinese culture. Also, owing to the timing of osmanthus blossoms, appreciating osmanthus flowers, and enjoying osmanthus-flavored wine or food are other traditional customs on the occasion. Throughout history, ordinary people have regarded the full moon as a symbol of family reunion. Chinese people's sentiments of nostalgia, gratitude for a bumper harvest, and aspiration for happiness have been stirred by the full-moon and embodied in the ways the Mid-Autumn Festival is celebrated, which makes the festival a colorful and precious cultural heritage.

重阳节在农历九月初九。《周易》中把"九"定为阳数，九月九日，两九相重，故而称重阳。在民俗观念中，九在数字中又是最大数，有长久、长寿的含义。1989 年，中国政府将重阳节定为"老年节"，表达了人们对老年人健康长寿的祝福。自 2013 年起实施的《老年人权益保障法》，明确规定每年农历九月初九为老年节，意味着重阳节自此成为中国法定的老年节。重阳节的重要传统习俗是赏菊和饮菊花酒。菊花酒的酿造方法颇为独特。古时，人们通常会在农历九月初九采摘新鲜的菊花和菊花叶，然后将它们同谷物混合酿制成酒，要到次年的同一天才饮用。重阳糕是重阳节的节令糕点，通常由面粉、红糖、水果、坚果等食材制作而成。在中国，"糕"与"高"同音，吃糕也有"登高"的寓意，这也与古时重阳节登高的习俗有关。重阳糕没有固定的样式，但通常做成九层，看起来像一座塔一样。

The Double Ninth Festival (Chongyang Festival) falls on the ninth day of the ninth month on the Chinese lunar calendar. In *The Book of Changes*, nine is regarded as the number of Yang (which means masculine). The ninth day of the ninth month is the day that has two Yang numbers, and "chong" in Chinese means double. Hence, the name Chongyang was created. In Chinese folklore, the number nine is the largest number. It's a homonym to the Chinese word "久" which contains the auspicious meaning of "a long and healthy life." In 1989, Chinese government designated the Double Ninth Festival as the "Festival for the Elderly" to express wishes for health and longevity of the senior citizens. The Law on the Protection of the Rights and Interests of the Elderly which has been in effect since 2013 clearly stipulates that every year's Double Ninth Festival is the legal festival for senior citizens in China. The important traditions of the Double Ninth Festival are appreciating chrysanthemums and drinking chrysanthemum wine. The chrysanthemum wine is unique in brewing. In ancient times, people usually picked fresh chrysanthemums and leaves on the ninth day of the ninth lunar month, and brewed the mixture of them and grains into wine, which would not be drunk until the same day next year. Chongyang cake is a festive cake for the Double Ninth Festival that is usually made of flour, brown sugar, fruits, and nuts among other ingredients. In China, the Chinese characters for "cake" and "height" are pronounced the same. Therefore, eating cake represents the meaning of "climbing to a height," which is also related to the ancient custom of climbing mountains to pray for good luck on this day. The Double Ninth Cake doesn't have a fixed style, but it is usually made into nine layers and looks like a tower.

冬至是中国传统二十四节气中的第22个节气，冬至当天，太阳几乎直射南回归线，北半球将经历一年中最短的白天和最长的黑夜。自此以后，白昼的时间变得越来越长，而夜晚则会越来越短。冬至也标志着一年中最寒冷时节的来临。在中国北方地区，吃饺子是冬至必不可少的习俗。南方地区的人通常会喝羊肉汤或吃汤圆来庆祝冬至。

Winter Solstice is the 22nd solar term in the 24 traditional Chinese solar terms. On the winter solstice, when the sun is almost directly above the Tropic of Capricorn, the Northern

Hemisphere will experience the shortest day and longest night of the year. From then on, the days become longer and the nights become shorter. The Winter Solstice also marks the arrival of the coldest days in the year. During Winter Solstice in northern China, eating dumplings is essential to celebrate the festival. In southern China, people usually celebrate the winter solstice by having mutton soup or eating Tangyuan.

腊八节，俗称腊八，是汉族传统节日，原是古代欢庆丰收、祭拜先祖和神灵的日子。如今，对腊八节的庆祝已不像古代时期那么隆重，但喝腊八粥的习俗仍旧保留了下来。腊八粥是在腊八节用多种食材熬制的一种粥，也叫七宝五味粥。腊八粥最早是用红豆煮成的，后经演变，食材越来越多样，并带有地方特色。腊八节喝腊八粥，有祛病迎祥、庆祝丰收的美好寓意。

Laba Festival, commonly known as Laba, is a traditional festival of Han nationality. Laba was an ancient sacrificial ceremony to celebrate the harvest and give thanks to ancestors and deities. Nowadays, the celebration of the Laba Festival is no longer as grand as it was in ancient times. However, the custom of having Laba porridge has been well preserved. Laba porridge, also known as the Porridge of Seven Treasures and Five Flavors, is made with a variety of ingredients on the Laba Festival. The earliest Laba porridge was cooked with red beans. Later, through evolution and with local characteristics, it has gradually become more and more diverse. Having Laba porridge on the Laba Festival carries the auspicious meaning of dispelling diseases, praying for prosperity and celebrating a bountiful harvest.

在中国的多元文化社会中，节日特色美食不仅是一种饮食表达，更是文化传承与美好祝福的载体。当家人欢聚一堂庆祝这些重要时刻时，美食的味道不仅承载着传统文化中的温暖，也寄托了人们对繁荣未来的期许。

In China's multicultural society, festive delicacies serve not merely as culinary expressions, but also as vessels of cultural heritage and best wishes. When families gather together to celebrate these significant moments, the flavors of these delicacies carry both the warmth of traditional culture and people's expectations for a prosperous future.

Exercises

1 Form the group and discuss the following questions.

(1) What are the Spring Festival couplets usually about?

(2) What traditional food do people usually eat on the Mid-Autumn Festival and what does the food symbolize?

(3) When is the Qingming Festival celebrated? What do Chinese people do to commemorate their departed family members?

❷ Choose the best answer for the following questions.

(1) During the Mid-Autumn Festival, people usually eat moon cakes. Eating moon cakes mainly represents _____ .

A. the reunion of family members   B. sweet love

C. living a happy life   D. great expectations

(2) Which of the following is the Qingming Festival custom?

A. Rowing a dragon boat.   B. Having an outing in spring.

C. Making dumplings.   D. Enjoying the full moon.

(3) In addition to eating moon cakes, what other food do people have on Mid-Autumn Festival?

A. Zongzi.   B. Osmanthus cake.

C. Glutinous rice ball.   D. Boiled dumpling.

(4) Which of the following options is not the custom of the Lantern Festival?

A. Eating Yuanxiao.

B. Enjoying watching lanterns.

C. Dragon and lion dances.

D. Sticking paper-cut for window decoration.

(5) Do you know when the earliest Zongzi were made?

A. In the Jin Dynasty.

B. During the Spring and Autumn period.

C. In the Northern and Southern Dynasties.

D. In the Shang and Zhou dynasties.

中国传统美食的制作方法
Ways to Make Traditional Chinese Delicacies

在丰富多彩的中国传统美食中，饺子、汤圆和春饼以其独特的风味和深厚的文化内涵成为最具代表性的经典佳肴。本章将介绍这三种美食的制作方法，开启中华美食制作之旅。

Among the rich and diverse traditional Chinese delicacies, dumplings, Tangyuan, and spring pancakes stand out as the most representative classic dishes due to their unique flavors and profound cultural significance. This chapter will guide you to explore the cooking methods of these three delicacies and start a journey of making Chinese cuisine.

1 | 饺子
Dumplings

饺子是中国传统美食之一，经常出现在节日的餐桌上。由于其形状与元宝颇为相似，吃饺子也被赋予了招财进宝的美好祈愿。

Dumplings are one of the traditional delicacies in China, often found on festive dining tables. As their shape resembles that of gold or silver ingots in ancient times, eating dumplings has been endowed with the auspicious wish of ushering in wealth and good fortune.

过年吃饺子的习俗在明清时期逐渐盛行起来，人们通常在除夕夜守岁时包饺子，在辞岁时食用，寓意着"更岁交子"，"饺子"这一名称便由此谐音而来。吃饺子的习俗，曾经主要盛行于中国北方地区，而今，饺子已成为全国各地常见的食品，同时也是中国传统美食在海外的重要代表，是中华文化的象征。

The custom of eating dumplings during Chinese New Year thrived in the Ming and Qing dynasties. People usually make dumplings while staying up on New Year's Eve and eat them when bidding farewell to the old year, signifying "the transition between the old and new years and ushering in the new year" ("更岁交子" in Chinese). The name "dumplings" ("饺子" in Chinese) is thus derived from the homophonic pronunciation of this phrase. The practice of eating dumplings was mainly prevalent in northern China in the past. Nowadays, however, dumplings have become ubiquitous throughout the nation. Meanwhile, they are also an important representative of traditional Chinese food abroad and a symbolic icon of Chinese culture.

饺子的馅料丰富多样，可荤可素，几乎任何食材都能用来做馅。常见的饺子肉馅包括猪肉、羊肉、牛肉、鸡肉、鱼肉和虾肉，这些馅料通常会与切碎的蔬菜混合在一起。常见的素菜馅包括大白菜、葱、韭菜、芹菜、蘑菇、黑木耳、胡萝卜和韭黄。这些食材被细细切碎后，与油、盐、五香粉以及其他调味料混合拌匀，制成饺子馅。在面皮上放一点馅料，把面皮捏合起来，一个饺子就包好了。

The fillings of dumplings are rich and varied, encompassing both meat and vegetables, and almost any ingredient can be used as stuffing. Common dumpling meat fillings include pork, mutton, beef, chicken, fish, and shrimp, which are usually mixed with chopped vegetables. Popular vegetable fillings include cabbage, spring onions, Chinese chives, celery, mushrooms, black fungus, carrots, and hotbed chives. These ingredients are chopped finely, mixed with oil, salt, five-spice powder, and other seasonings to create the fillings. To make dumplings, place a small amount of fillings on the dough wrapper and pinch the wrapper together.

包好的饺子可以水煮、蒸制或者煎制，其中水煮是最常见的做法。食用时，既可以直接吃，又可以蘸着酱油、醋、蒜泥等调料享用。此外，酸汤水饺也别有一番风味，深受人们喜爱。

The prepared dumplings can be boiled, steamed, or pan-fried, with boiling being the most common method. When eating, they can be enjoyed directly or with soy sauce, vinegar, mashed garlic, and other condiments. Additionally, dumplings in spicy and sour soup offer a unique flavor and are deeply loved by people.

饺子，这一简单的美食，承载着千年的历史、温暖的情谊和美好的寓意。它不仅是舌尖上的美味，更是维系家庭情感的纽带和传承中华文化的重要载体。对于绝大多数中国人来说，饺子的味道总能唤起对家的思念，承载着对美好生活的无限憧憬。

Dumplings, a simple delicacy, carry thousands of years of history, warm affection, and auspicious meaning. More than a culinary delight, they serve as a bond that strengthens family ties and a significant carrier for the inheritance of Chinese culture. For the vast majority of Chinese people, the taste of dumplings always evokes a longing for home and embodies endless hopes for a better life.

饺子馅料的选择可因个人喜好而定。本部分将以备受大众喜爱的韭菜鸡蛋馅饺子为例，来展示包饺子的详细步骤与过程。

扫描二维码获取韭菜
鸡蛋馅饺子制作方法
与教学视频
**Scan the QR-code to get
the methods and teaching
video of making dumplings
with Chinese chives and
egg filling**

The choice of dumpling fillings depends on personal preference. In this part, we will take the widely popular dumplings with Chinese chives and egg filling as an example to demonstrate the detailed steps and process of making dumplings.

所需材料：300 克面粉；46 克温水；200 克韭菜；2 个鸡蛋；蒜末；姜蓉；酱油；芝麻油；葱花；适量的盐和胡椒粉。

Material needed: 300 grams of wheat flour, 46 grams of warm water, 200 grams of Chinese chives, two eggs, finely chopped garlic, grated ginger, soy sauce, sesame oil, chopped green onions, and an appropriate amount of salt and pepper.

Exercises

1 **Answer the following questions.**

(1) Empanada in Spain, samosa in India, and gnocchi in Italy resemble Chinese dumplings. Do your countries have similar traditional foods?

(2) What are the possible reasons for the wide-spread popularity of dumplings around the world?

(3) What is the cultural motivation behind the practice of some people inserting special items like coins, candies, or peanuts into dumplings?

2 **Choose the best answer to each of the following questions.**

(1) Which festival in China are dumplings most closely associated with?

A. Mid-Autumn Festival.   B. Dragon Boat Festival.

C. Spring Festival.   D. Qingming Festival.

(2) In Chinese culture, what does the shape of dumplings resemble and symbolize?

A. The shape of dumplings resembles a crescent moon, symbolizing beauty.

B. The shape of dumplings is similar to the shape of gold and silver ingots, representing the hope for wealth and prosperity.

C. The shape of dumplings resembles a flower, symbolizing prosperity.

D. The shape of dumplings resembles a boat, symbolizing a smooth journey.

(3) Which of the following is NOT a common filling for traditional Chinese dumplings?

A. Apple and cinnamon.   B. Shrimp and Chinese chives.

C. Pork and cabbage.   D. Beef and scallion.

(4) Which of the following is a common ingredient in many dumpling dipping sauces?

    A. Maple syrup.   B. Soy sauce.

    C. Honey.   D. Whipped cream.

(5) The art of making dumplings has been passed down for generations. What is one of the cultural values it represents?

    A. It represents laziness as it takes a long time to make.

    B. It represents competition among families.

    C. It represents individualism as each person makes their own style of dumplings.

    D. It represents family heritage and unity.

2 | 元宵 / 汤圆
Yuanxiao/Tangyuan

元宵或汤圆是元宵节传统美食，是用糯米粉做成的圆团形食品，主要流行于汉族地区。

Yuanxiao or Tangyuan, a traditional food for the Lantern Festival, is a round-shaped food made of glutinous rice flour. It is mainly popular in areas inhabited by the Han ethnic group.

北宋之前，元宵是无馅的糯米实心团子，放入沸水中煮熟后，搭配酒酿、白糖、蜜枣、桂花等辅料一同食用。南宋时期开始有了糖馅元宵，此后更是演变出多种多样的馅料。在不断的发展历程中，元宵的口味也持续变化，其馅料主要分为甜、咸两类。甜馅一般由糖、豆沙、枣泥、桂花、果仁等制成；咸馅则多为荤菜馅料，通常采用肉或者肉与蔬菜混合制作而成。

Before the Northern Song Dynasty, Yuanxiao were solid glutinous rice balls without fillings, cooked in boiling water and served with auxiliary ingredients such as fermented glutinous rice, sugar, candied dates, and osmanthus flowers. During the Southern Song Dynasty, Yuanxiao with sugar fillings began to appear, and since then a wide variety of fillings have been created. In the course of continuous development, the taste of Yuanxiao has also been constantly changing. The fillings are mainly divided into two categories: sweet and salty. Sweet fillings are usually made of sugar, red bean paste, jujube paste, osmanthus, nuts, etc., while salty fillings are mostly meat fillings, usually made of meat or a combination of meat and vegetables.

元宵的制作方法在中国有南北差异。过去素有"南汤圆，北元宵"的说法，不过如今这种区分已不那么严格。南方人在制作汤圆时，通常先将糯米粉用水调和成皮，然后包上馅揉成圆球状。北方人制作元宵时，往往会先拌馅料，把各种馅料混合搅拌均匀后摊成大饼状，晾晒后再切成一个个方形小块，然后把馅块放入箩筐、竹筛或其他容器内，倒入糯米粉，不停地摇晃，其间加入清水使糯米粉黏附在馅块上，当馅料表面变成小圆球状时，元宵便制作完成了。

The production methods of Yuanxiao vary between the northern and southern regions of China. Traditionally, it was said that "Tangyuan is made in the south and Yuanxiao in the north", yet nowadays this difference has become less pronounced. When making Tangyuan in the south, one first mixes glutinous rice flour with water to form a wrapper, then encloses the filling and shapes it into a ball. In contrast, when making Yuanxiao in the north, the process begins with preparing the filling. Various fillings are thoroughly mixed and spread out into a flat cake shape, which is then dried and cut into small square pieces. Subsequently, these filling pieces are placed in a basket, bamboo sieve or other containers, and glutinous rice flour is poured in and shaken continuously. Water is intermittently added to ensure the glutinous rice flour adheres to the filling pieces. Once the surface of the filling takes on a small spherical appearance, the Yuanxiao is successfully made.

元宵或汤圆，以水煮食为主，亦能蒸、炸、煎、炒。其外形圆润，名称与"团圆"相近，带有全家团圆和睦的寓意，寄托着人们对圆满、美好生活的憧憬。如今，元宵或汤圆早已突破节日的限制，成为备受大众青睐的日常美食。

Yuanxiao or Tangyuan is typically prepared by boiling in water, and can also be steamed, deep-fried, pan-fried or stir-fried. With their round shape and names similar to "Tuanyuan" (signifying reunion), they stand as symbols of family reunion and harmony and embody people's longing for a perfect and blissful life. Nowadays, Yuanxiao or Tangyuan have broken through the limitations of being solely festival fare and are available in the market all year long, evolving into one of the daily delicacies favored by the public.

本部分将介绍黑芝麻花生馅汤圆的制作方法。

In this part, you will find the methods of making Tangyuan with black sesame and peanut filling.

扫描二维码获取黑芝麻
花生馅汤圆制作方法
与教学视频
Scan the QR-code to get
the methods and teaching
video of making Tangyuan
with black sesame and
peanut filling

所需材料：糯米粉；水；熟黑芝麻；熟花生；猪油；白糖。

Material needed: glutinous rice flour, water, roasted black sesame seeds, roasted peanuts, lard, and sugar.

Exercises

1 **Answer the following questions.**

(1) With the increasing popularity of healthy eating, how can the traditional recipe of Yuanxiao or Tangyuan be modified to meet the demands of health-conscious consumers?

(2) How can Yuanxiao or Tangyuan be incorporated into a modern Western diet to create a new fusion cuisine?

2 **Choose the best answer to each of the following questions.**

(1) Which festival is Yuanxiao or Tangyuan most closely associated with and symbolizes family reunion?

A. Dragon Boat Festival.   B. Lantern Festival.

C. Mid-Autumn Festival.   D. Qingming Festival.

(2) The shape of Yuanxiao or Tangyuan is usually round. What cultural meaning does this round shape convey in Chinese culture?

A. Abundance and wealth.   B. Longevity and health.

C. Harmony and completeness.   D. Bravery and strength

(3) When making Yuanxiao or Tangyuan, what is the main ingredient of the outer skin?

A. Corn starch.   B. Potato starch.

C. Wheat flour.   D. Glutinous rice flour.

(4) Which of the following is a typical way of serving Yuanxiao or Tangyuan in southern China?

A. With sweet osmanthus syrup.   B. With pickled cabbage soup.

C. With spicy beef broth.   D. With cheese sauce.

(5) Which of the following ingredients is not suitable for making Yuanxiao or Tangyuan?

A. Walnut.   B. Peanut.

C. Pepper.   D. Jujube paste.

3 | 春饼
Spring Pancake

春饼是中国的一种传统面食，是用面粉烙制或蒸制而成的圆形薄饼，人们常常将其与各类菜肴搭配卷食。春饼因在立春日食用的传统习俗而得名，也被称作薄饼、荷叶饼。

Spring pancakes are a kind of traditional wheaten food in China. They are round and thin pancakes made by baking or steaming flour. People often roll them up with various dishes to eat. Owing to the age-old custom of having them on the Beginning of Spring, they have acquired the name of spring pancakes. Additionally, they are also referred to as thin pancakes or lotus leaf pancakes.

春饼以薄、软为显著特点，其形状可大可小，食用时用饼裹菜。在古代，立春之际除自家食用春饼外，人们还相互赠送，以表迎春纳福之意。

Spring pancakes are notably characterized by their thinness and softness. They can be made in various sizes, and when eating, vegetables are wrapped within the pancake. In ancient times, on the day of the Beginning of Spring, apart from having spring pancakes at home, people also gave them to one another as a gesture of welcoming spring and inviting good luck.

吃春饼需咬，谓之"咬春"。古时人们认为"咬春"能去春困、避百病，还能得到春天万物复苏的吉祥之气。有的地方把吃春饼称作"食煎虫"，意为煎除百病。

Eating spring pancakes needs biting, which is called "biting spring." People in ancient times believed that "biting spring" can relieve spring fatigue, avoid illnesses, and bring good fortune associated with the revival of all things in spring. In some places, eating spring pancakes is called "eating fried insects," symbolizing frying away various illnesses.

春饼裹的馅料因时因地而异。最初的春饼是配合菜进食的，合菜以豆芽、菠菜、韭黄、粉线等食材一同炒成。宋时人们将可生食蔬菜切细，以春饼卷着食用。元代出现包馅后油炸的食用方法。到清代，春饼也有用炒菜作馅的。随着配方与技艺的精进，春饼在明清之际从民间进入宫廷，成为御膳之一，也成为满汉全席中的一道点心。现如今，春饼的配料更加丰富多样，人们可以根据自己的喜好选择春饼的配菜。吃春饼时，人们习惯将菜包起来后从头吃到尾，称"有头有尾"，有在春天祈望全年美好的寓意。

The fillings for spring pancakes vary depending on the time and place. Initially, spring pancakes were eaten together with vegetables that were stir-fried with bean sprouts, spinach, hotbed chives, rice vermicelli, and other ingredients. During the Song Dynasty, people chopped vegetables that could be eaten raw into fine pieces, and wrapped them in spring pancakes to eat. In the Yuan Dynasty, a method of frying the filled spring pancakes after wrapping emerged. By the Qing Dynasty, stir-fried dishes were also used as fillings. With the improvement of recipes and techniques, spring pancakes entered the imperial court from the dining tables of common folks during the Ming and Qing dynasties, becoming one of the imperial dishes and later a signature dim sum in the Manchu-Han Imperial Feast. In modern times, the ingredients for spring pancakes have become even more diverse, allowing people to choose their preferred accompaniments. When eating spring pancakes, it is customary to wrap the vegetables and eat them from the beginning to the end, which is called "having a good start and end," symbolizing the hope for good fortune throughout the year.

扫描二维码获取春饼
制作方法与教学视频
Scan the QR-code to
get the methods and
teaching video of making
spring pancakes

所需材料：面粉；盐；食用油；水。

Material needed: wheat flour, salt, cooking oil, and water.

Exercises

1 **Answer the following questions.**

(1) In what ways do the different names of spring pancakes, such as "thin pancake" and "lotus leaf pancake," reflect their characteristics and cultural associations?

(2) What is the relationship between the cultural meaning of "biting spring" and the ingredients and eating methods of spring pancakes?

(3) Explain the significance of spring pancakes being both a folk food and an imperial dish.

2 **Choose the best answer to each of the following questions.**

(1) Which of the following is a traditional filling for spring pancakes?

A. Strawberry jam.   B. Cream cheese.

C. Shredded pork with scallions.   D. Chocolate spread.

(2) What is the main ingredient of the spring pancake dough?

A. Wheat flour.   B. Cornmeal.

C. Rice flour.   D. Potato starch.

(3) Which of the following is NOT a reason why people eat spring pancakes on the Beginning of Spring?

A. To relieve spring fatigue.

B. To fend off evil spirits.

C. To bring health benefits and ward off various ailments.

D. To get the good fortune related to spring revival.

(4) When did spring pancakes enter the imperial court and become one of the imperial dishes?

A. During the Jin Dynasty.

B. During the Tang Dynasty.

C. During the Yuan Dynasty.

D. During the Ming and Qing dynasties.

(5) What is the traditional way of eating spring pancakes that implies a good omen?

A. Cutting them into small pieces and sharing them.

B. Wrapping the fillings and eating from the beginning to the end.

C. Dipping them into a sweet sauce and then eating.

D. Rolling them up without fillings and eating.

Chapter 6

中国画
Chinese Painting

中国画，亦称"国画"，是中国传统艺术中的璀璨明珠。中国画的画家们巧妙地运用水墨、颜料与宣纸等材料，通过墨色的浓淡、笔触的灵动与色彩的和谐，生动地表现出山水之壮丽、花鸟之生机、人物之情感，展现出独树一帜的审美韵味与博大精深的文化内涵。中国画的审美追求，深刻体现了中华民族对自然、社会与人生的深邃洞察与独特感悟。在中国传统文化版图中，中国画占据着举足轻重的地位，被誉为"东方艺术之瑰宝"。作为中国传统文化的重要象征之一，中国画在传承与弘扬中华优秀传统文化、培育民族精神以及增强文化自信方面，发挥着至关重要的作用。

Chinese painting, also known as Guohua, is a dazzling pearl of traditional Chinese art. The painters of Chinese painting skillfully utilize materials such as ink, pigments, and rice paper. Through the shades of ink, the agility of brushwork, and the harmony of colors, they delicately outline the grandeur of landscapes, the vitality of flowers and birds, and the emotions of people, demonstrating its unique aesthetic charm and profound cultural connotations. Its aesthetic pursuit profoundly embodies the deep insights and unique perceptions of the Chinese nation towards nature, society, and life. In the realm of traditional Chinese culture, Chinese painting occupies a pivotal position and is known as the "Treasure of Oriental Art." As one of the key symbols of traditional Chinese culture, Chinese painting plays a crucial role in inheriting and promoting China's excellent traditional culture, as well as nurturing national spirit and enhancing cultural confidence.

中国画发展概况
An Overview of the Development of Chinese Painting

中国画历史悠久，其源头可追溯至史前时期。那时的艺术家们，以岩石为纸，以矿物为墨，在幽深的洞穴中绘制出了一幅幅生动而质朴的壁画。这些壁画虽历经风雨侵蚀，却依然能够让人们窥见古代人类对于自然、对于生活的原始感知与独特表达。它们不仅是人类艺术史上的珍贵遗产，更是人们了解古代社会、探索人类精神世界的窗口。

Chinese painting boasts a long history. Its origin can be traced back to the prehistoric period, when artists used rocks as paper and minerals as ink to create vivid and rustic murals in deep caves. Although these murals have been eroded by wind and rain, they still allow us to glimpse the ancient humans' primitive perceptions and unique expressions of nature and life. They are not only valuable heritages in human art history, but also windows for us to understand ancient societies and explore the human spiritual world.

随着历史的车轮滚滚向前，人类社会步入了文明的新纪元。在这一进程中，中国画也经历了从萌芽到成熟的蜕变。从夏商周时期的青铜器纹饰，到秦汉时期的砖石壁画；从魏晋南北朝时期的士人山水画，到隋唐五代时期的宫廷绘画以及宋元明清时期文人画、宫廷画、民间画等多种风格的并蓄发展，中国画在不断吸收、融合与创新中，逐渐形成了自己独特的艺术风格和技法体系。

As the wheel of history rolls forward, human society has entered a new era of civilization. In this process, Chinese painting has undergone a transformation from its infancy to maturity. From the bronze patterns of the Xia, Shang, and Zhou dynasties, to the brick and stone murals of the Qin and Han dynasties; from the scholar landscape paintings of Wei, Jin, and the Northern and Southern Dynasties, to the court paintings of Sui, Tang, and the Five Dynasties and then to the diverse styles of literati paintings, court paintings, and folk paintings in the Song, Yuan, Ming, and Qing dynasties, Chinese painting has gradually formed its own unique artistic style and technique system through continuous absorption, integration, and innovation.

在这一过程中，中国画不仅注重笔墨的运用和意境的营造，更强调画家个人的情感与思想的融入。中国画追求"形神兼备""以形写神"的艺术境界。画家们通过精湛的笔墨技巧，将自然景物、人物形象等客观对象进行高度概括与提炼，进而表达出自己对于生命、宇宙、自然等深层次问题的思考和感悟。

In this process, Chinese painting not only focuses on the use of ink and brushwork and the creation of artistic conception, but also emphasizes the integration of the painter's personal emotions and thoughts. Chinese painting pursues the artistic realm of "both form and spirit" and "expressing spirit through form." Painters use exquisite brushwork and ink techniques to highly condense and refine objective objects, such as natural scenery and human figures, thus expressing their thoughts and insights on profound issues such as life, the universe, and nature.

此外，中国画还深受儒家、道家、禅宗等哲学思想的影响，形成了"诗书画印"相结合的艺术特色。画家们常常在画作上题诗落款、钤印盖章，以此来丰富画面的文化内涵和审美意趣。这种独特的艺术表现形式，不仅展现了中国传统文化的博大精深，也体现了中国画家对于艺术、人生、宇宙的独特理解和追求。

In addition, Chinese painting has been deeply influenced by philosophical ideas, such as Confucianism, Taoism, and Zen Buddhism, forming an artistic feature that combines poetry, calligraphy, painting, and seal engraving. Painters often inscribe poems, sign their names, and stamp their seals on their paintings to enrich the cultural connotations and aesthetic appeals of the pictures. This unique form of artistic expression not only demonstrates the profundity and extensiveness of traditional Chinese culture, but also embodies the unique understanding and pursuit of Chinese painters towards art, life, and the universe.

在漫长的历史长河中，中国画以其独特的艺术魅力和深厚的文化底蕴，吸引了无数国内外艺术爱好者的关注。它不仅是中华民族的文化瑰宝，也是世界艺术宝库中的一颗璀璨明珠。

Throughout the long river of history, Chinese painting has attracted the attention and affection of countless art enthusiasts both domestically and internationally with its unique artistic charm and profound cultural heritage. It is not only a cultural treasure of the Chinese nation but also a dazzling gem in the world's art treasury.

中国画的起源与发展经历了多个时期的演变和创新，每个时期都有其独特的艺术风格和代表作品。这些演变和创新不仅丰富了中国画的艺术内涵和表现手法，还提升了中国画在世界艺术领域中的地位和影响力。

The origin and development of Chinese painting have undergone multiple periods of evolution and innovation, with each period boasting its unique artistic style and representative works. These evolutions and innovations have not only enriched the artistic content and expression techniques of Chinese painting, but also promoted its status and influence in the field of world art.

中国画的历史可追溯至遥远的新石器时代。那时的人们以岩石为画布，用简洁而有力的线条，勾勒出狩猎、祭祀、舞蹈等鲜活的生活画面。这些岩画不仅是艺术领域的璀璨明珠，更是人们探究古代社会风貌、文化脉络与宗教信仰的珍贵资料。在这一时期，彩陶画亦绽放出绚丽的光彩。先民们巧妙地将五彩斑斓的图案绘制于陶器之上，既有抽象的几何纹饰，又不乏具象的动植物形象，展现了其超凡的想象力和精湛的技艺。

The history of Chinese painting can be traced back to the distant Neolithic Age. People of that period used rocks as canvases and outlined vivid life scenes such as hunting, sacrifice, and dancing with concise and powerful lines. These rock paintings are not only dazzling pearls in the field of art but also precious materials for us to explore the ancient social style, cultural context, and religious beliefs. At the same time, painted pottery also shone brightly in the pre-Qin period. The ancestors skillfully painted colorful patterns on pottery, including both abstract geometric decorations and concrete images of animals and plants, demonstrating their extraordinary imagination and exquisite craftsmanship.

中国古代岩画
Ancient Chinese rock paintings

半坡遗址距今约 6000 年，处于新石器时代仰韶文化时期，是黄河流域规模最大且保存最完整的母系氏族公社村落遗址，为研究新石器时代人类生活与社会组织提供了珍贵的实物资料。陕西半坡遗址出土的彩陶画，以红色为基调，搭配黑、白等色，线条灵动，构图精妙，生动展现了半坡人的生产、生活与图腾崇拜，堪称中国绘画史上的重要里程碑，是中华民族悠久历史文化的鲜活体现。

The Banpo Site dates back to about six thousand years ago and belongs to the Yangshao Culture period in the Neolithic Age. It is the largest and best-preserved matriarchal clan commune village site in the Yellow River Basin, providing precious physical materials for the study of human life and social organization in the Neolithic Age. The painted pottery paintings unearthed at the Banpo Site in Shaanxi Province are outstanding. Using red as the dominant hue, complemented by colors like black and white, these artworks feature lively and smooth lines and ingenious compositions. They vividly demonstrate the production activities, lifestyles, and totem worship of the people at Banpo. They can be regarded as an important milestone in the history of Chinese painting and a vivid reflection of the long history and splendid culture of the Chinese nation.

半坡遗址出土的人面鱼纹彩陶盆
Painted pottery basin with human face and fish design unearthed at the Banpo Site

在这一时期，半坡人与马家窑人匠心独运，创作出无数精美的岩画与彩陶画作品，并在创作过程中逐步凝练出别具一格的艺术表现手法。商代与西周时期的青铜器铭文与铜镜图案，则彰显了中国古代绘画在装饰艺术领域的卓越成就。而春秋战国时期竹简画与丝织品图案的涌现，更是展现了中国古代绘画在技法创新和题材拓展上的丰富面貌与多元可能。

西周青铜器上的图案花纹
Patterns and decorative designs on the bronze wares of the Western Zhou Dynasty

During this period, the Banpo people and Majiayao people displayed remarkable ingenuity in creating countless exquisite rock paintings and painted pottery works, and gradually refined their unique artistic expression techniques throughout their creative journey. The inscriptions on bronze vessels and the patterns on bronze mirrors from the Shang and Western Zhou dynasties demonstrated the remarkable achievements of ancient Chinese painting in the field of decorative art. During the Spring and Autumn and Warring States periods, the emergence of bamboo slip paintings and silk patterns further demonstrated the richness and diverse possibilities of ancient Chinese painting in technical innovation and subject matter expansion.

秦汉时期是中国画艺术发展史上一个极为重要的阶段。在这一时期，中国画艺术不仅在表现形式与技法上取得了显著的进步与突破，更在文化内涵与审美风格上形成了独具特色的风貌与特征。秦汉时期，中国画的表现形式主要聚焦于壁画与丝织品上的绘画，两者各具特色，共同构建了这一时期绘画艺术的繁荣景象。秦代壁画，作为皇家宫殿装饰的重要组成部分，其主题往往围绕着宏伟壮观的宫殿场景以及神秘莫测的神话传说展开。这些壁画不仅色彩鲜艳、对比强烈，给人以强烈的视觉冲击，更在构图上追求对称与平衡，展现出一种庄重而和谐的美感。在线条的运用上，秦代壁画倾向于简洁明快，通过精炼的笔触勾勒出物象的轮廓与动态，赋予画面以生动的气韵。

The Qin and Han dynasties were an extremely important period in the history of the development of Chinese painting art. During this period, Chinese painting art not only made significant progress and breakthroughs in forms of expression and techniques, but also formed unique styles and characteristics in cultural connotation and aesthetic style. In the Qin and Han dynasties, the forms of expression in Chinese painting were mainly murals and paintings on silk fabrics, both of which had their own characteristics and jointly built the prosperity of painting art in this era. Qin Dynasty murals, as an important part of the decoration of royal palaces, often revolved around magnificent palace scenes and mysterious myths and legends. These murals not only are colorful and contrasting, giving people a strong visual impact, but also pursue symmetry and balance in composition, showing a solemn and harmonious beauty. In terms of line use, Qin Dynasty murals tend to be concise and lively, using refined strokes to outline the contours and dynamics of objects, which gives the artwork a vivid charm.

汉代马王堆帛画
Silk painting from Mawangdui of the Han Dynasty

汉代的丝织品绘画则更加注重人物形象的刻画与故事情节的展现。这一时期的丝织品绘画作品，无论是图案设计还是色彩搭配，都更加细腻入微、丰富多彩。艺术家们通过流畅的线条和生动的笔触，将人物形象刻画得栩栩如生、形神兼备。汉代的马王堆帛画是丝织品绘画中的杰出代表，它以独特的艺术风格、精湛的技艺、细腻的线条、生动的形象和丰富的色彩展现了汉代社会的风貌和人文精神，深刻体现了汉代绘画艺术的魅力。这些珍贵的艺术遗产不仅揭示了古代社会的风貌与人文精神，更为世人提供了宝贵的艺术资源与文化启示。

Silk paintings from the Han Dynasty placed greater emphasis on the depiction of human figures and the representation of narrative scenes. During this period, the silk paintings, whether in terms of pattern design or color coordination, exhibited more delicate and diverse characteristics. Through flowing lines and vivid brushwork, artists captured the figures with lifelike detail and a perfect blend of form and spirit. The Mawangdui silk paintings from the Han Dynasty are outstanding examples of silk painting art, featuring unique artistic style and exquisite craftsmanship. They use fine lines, vivid imagery, and rich colors to depict the social ethos and humanistic spirit of the Han Dynasty, showcasing the charm of Han Dynasty painting art profoundly. These precious artistic legacies not only reveal the social landscape and humanistic spirit of ancient times but also provide us with valuable artistic resources and cultural insights.

魏晋南北朝是一个变革与创新交织的时代，绘画艺术在此时期迎来了前所未有的繁荣盛世。山水画与人物画双双步入成熟之境，更在技法、理念及审美追求上实现了质的飞跃，为后世留下了璀璨的艺术瑰宝与深远的文化烙印。这一时期的画家们将绘画技法推向了新的高度。他们不仅精通于细腻的线条勾勒与色彩的巧妙运用，更在构图、透视等艺术领域取得了显著的突破。在山水画中，画家们匠心独运，以墨色的浓淡干湿巧妙地表现远近层次，营造出一种深邃而悠远的意境，令人心旷神怡；在人物画中，画家们则更加注重人物性格与情感的细腻刻画，通过精湛的笔触与生动的表情，将人物形象刻画得栩栩如生。

Wei, Jin, and the Southern and Northern Dynasties were an era intertwined with change and innovation, ushering in an unprecedented prosperity in painting art. Both landscape painting and figure painting reached maturity, achieving a qualitative leap in techniques, concepts, and aesthetic pursuits, leaving behind brilliant artistic treasures and profound cultural imprints for future generations. Painters of this period pushed the art of painting to new heights. They were not only proficient in delicate line drawing and clever use of colors, but also made remarkable breakthroughs in the artistic fields of composition and perspective. In landscape paintings, painters ingeniously used the shades of ink and the wetness and dryness of brushwork to skillfully express distant and near layers, creating a profound and distant artistic conception that was exhilarating. In figure paintings, artists paid more attention to the delicate portrayal of personality and emotion, using exquisite brushwork and vivid expressions to bring characters to life.

在这一时期，众多杰出的画家与作品如雨后春笋般涌现。王羲之作为书法界的泰斗，其书法作品虽不属于绘画范畴，但他对线条美感的极致追求与独树一帜的风格，无疑对同时代的绘画艺术产生了深远而广泛的影响。顾恺之则是这一时期绘画艺术的璀璨明星。他的代表作《洛神赋图》不仅以高超的绘画技艺与细腻入微的情感描绘赢得了世人的赞誉，更以深邃的意境与独特的艺术风貌在中国绘画史上留下了浓墨重彩的一笔，成为不可多得的经典之作。

During this period, numerous outstanding painters and their works emerged like mushrooms after a spring rain. Wang Xizhi was a leading figure in calligraphy. His works, though not paintings, undoubtedly had a profound and extensive influence on painting of his time, due to his meticulous pursuit of the beauty of lines and unique style. Gu Kaizhi, on the other hand, was a shining star in the realm of painting during this era. His masterpiece, *The Goddess of the Luo River*, not only won worldwide admiration with its superb painting skills and delicate emotional portrayal, but also left an indelible mark in the history of Chinese painting with its profound artistic conception and unique artistic style, thus becoming a rare classic.

王羲之书法《兰亭集序》
Wang Xizhi's calligraphy work *Preface to the Poems Collected at Orchid Pavilion*

隋唐五代时期的绘画艺术则攀升至前所未有的巅峰。此时期的画作，技艺之精湛令人叹为观止，风格之多样更是令人目不暇接。山水画、人物画与花鸟画这三大艺术领域均实现了飞跃性的发展。这一时期的山水画家们不再停留于对自然景观的表象描绘，而是深入挖掘并展现山水所蕴含的深远意境。他们凭借精湛的笔墨技法，将山川的巍峨壮丽、江河的奔腾不息、云雾的缭绕缥缈等自然景致精妙地融入画中，营造出一种超凡脱俗、引人入胜的艺术境界。以唐代著名山水画家李思训为例，他的作品以金碧辉煌、气势恢宏而著称。他擅长运用青绿山水技法，将山石、树木、云雾等自然元素，以斑斓的色彩和细腻的笔触加以呈现，使得画面既具有强烈的视觉冲击力，又展现出和谐统一的美感。李思训的代表作品有《江帆楼阁图》《九成宫纨扇图》等。这些作品充分展现了他独特的青绿山水技法，以及他对于山水深远意境的深刻理解。

The painting art in Sui, Tang, and the Five Dynasties period reached an unprecedented peak. The exquisite craftsmanship of the paintings during this period is breathtaking, and the diversity of styles is overwhelming. The three major artistic fields of landscape painting, figure painting, and flower-and-bird painting all achieved leapfrog development. The landscape painters of this period no longer limited themselves to depicting the superficial appearances of natural scenery, but instead delved deeply into and presented the profound artistic conception embodied in landscapes. With exquisite brushwork techniques, they subtly integrated the majestic grandeur of mountains and rivers, the ceaseless flow of rivers, the misty entanglement of clouds and mists, and other natural sceneries into their paintings to create an extraordinary and fascinating artistic realm. Take the famous Tang Dynasty landscape painter Li Sixun as an example. His works are renowned for their splendid brilliance and magnificent momentum. He excelled at using the green landscape technique to present natural elements such as rocks, trees, clouds, and mists with vivid colors and delicate brushstrokes, making the paintings both visually impactful and harmoniously unified. Representative works of Li Sixun include *Riverbank with Sailboats and Pavilions* and *Nine Layers Palace Silk Fan Painting*. These works fully demonstrate his unique green landscape technique and his deep understanding of the profound artistic conception of landscapes.

隋唐五代的人物画也取得了极高的艺术成就。画家们在追求人物形象准确刻画的同时，更加注重人物的生动传神。他们通过细腻的笔触和精准的色彩运用，将人物的内心世界和性格特征展现得淋漓尽致。阎立本是这一时期的杰出代表，其《步辇图》是人物画中的经典之作。该作品以唐太宗接见吐蕃使臣禄东赞的历史事件为题材，通过细腻的线条和丰富的色彩，生动展现了唐太宗的威严与从容和禄东赞的虔诚与智慧。画面构图严谨，人物比例协调、形神兼备，给人以强烈的视觉震撼和心灵共鸣。

The figure painting of Sui, Tang and the Five Dynasties also achieved great artistic success. While pursuing the accurate depiction of character images, painters paid more attention to vivid character expressions. Through delicate brushwork and precise color application, they vividly displayed the inner world and personality characteristics of the characters. Yan Liben was an outstanding representative of this period. His *Emperor Taizong Receiving the Tibetan Envoy* is a classic work of figure painting. This work is based on the historical event of Emperor Taizong of the Tang Dynasty receiving Lu Dongzan, the envoy of

Tubo (Tibetan regime in ancient China). Through delicate lines and rich colors, it vividly depicts the majesty and calmness of Emperor Taizong and the piety and wisdom of Lu Dongzan. The composition of the picture is rigorous, the proportion of the characters is coordinated, and the form and spirit are both possessed, which gives people a strong visual shock and spiritual resonance.

隋唐五代的花鸟画也取得了显著发展。画家们以自然界中的花鸟鱼虫为题材，通过细腻的笔触和生动的色彩，灵动地展现了它们的形态、动态和神韵。这些作品不仅体现了画家们高超的绘画技艺，更寄托了他们对自然美的热爱和向往。五代时期画家黄筌的《写生珍禽图》便是花鸟画的典范之作。

The flower-and-bird painting of Sui, Tang, and the Five Dynasties also achieved remarkable development. Painters took flowers, birds, fish, and insects in nature as their themes. Through delicate brushstrokes and vivid colors, their shapes, movements, and charm were vividly displayed. These works not only demonstrated the painters' superb painting skills, but also embodied their love and yearning for natural beauty. Huang Quan, a painter of the Five Dynasties period, produced *Scroll of Rare Birds Sketched from Life*, which stands as a model work of flower-and-bird painting.

宋元时期，社会经济的繁荣和文化氛围的宽松使得绘画艺术进入了全面发展阶段。这一时期，山水画、人物画、花鸟画三大画科均取得了令人瞩目的成就，各自展现出独特的艺术魅力。

During the Song and Yuan dynasties, with the prosperity of the social economy and the relaxed cultural atmosphere, painting art entered a stage of all-round development. During this period, the three major genres: landscape painting, figure painting, and flower-and-bird painting all achieved remarkable achievements, each displaying unique artistic charm.

在山水画领域，宋元画家们将自然之美与人文情怀完美融合，创造出了一幅幅意境深远、气韵生动的山水画卷。他们不仅注重表现山川的壮丽景色，更通过细腻的笔触和巧妙的构图，传达出对自然之美的深刻感悟和对人生哲理的独到见解。范宽是北宋山水画的杰出代表，其《溪山行旅图》以雄浑壮阔的笔调，展现了北方山水的磅礴气势和苍茫意境，被誉为中国山水画史上的经典之作。

范宽《溪山行旅图》
Fan Kuan's *Travelers among Mountains and Streams*

In the field of landscape painting, the painters of the Song and Yuan dynasties perfectly integrated the beauty of nature with humanistic feelings, creating a series of landscape paintings with profound artistic conception and vivid charm. They not only focused on expressing the magnificent scenery of mountains and rivers, but also conveyed their profound perception of the beauty of nature and unique insights into the philosophy of life through delicate brushstrokes and ingenious compositions. As an outstanding representative of the landscape painting of the Northern Song Dynasty, Fan Kuan's *Travelers among Mountains and Streams* depicts the magnificent momentum and vast artistic conception of the northern landscapes with vigorous and magnificent brushwork, and is hailed as a classic work in the history of Chinese landscape painting.

人物画方面，宋元画家们致力于捕捉人物的神态与情感，通过精湛的技法和生动的造型，塑造出一个个栩栩如生的人物形象。他们不仅注重表现人物的形貌特征，更善于通过细节刻画和氛围营造，传达出人物的性格特点和内心世界。

In terms of figure painting, the painters of the Song and Yuan dynasties were committed to capturing the expressions and emotions of the characters, creating life-like characters through exquisite techniques and vivid shapes. They not only focused on expressing the physical characteristics of the characters, but were also adept at conveying the personality traits and inner world of the characters through detailed portrayal and atmosphere creation.

花鸟画作为中国传统绘画的重要组成部分，在宋元时期同样取得了显著成就。画家们以细腻的笔触和丰富的色彩，描绘出花卉的娇艳、鸟禽的灵动，以及它们与自然环境之间的和谐共生。宋徽宗赵佶对花鸟画的发展作出了卓越贡献。他不仅完善了皇家画院制度，招揽天下绘画才俊，还亲自参与创作，推动了花鸟画向更为精致、细腻的方向发展。他善于以细腻入微的笔触和丰富多彩的色调捕捉花卉的娇艳瞬间和鸟禽的灵动姿态，他的花鸟画作品不仅展现了自然之美，更寄托了他对生命的热爱与对艺术的追求。

As an important part of traditional Chinese painting, flower-and-bird painting also made remarkable achievements during the Song and Yuan dynasties. Painters used delicate brushstrokes and rich colors to depict the charm of flowers, the vitality of birds, and the harmonious coexistence between them and the natural environment. Emperor Huizong Zhao Ji made outstanding contributions to the development of flower-and-bird painting. He not only consolidated and refined the system of the Imperial Academy of Painting and recruited talented painters from all over the country, but also personally participated in the creation, promoting the development of flower-and-bird painting towards a more delicate and exquisite direction. He was good at capturing the charming moments of flowers and the lively poses of birds, using delicate brushstrokes and rich and colorful tones. His flower-and-bird painting works not only show the beauty of nature, but also embody his love for life and pursuit of art.

明清时期的绘画技法在继承前代传统的基础上实现了创新与突破。画家们不再拘泥于传统的技法束缚，而是勇于探索、敢于尝试，将笔墨纸砚的运用推向了新的艺术高度。他们通过巧妙的构图、细腻的笔触、丰富的色彩以及深邃的意境，展现出了各自独特的艺术风格。沈周是"吴门画派"的领军人物，其《庐山高图》一画以雄浑的笔墨、深邃的意境，生动地描绘了庐山的壮美景色，展现了画家对自然之美的深刻感悟与独特表达。

The painting techniques of the Ming and Qing dynasties, on the basis of inheriting the traditions of previous generations, achieved innovations and breakthroughs. Painters were no longer constrained by traditional techniques, but bravely explored and dared to try, pushing the use of ink, brush, paper, and inkstone to new heights. Through ingenious composition, delicate brushwork, rich colors, and profound artistic conception, they demonstrated their unique artistic styles. Shen Zhou was the leader of the "Wu School of Painting." His painting *Lofty Mount Lu* vividly depicts the magnificent scenery of Lushan Mountain with vigorous ink and profound artistic conception, demonstrating the painter's profound perception and unique expression of natural beauty.

明清时期绘画艺术的多元化发展，离不开当时特定的文化与社会背景。随着商品经济的繁荣和市民阶层的兴起，人们对于精神文化的需求日益增加。绘画艺术作为传统文化的重要组成部分，自然成为人们追求精神寄托与审美享受的重要途径。同时，随着文人雅士的积极参与和推动，绘画艺术逐渐摆脱了宫廷贵族的束缚，走向了更广阔的民间社会。这种文化与艺术的普及，为绘画艺术的多元化发展提供了肥沃的土壤和广阔的发展空间。

The diversified development of painting art in the Ming and Qing dynasties cannot be separated from the specific cultural and social backgrounds at that time. With the prosperity of the commodity economy and the rise of the citizen class, people's demand for spiritual and cultural enrichment increased day by day. As an important part of traditional culture, painting art naturally became an important way for people to pursue spiritual sustenance and aesthetic enjoyment. At the same time, with the active participation and promotion of literati and scholars, painting art gradually broke away from the shackles of royal aristocrats and moved towards a broader civil society. This popularization of culture and art provided fertile soil and vast space for the diversified development of painting art.

近现代时期，中国画不再局限于传统的技法与题材，而是勇敢地吸收西方绘画的精髓，形成了独具特色的艺术风貌。艺术家们不再拘泥于传统的笔墨纸砚，而是大胆尝试新的材料（如水彩、油画颜料等）与技法，使画面效果更加多样化。同时，他们注重将西方绘画的写实精神与中国画的意境追求相结合，创造出既有西方绘画的精细描绘，又不失中国画神韵的作品。在这一变革过程中，涌现出了一批杰出的艺术家，他们用自己的创作实践推动了中国画的发展。其中，齐白石、徐悲鸿、张大千无疑是这一时期的代表人物。

In modern times, Chinese painting has gone beyond traditional techniques and themes, boldly absorbing the essence of Western painting to form a unique artistic style. Artists are no longer confined to traditional brushes, ink, paper, and inkstones. Instead, they boldly experiment with new materials (such as watercolors and oil paints) and techniques, to diversify visual effects. At the same time, they focus on integrating the realistic spirit of Western painting with the pursuit of artistic conception in Chinese painting, creating works that embody both the meticulous portrayal of Western painting and the artistic charm of Chinese painting. In this process of transformation, a group of outstanding artists emerged, who promoted the development of Chinese painting through their own creative practices. Among them, Qi Baishi, Xu Beihong, and Zhang Daqian are undoubtedly the representatives of this period.

齐白石作为近现代中国画坛的巨匠，以独特的艺术风格和深厚的艺术造诣赢得了广泛赞誉。他的代表作《虾》通过精湛的笔墨技巧展现了虾的灵动与神韵。齐白石的作品充满了生活气息，他善于从日常生活中汲取灵感，赋予平凡之物以艺术生命力。徐悲鸿则以其深厚的写实功底和强烈的民族情感著称。他的代表作《马》以雄健有力的笔触和生动传神的形象，展现了马的精神风貌和力量之美。徐悲鸿的作品不仅具有高度的艺术价值，更蕴含着深厚的文化内涵和民族精神。张大千的作品风格多样，既有传统中国画的韵味，又有西方绘画的元素，独具风格。他以广博的学识和精湛的技艺，在山水画、花鸟画等领域均取得了卓越成就。

As a giant in modern Chinese painting, Qi Baishi has won widespread acclaim for his unique artistic style and profound artistic attainments. His masterpiece *Shrimp* conveys the agility and charm of the shrimp through exquisite brushwork skills. Qi Baishi's works are imbued with the breath of life, and he is adept at drawing inspiration from daily life, giving artistic vitality to ordinary objects. Xu Beihong, on the other hand, is renowned for his profound realistic skills and strong national sentiment. His masterpiece *Horse* demonstrates the spirited demeanor and powerful beauty of the horse through vigorous and vivid brushstrokes. Xu Beihong's works not only possess high artistic value but also embody profound cultural connotations and national spirit. Zhang Daqian's artistic style is diverse, incorporating both the charm of traditional Chinese painting and elements of Western painting to create his own unique style. With his extensive knowledge and exquisite skills, he has achieved remarkable accomplishments in landscape painting, flower-and-bird painting, and other fields.

近现代中国画在受到西方绘画影响的同时，也实现了自身的创新与变革。这一过程不仅丰富了中国画的技法与形式，更推动了中国画与现代审美观念的融合。随着全球化的不断深入和文化交流的日益频繁，中国画将继续保持其开放包容的姿态，不断吸收新的艺术元素和观念，创造出更加丰富多彩的艺术作品。

Modern Chinese painting, influenced by Western painting, has undergone significant innovation and transformation. This process has not only enriched the techniques and forms of Chinese painting, but also promoted its integration with modern aesthetic concepts and driven its development. With the continuous deepening of globalization and the increasingly frequent cultural exchanges, Chinese painting will continue to maintain an open and inclusive attitude, constantly absorbing new artistic elements and concepts to create more colorful art works.

Exercises

1 **Answer the following questions.**

(1) What were the main themes of the murals in the Qin Dynasty, and how did they reflect the society of that time?

(2) What did the painters of Sui, Tang, and the Five Dynasties period particularly focus on when depicting human figures in their paintings?

(3) How has modern Chinese painting evolved in relation to Western painting, and what is its future direction?

Choose the best answer to each of the following questions.

(1) What is the significance of the painted pottery from the Banpo site in Shaanxi Province?

A. It is the earliest form of Chinese painting.

B. It is a significant milestone in the history of Chinese painting.

C. It is the only form of pottery that has been discovered.

D. It is not related to the Banpo people.

(2) What was the main focus of Qin Dynasty murals in terms of subject matter?

A. Palace scenes and myths.   B. Natural landscapes.

C. Everyday life of common people.   D. Abstract patterns.

(3) Which of the following best describes the style of Han Dynasty silk paintings?

A. Bold and geometric.   B. Abstract and symbolic.

C. Monochromatic and somber.   D. Delicate and diverse.

(4) Which of the following works is mentioned as a classic example of figure painting from Sui, Tang, and the Five Dynasties period?

A. *Scroll of Rare Birds Sketched from Life* by Huang Quan.

B. *Emperor Taizong Receiving the Tibetan Envoy* by Yan Liben.

C. *Travelers among Moutains and Streams* by Fan Kuan.

D. *Riverbank with Sailboats and Pavilions* by Li Sixun.

(5) Who was the emperor who made significant contributions to the development of flower-and-bird painting during the Song and Yuan dynasties?

A. Emperor Huizong Zhao Ji.   B. Emperor Kangxi.

C. Emperor Qianlong.   D. Emperor Taizu Zhao Kuangyin.

中国画的分类
Classification of Chinese Painting

在浩瀚的中国画艺术海洋中，根据不同的分类标准和视角，中国画可以分为多个类别，每一类都蕴含着丰富的文化内涵和独特的艺术魅力。

In the vast ocean of Chinese painting art, Chinese painting can be divided into multiple categories based on different classification standards and perspectives, each of which contains rich cultural connotations and unique artistic charm.

从题材的角度来看，中国画可以分为山水画、花鸟画和人物画三大类。

From the perspective of subject matter, Chinese painting can be divided into three major categories: landscape painting, flower-and-bird painting, and figure painting.

山水画不仅是一种绘画形式，更是一种哲学思想的体现，追求着"天人合一"的至高境界。画家们以自然山水为蓝本，挥洒笔墨，勾勒出一幅幅雄浑壮丽、意境深远的山水画卷。在山水画的创作中，画家们巧妙地运用墨色的浓淡干湿和线条的疏密曲直，来表现山川的雄伟壮丽和云雾的缥缈朦胧。这种表现手法不仅体现了画家们高超的技艺，更蕴含了他们对自然之美的深刻感悟和无限向往。墨色的浓淡变化，如同自然界的阴晴雨雪，给人以丰富的视觉享受；线条的疏密曲直，则如同山川的起伏跌宕，引导着观者的思绪飘向远方。

Landscape painting is not just a form of painting; it is also an embodiment of philosophical thought, pursuing the supreme state of "The Unity of Heaven and Man." Painters, taking the natural landscape as their model, wield their brushes to create a series of majestic and grand, profoundly meaningful landscape scrolls. In the creation of landscape paintings, artists skillfully use the variations in ink density, dryness, and wetness, as well as the spacing and curvature of lines, to depict the grandeur of mountains and rivers and the ethereal beauty of clouds and mist. This expressive technique not only reflects the artists' superb skills but also embodies their profound appreciation and boundless longing for the beauty of nature. The changes in ink density are like the weather's shifts between sunshine, clouds, rain, and snow, offering a rich visual feast. Meanwhile, the spacing and curvature of lines are like the undulating contours of mountains and rivers, guiding viewers' thoughts to drift into the distance.

历朝历代，无数画家倾尽心血，创作出了令人叹为观止的山水画作品。这些作品不仅展示了画家们的艺术才华和审美追求，更记录了中国的历史变迁和文化传承。其中，北宋画家范宽的《溪山行旅图》和元代画家黄公望的《富春山居图》被誉为传世佳作。范宽的《溪山行旅图》以其雄浑磅礴的气势和细腻入微的笔触，展现了北方山川的壮丽景色；黄公望的《富春山居图》则以淡雅清新的风格和深远悠长的意境，表现了江南山水的柔美与韵味。这两幅作品不仅是中国山水画的杰出代表，更是中华民族文化宝库中的珍贵财富。

Throughout the ages, countless painters have poured their hearts and souls into creating an astonishing array of landscape paintings that leave one in awe. These works not only showcase the artistic talents and aesthetic pursuits of the painters but also record the historical changes and cultural heritage of China. Among them, *Travelers among Mountains and Streams* by Fan Kuan, a painter in the Northern Song Dynasty, and *Dwelling in the Fuchun Mountains* by Huang Gongwang, a painter in the Yuan Dynasty, are hailed as masterpieces for the ages. Fan Kuan's *Travelers among Mountains and Streams* is celebrated for its majestic and powerful presence and meticulous brushwork, which captures the grandeur of the northern landscape. Huang Gongwang's *Dwelling in the Fuchun Mountains*, on the other hand, is known for its elegant and fresh style and its profound and enduring artistic conception, depicting the gentle beauty and charm of the landscapes in the Jiangnan Region. These two artworks are not only outstanding representatives of Chinese landscape painting but also precious treasures within the cultural repository of the Chinese nation.

花鸟画以绚烂多姿的花卉、翱翔翩跹的鸟禽、悠游自在的虫鱼为描绘对象，不仅展现了自然界的勃勃生机，更寄托了画家们对美好生活的深切向往和对自然之美的无限热爱。宋代赵昌的《写生蛱蝶图》以细腻的笔触描绘蝴蝶与花卉，展示了画家对自然和谐之美的感悟。清代恽寿平的《牡丹图》则淋漓尽致地展现了牡丹的华贵，融入环境元素，使画面生动和谐。花鸟画不仅具有独特的艺术魅力，还蕴含着深厚的文化和情感价值，是画家抒发情感、与自然对话的媒介，具有超越时空的艺术生命力。

Flower-and-bird painting captures the vibrant beauty of flowers, the graceful flight of birds, and the serene movements of insects and fish. It not only displays the vitality of nature but also embodies painters' profound yearning for a beautiful life and their boundless love for natural beauty. Zhao Chang's *Painting of Live Butterflies and Flowers* from the Song Dynasty, with its delicate brushwork depicting butterflies and flowers, showcases the painter's appreciation of the harmony of nature. Yun Shouping's *Peony Painting* from the Qing Dynasty vividly displays the elegance of peonies, incorporating environmental elements to create a lively and harmonious composition. Flower-and-bird painting is not only unique in its artistic charm but also carries profound cultural and emotional value. It serves as a medium for painters to express their emotions and converse with nature, possessing an artistic vitality that transcends time and space.

随着时代的发展和社会的进步，花鸟画也在不断创新与发展。现代画家们在继承传统的基础上，融入了更多的现代元素和审美观念，使得花鸟画在表现形式、技法运用及题材选择等方面都呈现出了更加多元化和个性化的特点。这种创新与发展不仅丰富了花鸟画的艺术内涵和外延，也为这一古老的艺术形式注入了新的活力和生机。花鸟画作为中国传统绘画的重要组成部分，以其独特的艺术魅力和深厚的文化内涵赢得了世人的喜爱和赞誉。

With the development of the times and the progress of society, flower-and-bird painting is constantly innovating and evolving. Modern painters, while inheriting traditions, incorporate more modern elements and aesthetic concepts, resulting in a more diverse and personalized character in terms of expression, technique application, and subject matter selection. This innovation and development not only enriches the artistic connotations and extensions of flower-and-bird painting, but also injects new vitality into this ancient art form. As an important part of traditional Chinese painting, flower-and-bird painting has won the love and acclaim of people worldwide with its unique artistic charm and profound cultural depth.

人物画自古以来便以其独特的艺术魅力吸引着无数画家与观赏者的目光。画家们以人物形象为核心，用精湛的技艺细腻地勾勒出人物的轮廓、衣纹乃至肌肤的质感，用丰富的情感生动地刻画人物的表情与眼神，深刻揭示了人物的性格特征与内心世界，展现了人类情感的细腻与复杂。

Figure painting has attracted the attention of countless artists and viewers with its unique artistic charm since ancient times. Focusing on figures, painters meticulously outline contours, clothing folds, and even skin texture through exquisite skills. Moreover, they vividly portray the expressions and eyes of figures with rich emotions, thereby profoundly revealing the character traits and inner world of the subjects, and showcasing the subtlety and complexity of human emotions.

唐代张萱的《捣练图》展现了宫廷女性捣练丝帛的场景，人物表情丰富，体现了画家对生活的细致观察和深刻理解。这幅画不仅展现了唐代社会的风貌，也探索了女性的内心世界。宋代李唐的《采薇图》描绘了伯夷、叔齐的故事，通过人物的形象传达了对忠贞美德的敬意。除了这两幅经典之作外，中国历史上还有许多优秀的人物画作品，如东晋顾恺之的《洛神赋图》、明代唐寅的《秋风纨扇图》等，它们都以各自独特的方式，展现了人物画的艺术魅力与思想深度。在当今社会，随着科技的进步与文化的交流，人物画艺术也在不断创新与发展。现代画家们在继承传统的基础上，融入了更多现代元素与表现手法，使得人物画呈现出更加多元化的风貌。

Women Preparing Silk by Zhang Xuan in the Tang Dynasty depicts the scene of palace women pounding silk fabrics, where their rich facial expressions reflect the painter's meticulous observations and profound understanding of life. This painting not only records Tang society but also explores the inner world of women. *Picking Vetches* by Li Tang of the Song Dynasty illustrates the story of Boyi and Shuqi, conveying respect for the virtue of loyalty through their images. In addition to these masterpieces, there are many other outstanding figure paintings in Chinese history, such as Gu Kaizhi's *The Goddess of the Luo River* from the Eastern Jin Dynasty and Tang Yin's *Autumn Breeze and Silk Fan* from the Ming Dynasty. Each of these works uniquely showcases the artistic charm and intellectual depth of figure painting. In today's society, with the advancement of technology and increasing cultural exchange, figure painting art continues to innovate. Modern painters, while inheriting traditions, incorporate more modern elements and techniques of expression, resulting in a more diverse style of figure painting.

除了按题材分类外，中国画还可以根据技法分为工笔画和写意画两大类。

In addition to being classified by subject matter, Chinese paintings can also be classified into two major categories based on technique: fine brushwork painting and freehand brushwork painting.

工笔画，顾名思义，注重的是"工"与"细"，即精湛的技艺与细腻的表现力。工笔画的核心在于对细节的极致刻画和对色彩的精妙运用。画家们以超乎常人的耐心和毅力，运用精细入微的线条，将物象的形态、结构乃至纹理都表现得淋漓尽致。工笔画在色彩的运用上也极具特色。它不拘泥于自然色彩的再现，而是追求色彩的丰富性和层次感。画家们通过巧妙的色彩搭配和过渡，使得画面色彩既饱满又和谐，既鲜艳又不失雅致。这种对色彩的精妙运用，不仅增强了画面的视觉效果，也赋予了作品更为深邃的情感内涵。

As the name suggests, fine brushwork painting emphasizes "meticulousness" and "delicacy," that is, fine craftsmanship and exquisite expressiveness. The core of fine brushwork painting lies in the ultimate portrayal of details and the exquisite use of colors. With extraordinary patience and perseverance, artists use delicate lines to express the shape, structure, and even texture of objects to the fullest extent. Fine brushwork painting is also highly distinctive in its use of colors. It does not confine itself to the imitation of natural colors, but instead pursues the richness and depth of hues. Through clever color combinations and transitions, painters achieve a full yet harmonious palette that is vibrant yet elegant. This exquisite use of color not only enhances the visual impact of the artwork but also imbues it with deeper emotional depth.

宋代王希孟的《千里江山图》是工笔山水画作品的典型代表。这幅作品以长卷的形式，描绘了连绵不绝的江山景色。画面中的山峰、溪流、云雾、林木等物象，都被画家以精细的线条和丰富的色彩表现得栩栩如生。更为难得的是，画家在表现这些物象的同时，还巧妙地融入了光影效果，使得画面更加立体生动，令人叹为观止。除了《千里江山图》之外，中国历史上还有许多著名的工笔画作品，如唐代周昉的《簪花仕女图》、宋代张择端的《清明上河图》等，都是工笔画的杰出代表。这些作品不仅展现了画家们高超的技艺和深厚的艺术修养，也为后世留下了宝贵的历史文化遗产。

Thousand Li of Rivers and Mountains by Wang Ximeng of the Song Dynasty is a typical example of a meticulous landscape painting. This work, in the form of a long scroll, depicts a continuous landscape of rivers and mountains. The mountains, streams, mists, and forests in the painting are all rendered with fine lines and rich colors, vividly bringing the scene to life. What is even more remarkable is that the artist skillfully incorporated the effects of light and shadow while depicting these objects, making the painting more three-dimensional and vivid, thereby leaving viewers in awe. In addition to *Thousand Li of Rivers and Mountains*, there are many other famous examples of fine brushwork painting in Chinese history. For instance, *The Ladies Wearing Flowers* by Zhou Fang of the Tang Dynasty and *Along the River during the Qingming Festival* by Zhang Zeduan of the Song Dynasty are both outstanding representatives of this genre. These works not only showcase the artists' superb skills and profound artistic cultivation but also leave us with valuable historical and cultural heritage.

写意画是中国传统绘画的重要组成部分，与工笔画齐名。它强调画家情感的表达和笔墨趣味，以简洁线条和淡墨勾勒物象，激发观者想象。画家通过自由笔触和深墨色，将自然、哲理和情感结合，营造出超越现实的意境美。这种美既是对自然的提炼，又是对内心世界的深入展现。

Freehand brushwork painting is an important component of traditional Chinese painting, alongside fine brushwork painting. It emphasizes the expression of the painter's emotions and the aesthetic appeal of brushwork and ink, outlining objects with concise lines and light ink, which stimulates the viewers' imagination. The painters combine nature, philosophy, and emotions through free brushstrokes and ink colors, creating a transcendent beauty that surpasses reality. This beauty is both a refinement of nature and a profound expression of the inner world.

明代画家徐渭的《墨葡萄图》是写意画的典范，以墨色变化展现葡萄和藤蔓的生动形象。这幅画不仅是静物描绘，也反映了徐渭的个人经历和情感。葡萄虽无色，却显现出生命力和坚韧；藤蔓的自由生长象征着画家内心的斗争。清代八大山人的《山水册》也是写意画的杰作，以独特的艺术风格和深邃的思想，充分展现了中国山水画的意境。画中以简洁线条和淡墨勾勒出意境深远的山水，既真实描绘自然，又反映画家内心世界。通过笔墨和意境的结合，八大山人将个人对生命和自然的感悟融入作品，赋予画作生动的哲思。

Ink Grapes by the Ming Dynasty painter Xu Wei is a paragon of freehand brushwork painting, showcasing the vivid images of grapes and vines through variations in ink color. This painting is not just a still life depiction but also reflects Xu Wei's personal experiences and emotions. Although the grapes are colorless, they exude vitality and resilience; the free growth of the vines symbolizes the inner struggles of the artist. *The Landscape Album* by the Qing Dynasty artist Bada Shanren is also a masterpiece of freehand brushwork painting, fully demonstrating the artistic conception of Chinese landscape painting with its unique artistic style and profound thoughts. The painting uses concise lines and light ink to depict landscapes with profound artistic conceptions, both portraying nature realistically and reflecting the inner world of the painter. Bada Shanren integrated his personal insights into life and nature through the combination of brushwork and artistic conception, endowing his paintings with vivid philosophical depth.

写意画之所以能够在中国绘画史上占据举足轻重的地位，除了其独特的艺术表现形式之外，更在于它所蕴含的文化内涵与精神追求。它不仅仅是一种绘画技法或艺术风格，更是一种文化精神的体现与传承。

The reason why freehand brushwork painting holds a pivotal position in the history of Chinese painting, apart from its unique artistic expression, lies in the cultural connotations and spiritual pursuits within it. It is not just a painting technique or an artistic style, but a manifestation and inheritance of Chinese cultural spirit.

中国画还可以根据地域分为南宗画和北宗画。南宗画是以南方地区为主要影响地域的中国画，包括江南水墨画、岭南画派等。

Chinese paintings can also be categorized by region into the southern school painting and the northern school painting. The southern school painting, primarily influenced by the southern regions in China, encompasses Jiangnan ink wash paintings, the Lingnan school of painting, and others.

江南水墨画温婉细腻。它以水调墨，以宣纸为载体，通过墨色的浓淡干湿来展现江南水乡的柔美与宁静。画面中，小桥流水、粉墙黛瓦、烟雨蒙蒙，每一处细节都透露出江南独有的温婉与细腻。五代南唐画家董源的《潇湘图》是江南水墨画的杰出代表，画家用细腻的笔触和淡雅的墨色，将早春时节的江南山水灵动地描绘出来。画中远山如黛，近水含烟，仿佛能让人置身其中，感受宁静与美好。此外，明代画家文徵明的《江南春图》也是江南水墨画的代表作之一，他以精湛的技艺和深厚的文化底蕴，将江南的春色表现得淋漓尽致。

Jiangnan ink wash paintings are known for their gentle and exquisite style. Using water to modulate ink and rice paper as the carrier, these works capture the beauty and tranquility of the Jiangnan water towns through the varying shades of ink—light and dark, dry and wet. In the depicted scenes, small bridges, flowing streams, whitewashed walls with black-tiled roofs, and misty rain all reveal the unique grace and subtlety of Jiangnan. In these ink wash paintings, *Xiao Xiang Tu* by Dong Yuan, a painter of the Southern Tang during the Five Dynasties period, is one of the best representatives. With fine brushwork and soft ink tones, the painter brought to life the landscapes of Jiangnan in early spring. The distant mountains are like indigo eyebrows, and nearby waters are misty, as if one could step into the painting and feel its serenity and beauty. Additionally, *Spring in Jiangnan* by the Ming Dynasty painter Wen Zhengming is also a representative work of Jiangnan ink wash painting. With his exquisite skill and profound cultural heritage, Wen Zhengming vividly captured the spring beauty of Jiangnan.

与江南水墨画的温婉细腻不同，岭南画派以豪放不羁、色彩鲜明而著称。岭南地区地处中国南疆，气候温暖湿润，植被茂盛，这为岭南画派提供了丰富的创作素材。岭南画家们善于运用鲜艳的色彩和大胆的笔触，将岭南的自然风光和人文景观表现得生动而富有活力。他们的作品展现了岭南的青山绿水、繁花似锦，以及充满生活气息的人物和场景。

Unlike the gentle and delicate ink wash paintings of the Jiangnan region, the Lingnan school is known for its unrestrained and vivid use of colors. Located in the southern frontier of China, the Lingnan area has a warm and humid climate with lush vegetation, providing abundant inspiration for the Lingnan school's artistic creation. Lingnan painters excel in using bright colors and bold brushstrokes to vividly depict the natural landscapes and cultural scenes of Lingnan. In their works, one can see green mountains and clear waters, the profusion of flowers, as well as figures and scenes that brim with the vibrancy of life.

南宗画对中国画的发展产生了深远影响。它不仅为后来的画家们提供了丰富的创作素材和灵感来源，还推动了中国画在技法、风格等方面的不断创新与发展。如今，南宗画已成为中国传统绘画的重要组成部分，被越来越多的人喜爱和传承。

The southern school painting has had a profound impact on the development of Chinese painting. It not only has provided later generations of artists with abundant creative materials and sources of inspiration, but also propels the continuous innovation and development of Chinese painting in terms of techniques and styles. Today, the southern school painting has become an important part of traditional Chinese painting, cherished and passed down by an increasing number of people.

北宗画是以北方地区为主要影响地域的中国画，包括北方山水画、工笔画等。

The northern school painting, primarily influenced by the northern regions in China, includes northern landscape painting, fine brushwork painting and, so on.

北方山水画是北宗画的重要组成部分，取材于北方山水，艺术风格雄浑。与南方山水画风格不同，北方山水画强调山的壮丽和水的激荡，反映了自然的力量。这种风格也与北方地理紧密相关。在宋代范宽的《溪山行旅图》中，高耸的山峰和曲折的山路，构成了一幅宏伟的自然画卷。北宗画派的工笔画以精细笔触和丰富色彩而闻名，展现了人物、花鸟、鱼虫等题材的细腻美。画家深入观察研究对象，准确捕捉对象的形态、结构和神韵，并运用高超技艺和想象力将其生动呈现。如明代仇英的《汉宫春晓图》生动描绘了宫廷生活，让人有身临其境之感。

Northern landscape painting, as a key component of the northern school, draws its inspiration from the landscapes of the north, exhibiting a robust artistic style. Unlike the southern painting style, the northern style emphasizes the grandeur of mountains and the turbulence of water, reflecting the power of nature. This artistic style is also closely related to the northern geographic features. Fan Kuan's *Travelers among Mountains and Streams* from the Song Dynasty, with its towering peaks and winding mountain paths, creates an awe-inspiring natural panorama. The fine brushwork painting style of the northern school is renowned for its fine brushwork and rich colors, revealing the delicate beauty of subjects like figures, flowers, birds, fish, and insects. Painters must deeply observe and study their subjects, accurately capture form, structure, and essence, and employ superior technique and imagination to vividly present them. For instance, Qiu Ying's *Spring Dawn in the Han Palace* from the Ming Dynasty vividly depicts palace life, making people feel as if they are experiencing the splendor of the Han Palace firsthand.

北宗画之所以在中国画坛中独树一帜，是因为其独特的艺术风格、精湛的绘画技艺及深厚的文化内涵。作为中国传统文化的重要组成部分，它不仅反映了中华民族对自然和宇宙的深刻理解，还向世界展示了中华文化的魅力。在现代社会，北宗画也在创新中焕发新生，为当代艺术发展注入新动力。作为中国画坛的瑰宝，北宗画不仅提供了艺术享受和精神滋养，还助力于中华优秀传统文化的传承和弘扬。

The northern school painting stands out in the Chinese painting world due to its unique artistic style, exquisite craftsmanship, profound cultural connotations, and high artistic value. As an important part of traditional Chinese culture, it not only reflects the profound understanding of nature and the universe by the Chinese nation but also showcases the charm of Chinese culture to the world. In modern society, the northern school painting is regaining new vitality through innovation, injecting impetus into the development of contemporary art. As a treasure in the Chinese painting world, the northern school painting not only offers artistic enjoyment and spiritual nourishment but also contributes to the inheritance and promotion of China's excellent traditional culture.

Exercises

1 Answer the following questions.

(1) What is the significance of figure painting in Chinese art according to the passage?

(2) Why does freehand brushwork painting hold a pivotal position in the history of Chinese painting?

(3) What is the significance of northern landscape painting in traditional Chinese culture?

2 Decide whether each of the following statements is true (T) or false (F).

(1) The Tang Dynasty's *Women Preparing Silk* by Zhang Xuan depicts a scene of palace women pounding silk fabrics.

(2) Gu Kaizhi's *The Goddess of the Luo River* was created in the Tang Dynasty.

(3) Modern painters incorporate more modern elements and techniques of expression into figure painting.

(4) Freehand brushwork painting is merely a painting technique without any cultural significance.

(5) Qiu Ying's *Spring Dawn in the Han Palace* accurately captures the essence of palace life.

(6) Northern landscape painting is not influenced by the profound understanding of nature by the Chinese nation.

❸ Choose the best answer to each of the following questions.

(1) What does Zhang Xuan's *Women Preparing Silk* primarily depict?

　　A. A scene of palace women pounding silk fabrics.

　　B. The story of Boyi and Shuqi.

　　C. The goddess of the Luo River.

　　D. Autumn breeze and silk fan.

(2) What is conveyed through the figures in Li Tang's *Picking Vetches*?

　　A. The characters' firm expression.

　　B. The brilliance of humanity and the power of morality.

　　C. The artistic charm of figure painting.

　　D. The social landscape of the Ming Dynasty.

(3) How do modern painters innovate in figure painting?

　　A. By incorporating more modern elements and techniques.

　　B. By strictly adhering to traditional methods.

　　C. By focusing solely on the social landscapes.

　　D. By documenting historical figures.

(4) What does *The Landscape Album* by Bada Shanren showcase?

　　A. A colorful depiction of nature.

　　B. A unique artistic style with profound thoughts.

　　C. A simple landscape with no artistic conception.

　　D. A realistic portrayal of the artist's life.

(5) What is the main subject of Fan Kuan's *Travelers among Mountains and Streams*?

　　A. Palace life.　　　　　　　　　　B. Portraits of figures.

　　C. Mountainous landscapes.　　　　　D. Still life with flowers and birds.

(6) What is the northern school painting renowned for?

　　A. Its abstract style.

　　B. Its focus on urban scenes.

　　C. Its use of monochrome ink.

　　D. Its fine brushwork and rich colors.

中国画工具和材料
Tools and Materials for Chinese Painting

中国画工具的发展历程是中华文明悠久历史的见证。在新石器时代，人们便开始用简易工具在陶器上绘图。汉代纸张的出现对绘画工具的发展产生了革命性的影响。唐代笔、墨、纸、砚的应用臻于成熟，特别是宣纸的广泛使用极大促进了水墨画的发展。宋代在砚台制作技术上取得了重大突破，端砚、歙砚等名砚成为收藏品。元明清时期，颜料种类增多，色彩世界更加丰富。笔、墨、纸、砚、颜料这五种在绘画中常用的工具或材料被称为"绘画五宝"。中国画工具的演进与社会文化的发展和科技的进步紧密相关，折射出各个时代的审美取向。

The development of Chinese painting tools reflects the long history of Chinese civilization. As early as the Neolithic Age, people began using simple tools to draw on pottery. The advent of paper in the Han Dynasty had a revolutionary impact on the development of painting tools. During the Tang Dynasty, the application of brushes, ink, paper, and inkstones reached maturity. In particular, the widespread use of rice paper greatly promoted the development of ink wash painting. In the Song Dynasty, significant breakthroughs were made in inkstone-making technology, and famous inkstones such as Duan inkstones and She inkstones became collectibles. In the Yuan, Ming, and Qing dynasties, the variety of pigments increased, enriching the palette of colors. The five commonly used tools or materials in Chinese painting, namely brushes, ink, paper, inkstones, and pigments, are known as the "Five Treasures of Painting." The evolution of Chinese painting tools is closely related to social and cultural development and the progress of science and technology, reflecting the aesthetic tastes of different eras.

在中国画的璀璨世界里，笔这一简单而又神奇的工具，被誉为绘画五宝之首，是艺术家们心灵与情感的直接载体。狼毫笔、羊毫笔与兼毫笔则如同三位性格迥异的画师，各自以其独特的笔触与韵味，共同绘就了中国画的辉煌篇章。

In the resplendent world of Chinese painting, the brush, this simple yet magical tool, is hailed as the foremost of the five treasures of painting, serving as the direct medium for the artist's soul and emotions. The wolf-hair brush, goat-hair brush, and mixed-hair brush are like three painters with distinct personalities. Each contributes its unique touch and charm, collectively painting the splendid chapters of Chinese art.

狼毫笔以其刚劲有力、弹性卓越的特质，成为中国画中勾勒线条与描绘细节的不二之选。其笔尖锋利，能够轻松达到力透纸背的效果，留下深浅不一、富有变化的墨痕。在工笔画这一精细入微的艺术形式中，狼毫笔更是大显身手，无论是花鸟鱼虫的细腻纹理，还是人物衣饰的繁复图案，都能用狼毫笔精妙地勾勒出来。古代宫廷画家在创作皇家御用画作时，常会根据题材与技法的需求选用狼毫笔。

The wolf-hair brush, with its strong and resilient characteristics, has become the preferred choice for outlining lines and detailing in Chinese painting. Its sharp tip is capable of easily penetrating the rice paper, leaving behind ink marks of varying depths and rich nuances. In the meticulous art form of fine brushwork painting, the wolf-hair brush truly excels. Whether it's the delicate textures of flowers, birds, fish, and insects, or the complex patterns of human garments and accessories, everything can be delicately outlined with wolf-hair brushes. Ancient court painters often selected wolf-hair brushes according to the requirements of subject matter and technical approaches when creating paintings for imperial use.

相较于狼毫笔的刚烈，羊毫笔柔软细腻、吸水性强。在泼墨山水画中，羊毫笔仿佛一位轻盈的舞者，以其独特的韵律在宣纸上翩翩起舞，营造出云雾缭绕、水波荡漾的梦幻意境。其柔软的笔尖能够吸附大量墨汁，随着画家的手腕轻转，便能在纸上留下层层叠叠、浓淡相宜的墨色变化。正是这种独特的吸水性能与表现力，使得羊毫笔成为山水画家们抒发情感、表达意境的重要工具。

Compared to the firmness of the wolf-hair brush, the goat-hair brush has a gentle and delicate nature and superior water-absorbing properties. In ink wash landscape paintings, the goat-hair brush glides across rice paper with unique rhythm, like a graceful dancer, creating a dreamy atmosphere of misty clouds and rippling waters. Its soft tip can absorb a large amount of ink, and with a light turn of the painter's wrist, it leaves behind layers of ink shades that are perfectly balanced in depth and lightness. It is this unique water-absorbing capability and expressiveness that makes the goat-hair brush an essential tool for landscape painters to express emotions and convey artistic conceptions.

兼毫笔的出现弥补了狼毫笔与羊毫笔的不足。兼毫笔，顾名思义，就是将狼毫与羊毫按一定比例混合制成的毛笔。它既保留了狼毫的弹性与锋利，又兼具羊毫的柔软与吸水性，使得画家在创作过程中能更加自如地切换技法与风格，实现更为丰富多样的艺术效果。宋代画家范宽，便是兼毫笔运用的高手之一。他在创作《溪山行旅图》时，巧妙地运用了兼毫笔的特性，既凭借狼毫之刚劲勾勒出山石树木的轮廓与结构，又凭借羊毫之柔软渲染出云雾水波的柔美与灵动，使得画面既富有力量感又不失温婉之美，展现了山水画深邃而灵动的艺术魅力。

The emergence of mixed-hair brush compensates for the deficiencies of wolf-hair and goat-hair brushes. As the name suggests, the mixed-hair brush is made by mixing wolf-hair and goat-hair in a certain proportion. It retains the elasticity and sharpness of wolf-hair, while also possessing the softness and water-absorption of goat-hair, allowing artists to switch techniques and styles more freely during the creative process, and resulting in a richer variety of artistic effects. One of the masters in the use of the mixed-hair brush was the Song Dynasty painter Fan Kuan. In creating *Travelers among Mountains and Streams*, he cleverly utilized the characteristics of the mixed-hair brush, using the tough and firm wolf-hair to outline the contours and structures of mountains, trees, and rocks, and using soft goat-hair to render the gracefulness and agility of clouds and water. This approach made the entire painting both powerful and gentle, showcasing the profound and lively artistic charm of landscape painting.

墨在中国传统艺术中同样有着举足轻重的地位。它不仅仅是书写与绘画的工具，更是文化、历史与技艺的载体。在国画创作中，对墨的使用并非简单的"一黑到底"，而是要有丰富的层次与变化。墨色根据浓淡干湿大致可以分为焦、浓、重、淡、清五种类型。这五种墨色各自拥有独特的魅力和表现力。通过五种墨色的巧妙运用和组合变化，画家们能够创造出丰富多彩、意境深远的国画作品。

Ink also plays a crucial role in traditional Chinese art. It is not just a tool for writing and painting, but also a carrier of culture, history, and craftsmanship. In the creation of Chinese paintings, the use of ink is not merely a uniform black but contains a rich range of tones and variations. Depending on the concentration, dryness, and moisture of the ink, it can be broadly categorized into five types: burnt, thick, dark, light, and clear. Each of these five ink shades possesses unique charm and expressiveness. Through the skillful use and combination of these five ink shades, painters can create a diverse array of Chinese paintings that are rich in color and profound in artistic conception.

在山水画中，焦墨常被用于勾勒山石的轮廓。那些由焦墨勾勒出的山石，线条刚劲有力，棱角分明，仿佛能穿透岁月的尘埃，展现出大自然最原始、最质朴的力量。当焦墨与淡墨、湿墨等墨色相结合时，能营造出一种层次分明、虚实相生的意境，使得画面更加生动传神。除了山水画外，焦墨在花鸟画和人物画中也有着广泛应用。在花鸟画中，焦墨常被用于表现老树的枝干。那些历经风霜、树皮斑驳的老树，在焦墨的勾勒下显得更加苍劲有力，仿佛能感受到它们与时间的抗争和生命的顽强。在人物画中，焦墨则常被用于描绘人物的须发、衣纹等细节部分，使得人物形象更加生动逼真，充满了生活气息。

In landscape painting, burnt ink is often used to outline the contours of mountains and rocks. Contours outlined by burnt ink are strong and angular, as if they could penetrate the dust of the ages, revealing the most primitive and simple power of nature. When burnt ink is combined with light ink, wet ink, and other shades, it can create an artistic conception with clear layers and a blend of reality and illusion, making the painting more lively and expressive. Besides landscape painting, burnt ink is also widely used in flower-and-bird painting and figure painting. In flower-and-bird painting, burnt ink is often used to depict the branches of old trees. Those weathered old trees with mottled bark appear more vigorous and powerful when outlined in burnt ink, as if one could feel their struggle against the passage of time and the tenacity of life. In figure painting, burnt ink is often used to depict details such as the hair and clothing folds of figures, thus making the figures more lifelike and full of life.

浓墨常常用来描绘近景的山石、树木等主体物象。山石的坚硬、树木的苍翠，在浓墨的渲染下更显生机，充满力量。在国画中，浓墨与淡墨的巧妙结合，能创造出一种令人叹为观止的艺术效果。淡墨轻盈、柔和，如同清晨的薄雾，为画面增添了几分朦胧与梦幻；浓墨则深邃、浓重，为画面注入了厚重的质感和强烈的生命力。两者相互映衬、相互交融，营造出一种丰富的层次感和空间感。

Thick ink is often used to depict main objects such as mountains, rocks, trees, and other elements in the foreground. The solidity of mountains and rocks, as well as the lushness of the trees, appears even more vigorous when rendered with thick ink. In traditional Chinese painting, the skillful combination of thick and light ink creates a breathtaking art effect. Light ink is delicate and soft, like the morning mist, adding a touch of vagueness and dreaminess to the painting; while thick ink, with its profound and intense quality, injects a sense of substantial texture and strong vitality into the painting. The two complement each other, blending to create a rich sense of depth and spatiality.

重墨的运用是一种极为重要的表现手法，它通常用来突出画面中的焦点部分，或者用来强调某些关键的细节之处。通过厚重而深邃的墨色和力度十足的笔触，重墨能够赋予画面一种强烈的视觉冲击力和情绪感染力。此外，重墨的使用还能够增强画面的立体感和空间感。通过在某些特定部位施加重墨，画家们可以有效地突出主体，使画面的焦点更加明确，同时也能通过墨色的深浅变化来营造出一种深远的空间感。这种空间感的营造不仅能够使画面显得更加生动和真实，还能够引导观者的视线，使其在欣赏画作时能够更加深入地理解和感受画家所要传达的艺术意境。

The use of dark ink is an extremely important technique. Painters often employ it to highlight the focal points of the scene or to emphasize certain key details. Through thick and profound ink colors and powerful brushstrokes, dark ink can create a strong visual impact and convey deep emotional expressiveness in a painting. Moreover, its application can enhance the three-dimensional effect and sense of space in a painting. By applying dark ink to specific areas, painters can effectively highlight the main subject, making it the clear focal point of the painting. At the same time, variations in ink density create a strong sense of depth in space. The creation of this spatial effect not only makes the painting appear more vivid and realistic but also guides the viewer's gaze, allowing for a deeper understanding and appreciation of the artistic conception that the painter intends to convey.

淡墨常常被画家巧妙地运用于描绘遥远的山峦、缥缈的云雾以及其他远景中的物象。淡墨的运用能够营造出一种淡雅而清新的氛围，使得整个画面呈现出一种超凡脱俗的美感。这种技法的运用不仅丰富了国画的表现力，还能带给观者一种心灵上的宁静与愉悦。

Light ink is often skillfully used by painters to depict distant mountains, ethereal clouds, and other objects in the background. Through the use of light ink, artists can create an elegant and fresh atmosphere, giving the entire painting an ethereal beauty. The application of light ink not only enriches the expressiveness of traditional Chinese painting, but also allows viewers to experience mental tranquility and joy while appreciating the artworks.

清墨常常用于描绘细腻而微妙的景象，如水面的倒影、月夜的清辉等。清墨所特有的清澈透明的墨色，配合细腻的笔触能够赋予画面一种生动逼真、富有诗意的美感。画家通过这种技法来捕捉自然界的细微之美，将这些美景以一种更加细腻和生动的方式呈现给观者。这种技艺的展现，不仅让画面呈现出一种静态的美感，更赋予了画面一种动态的生命力，使观者仿佛能够感受到画面中所描绘的自然景象的呼吸与流动。

Clear ink is often used to depict delicate and subtle scenes, such as reflections on the water surface or the serene glow of moonlight. The unique transparency of clear ink in color, combined with fine brushwork, can endow the painting with vivid, lifelike, and poetic beauty. Through this technique, artists capture the subtle beauty of nature and present it to viewers in a more delicate and lively way. The display of this skill not only presents a static aesthetic beauty in the painting but also infuses the artwork with dynamic vitality, making viewers feel as if they can sense the breath and flow of the depicted natural scenes.

在中国传统绘画艺术中，纸张的选择对于作品的最终呈现具有至关重要的作用。

中国画纸张的分类繁多，每一种都有其特定的用途和表现力。其中，宣纸作为中国画中最为常见且不可或缺的材料之一，其独特的质地和特性对于画面效果和艺术品质的影响尤为显著。宣纸主要分为生宣、熟宣和半生半熟宣三种类型，每一种类型都有各自的特点和适用场景。

In traditional Chinese painting art, the choice of paper plays a crucial role in the final presentation of the artwork. Chinese painting papers are classified into a wide variety, each with its specific uses and expressive qualities. Among these, rice paper, as one of the most common and indispensable materials in Chinese painting, has a unique texture and characteristics that significantly affect the visual impact and artistic quality of the painting. The classification of rice paper mainly falls into three types: raw rice paper, processed rice paper, and semi-raw semi-processed rice paper, each with its distinctive features and suitable applications.

生宣纸因其卓越的吸水性能和柔软的质地而闻名，它能够完美地吸收墨水和各种颜料，从而使得绘制出的画面呈现出一种天然的晕染效果。这种独特的纸张特别适用于表现水墨画的生动流畅，因此在写意画的创作中被广泛应用和推崇。

Raw rice paper is renowned for its superior water absorption and soft texture, which allows it to perfectly absorb ink and various pigments, resulting in a naturally blurred effect in the drawn images. This unique paper is ideal for expressing the fullness and fluidity of ink wash paintings, and is therefore widely used and esteemed in freehand brushwork painting.

熟宣纸是一种经过特殊加工处理的宣纸，其表面涂有一层胶质，这种特殊的处理方式大大降低了纸张的吸水性。正是因为这种低吸水性的特点，熟宣纸能够更好地控制墨水和颜料的流动，使得画家在作画时能够更加自如地掌握色彩的分布和线条的粗细。这种纸张特别适用于工笔画，因为工笔画要求线条精细、色彩层次分明，每一笔都需要精确到位。熟宣纸能够帮助画家精确地描绘细节，保持色彩的稳定和清晰，避免色彩的过度扩散和模糊。这种纸张的特性使得作品在表现精细和严谨方面具有独特的优势，能够更好地展现工笔画的精致和细腻，使画面更加生动和逼真。

Processed rice paper is a special kind of rice paper that has been processed with a layer of glue on its surface, significantly reducing the paper's absorbency. Due to its low absorbency, processed rice paper better controls the flow of ink and pigments, allowing painters to more freely manage the distribution of colors and the thickness of lines. This paper is particularly suitable for fine brushwork painting, which requires fine lines and distinct color layers, with each stroke being precisely placed. Processed rice paper helps artists to accurately depict details, maintain color stability and clarity, and prevent excessive color spreading and blurring. The properties of this paper give it a unique advantage in expressing fine and precise details, better showcasing the delicacy and subtlety of fine brushwork paintings, making the images more vivid and realistic.

半生半熟的宣纸，顾名思义，介于生宣和熟宣这两种宣纸之间。这种宣纸既保留了一定的吸水性，又具有一定的抗水性，因此在使用上具有更大的灵活性和多样性。这种宣纸的特性使得它在创作中能够兼顾写意的自由和工笔的精细，为画家提供了更多的表现空间和创作自由度。

As the name suggests, semi-raw semi-processed rice paper is a unique type of rice paper that lies between raw and processed rice paper. It retains certain degree of absorbency while also possessing water resistance, offering greater flexibility and versatility in application. This characteristic allows the rice paper to balance the spontaneity of freehand brushwork with the precision of fine brushwork, providing artists with more expressive space and creative freedom.

在绘画五宝中，砚台作为研磨墨汁的工具，其材质与造型不仅影响着墨色的品质，也承载着深厚的文化意蕴。端砚，产自广东肇庆，以细腻的石质和天然的纹理著称，被誉为"砚中之宝"。用端砚研磨出的墨汁细腻均匀，适于精细的线条勾勒和层次丰富的渲染。歙砚产自安徽歙县，以青黑色的石质和金星点点的纹理而闻名，其研磨出的墨汁颜色深沉，适于表现中国画中的深邃与厚重。洮河砚产于甘肃洮河，其石质温润，色泽淡雅，研磨出的墨汁颜色柔和，特别适于表现淡墨山水和清新雅致的画风。这些砚台的特色不仅体现在材质上，更在于它们各自独特的造型设计和文化内涵，如端砚的砚池深浅适宜，歙砚的砚盖精雕细琢，洮河砚的砚形简约大方。在选择砚台时，艺术家们会根据自己的绘画风格和对墨色的需求，挑选出最适合的砚台，以期达到笔墨纸砚与颜料的完美结合，创作出具有独特韵味的中国画作品。

Among the five treasures of Chinese painting, the inkstone, as a tool for grinding ink, not only affects the quality of ink color through its material and shape, but also carries profound cultural connotations. The Duan inkstone produced in Zhaoqing, Guangdong, is renowned for its fine stone texture and natural patterns, and is hailed as the premier inkstone among all varieties. The ink ground with a Duan inkstone is smooth and even, making it suitable for delicate brush lines and multi-layered ink washes. The She inkstone comes from Shexian, Anhui, and is famous for its dark gray stone speckled with golden stars. Its ink color is deep and well-suited for expressing the profundity and weightiness in Chinese paintings. The Taohe inkstone is produced along the Tao River in Gansu, with a stone texture that is warm and has a pale, elegant color, grinding ink that is soft and particularly suitable for expressing light ink landscapes and fresh, elegant painting styles. The uniqueness of these inkstones is not only reflected in their materials but also in their distinctive design and cultural connotations, such as the Duan inkstone's well-proportioned inkwell, the exquisitely carved lid of the She inkstone, and the simple yet elegant shape of the Taohe inkstone. When choosing an inkstone, artists select the one that best suits their painting style and ink color needs, aiming to achieve the perfect combination of brush, ink, paper, inkstone, and pigments to create Chinese painting works with unique charm.

砚台不仅是研磨墨汁的工具，更是文人墨客情感寄托的载体。研墨的技巧直接关系到墨色的深浅与层次感，进而影响整个作品的韵律与表现力。传统上，研墨讲究"水少墨多"，即在砚台中加入少量清水，然后用墨锭在砚面上以均匀的力度研磨，直至墨汁达到理想的浓度。据《文房四谱》记载，研墨时需"如磨刀石，不急不缓"，这表明研墨时需要耐心与细致。砚台的清洁与维护同样重要，使用完毕后，应立即用清水冲洗干净，避免墨汁干结，损害砚台的表面。对于端砚、歙砚等名贵砚台，还需用柔软的布料轻轻擦拭，保持其天然的光泽与纹理。正如古人所言："砚之为用，非独墨也，亦以养心。"砚台的保养不仅是对工具的尊重，更是艺术创作态度的体现。

An inkstone is not only a tool for grinding ink but also a vessel for literati and scholars to express their emotions. The skill of grinding ink directly affects the depth and layering of the ink color, which in turn influences the rhythm and expressiveness of the entire work. Traditionally, the art of grinding ink emphasizes "less water, more ink," meaning adding a small amount of water to the inkstone and then grinding the ink stick on its surface with uniform pressure until the ink reaches the desired consistency. According to *Manuals on the Four Treasures of the Study*, grinding ink requires technique similar to sharpening a knife on a stone—neither too fast nor too slow—indicating the patience and meticulousness needed for the process. Cleaning and maintaining the inkstone are equally important. After being used, it should be immediately rinsed with clean water to prevent the ink from drying and damaging the surface of the inkstone. For precious inkstones like Duan inkstones and She inkstones, they should be gently wiped with a soft cloth to preserve their natural luster and grain after rinsing. As an ancient saying goes, the use of an inkstone is not just for grinding ink, but also for cultivating the mind. The maintenance of an inkstone not only shows respect for the tool but also reflects one's attitude towards artistic creation.

中国画颜料种类繁多，其中包括汁绿、墨青、褐色、紫色、鹅黄、深红、粉色、赭黄、朱红、青灰、豆绿、土黄等，这些色彩相互交织，构建了中国画丰富而多变的色彩体系。就其原材料而言，中国画颜料大致可分为矿物质颜料、植物颜料和化学合成颜料这三大类别。

Chinese painting pigments boast a rich diversity, encompassing hues like juice green, ink blue, brown, purple, goose yellow, deep red, pink, ochre yellow, vermilion, bluish gray, pea green, earthy yellow, and numerous others. These colors interweave with each other, constructing a rich and varied color system of Chinese painting. In terms of raw materials, Chinese painting pigments can generally be divided into three main categories: mineral pigments, plant-based pigments, and chemically synthesized pigments.

矿物质颜料普遍具有色泽厚重艳丽、不透明及覆盖力强的显著特性，并且能够长久保持色彩的鲜艳度与稳定性，如石绿、朱砂、雄黄等，不过在实际的绘画操作过程中，往往需要先用植物颜料进行打底，以便更好地展现矿物质颜料的色彩优势与表现效果。植物颜料包括花青、藤黄、胭脂等，其特点在于色彩透明度高、渗化性好，能够使画面呈现出柔和、自然且细腻的过渡效果，然而其遮盖力相对较弱，所以在色彩叠加与覆盖运用时，需要画家具备高超的技巧和敏锐的色彩感知能力。化学合成颜料是现代工业生产的产物，旨在模拟传统颜料的特性，不过在色泽表现的精准度及稳定性方面，与传统颜料相比存在一些细微的差异。

Mineral pigments including Shilü, Zhusha, Xionghuang, etc., possess remarkable characteristics such as thick and vibrant colors, opacity, and high coverage. They can maintain the vividness and stability of the color for a long time. However, in the actual painting process, it is often necessary to first apply a base layer of plant pigments to better display their color advantages and performances. Plant-based pigments, including Huaqing, Tenghuang, Yanzhi, etc., are characterized by high color transparency and good permeability, enabling the painting to present a soft, natural, and delicate transition effect. However, their covering power is relatively weak. Therefore, when it comes to color superimposition and coverage application, painters need to possess excellent skills and a keen sense of color perception. Chemically synthesized pigments are the outcome of modern industrial manufacturing processes. They are created to replicate the attributes of traditional pigments. Nevertheless, in terms of color presentation accuracy and stability, there exist several minor discrepancies when contrasted with traditional pigments.

在绘画创作中，画家会依据画面的主题构思、风格以及个人审美和创作习惯来选择使用各类中国画颜料，并通过巧妙的色彩搭配、独特的表现技法以及细腻的情感融入，创作出生动传神的国画作品。

During the process of painting creation, painters select various Chinese painting pigments based on the thematic concept, stylistic orientation, as well as their individual aesthetic sensibilities and creative practices. Through skillful color combination, unique expressive techniques, and infusion of delicate emotions, they can create vivid and expressive traditional Chinese painting works that truly captivate the viewers.

配色颜料是用来调配色彩的颜料。在传统中国画里，色彩运用极为讲究"五色"，即青、赤、黄、白、黑。这五种颜色不但各自蕴含独特的象征意义，而且在相互搭配时，也严格遵循和谐与平衡的原则。例如，青色与赤色的组合，象征着阴阳调和，常用于表现山水画中的山与水，形成鲜明对比而又不失协调。在画面的构图与意境营造上，国画家们往往采用"留白"手法，通过在画面上留出未着色的部分来营造意境，给观者留下想象空间，通过虚实对比突出主体。"留白"体现了道家的"有无相生"与儒家的"中庸平衡"，即"实"（色彩、线条）与"虚"（留白）相依的哲学思想。

Color-mixing pigments refer to those used for color combination. In traditional Chinese painting, great attention is paid to the "five colors," namely cyan, red, yellow, white, and black. These five colors not only have unique symbolic meanings but also follow the principles of harmony and balance when combined with one another. For example, the combination of cyan and red symbolizes the balance of Yin and Yang and is often used to depict mountains and water in landscape paintings, creating a striking contrast while maintaining harmony. For a painting's composition and the creation of its artistic conception, traditional Chinese painters often employ the technique of "leaving white." By leaving uncolored areas on the painting's surface, they craft the artistic conception, leave room for viewers' imagination, and highlight the main subject through the contrast between "void" (leaving white) and "solid" (colors and lines). "Leaving white" embodies the philosophical ideas of Taoism's "interdependence of 'being' and 'non-being'" and Confucianism's "doctrine of the mean and balance"— a philosophy where "solid" (colors and lines) and "void" (leaving white) are mutually dependent.

在国画中，三原色红、黄、蓝是色彩调配的基础。红色加蓝色可以调出紫色，不同红色和蓝色的组合会得到不同效果的紫色，例如大红与普蓝混合可以得到鲜艳的紫红色，而深红与湖蓝混合则可以得到较深的蓝紫色。调色时，红色和蓝色的混合比例会影响最终得到的紫色深浅和色调。若想要偏向红色的紫色，可以增加红色的比例；

若想要偏向蓝色的紫色，则可以增加蓝色的比例。此外，若要调出淡紫色，可以在调好的紫色基础上加入适量的白色颜料；若要调出深紫色，可以加入少量的黑色颜料，但需注意黑色的加入量要谨慎控制，以免颜色变得过于暗淡或接近黑色。

In traditional Chinese painting, the three primary colors—red, yellow, and blue—form the basis of color mixing. Red mixed with blue can produce purple. Different combinations of red and blue will yield various shades of purple. For instance, mixing bright red with dark blue might create a vivid purplish red, whereas deep red mixed with light blue could produce a darker blue-purple. The ratio of red to blue in the mixture will affect the depth and hue of the final purple. To achieve a red-leaning purple, increase the proportion of red; for a blue-leaning purple, increase the proportion of blue. To create a light purple, add an appropriate amount of white paint to the mixture. For a dark purple, add a small amount of black paint, but be cautious with the amount of black to avoid making the color too dull or too close to pure black.

红色与黄色结合可以调出不同的橙色，这是一种鲜艳且温暖的颜色。调出橙色时，可以根据需要调整红色和黄色的比例，以获得不同色调的橙色。如果红色与黄色等量混合，通常会产生纯正的橙色。若希望橙色偏向黄色，可以适当增加黄色的比例；相反，如果希望橙色偏红一些，可以稍微增加红色的比例。这种色彩变化为艺术家们提供了丰富的选择，使他们能够根据需要调整色彩，创造出独特的视觉效果。

The combination of red and yellow can produce various shades of orange, a bright and warm color. When mixing orange, adjust the ratio of red to yellow according to need to achieve different hues of orange. If red and yellow are mixed in equal amounts, they typically produce a pure shade of orange. To make the orange lean towards yellow, increase the proportion of yellow. Conversely, if a slightly redder orange is desired, one can add a bit more red. This color variation provides artists with a rich palette of options, allowing them to adjust hues as needed and create unique visual effects.

蓝色和黄色相混合可以调出不同的绿色，通常建议按照一定比例混合黄色和蓝色颜料，例如常见的 2:1 的比例，即两份黄色与一份蓝色，但具体比例可根据所需绿色的深浅和色调进行调整。调色时，可以先将黄色颜料加水稀释，然后蘸取蓝色进行调色。画笔只需蘸取少量蓝色，就能得到偏绿的黄色，逐渐加入更多的蓝色则可以得到更深的绿色。在此过程中，需要不断观察颜色的变化，并适时调整两种颜料的比例，直到调出满意的绿色。此外，还可以通过添加其他颜色来调整绿色的色调。例如，加入少量红色或紫色可以使绿色更加鲜艳，加入白色颜料可以使绿色变得更加明亮，而加入黑色颜料则可以使绿色变得更加深沉。

Different shades of green can be created by combining blue and yellow. It is generally recommended to mix yellow and blue pigments in a certain ratio, such as the common 2:1 ratio, which means two parts yellow to one part blue. However, the specific ratio can be adjusted according to the desired depth and tone of the green. When mixing colors, you can first dilute the yellow pigment with water, then add blue to create green. A small amount of blue on the brush will yield a greenish yellow, and gradually adding more blue will result in a deeper green. During this process, it is necessary to continuously observe color changes and adjust the ratio of the two pigments until a satisfactory green is achieved. Additionally, other colors can be added to adjust the hue of green. For example, adding a small amount of red or purple can make the green more vivid. Adding white pigment lightens the green and enhances its luminosity, while adding black pigment deepens the green.

水彩颜料是一种透明的水性颜料，它具有极高的透明度和可用水稀释的特性。这种颜料能够创造出色彩鲜艳、明亮的效果，非常适合绘制写意花鸟和风景画。水彩画以其轻盈、灵动、富有变化的特点，成为许多艺术家表达情感和描绘自然景观的首选。

Watercolor paints are a type of transparent, water-based paint with high transparency and dilutability in water. These paints can create vivid and bright color effects, making them ideal for painting freehand flowers, birds, and landscapes. Watercolor paintings are favored by many artists for expressing emotions and depicting natural scenes due to their lightness, agility, and versatility.

Exercises

① **Answer the following questions.**

(1) What's the significance of the combination of different ink colors in creating the artistic conception of a Chinese painting?

(2) What role does the choice of rice paper play in determining the style and effect of a Chinese painting?

(3) In what ways does the use of ink in Chinese painting reflect the concept of "less is more" in art?

❷ Decide whether each of the following statements is true (T) or false (F).

(1) The wolf-hair brush is mainly for outlining lines and depicting details due to its strong and resilient characteristics.

(2) Only professional painters need to consider the choice of rice paper type in Chinese painting.

(3) Mineral pigments are more commonly used than plant pigments in modern Chinese painting.

(4) Processed rice paper is more suitable for detailed painting as it can control the ink and pigment well, while raw rice paper is more suitable for freehand brushwork.

(5) The "leaving white" technique in Chinese painting is only used for aesthetic purposes and has no philosophical implications.

Section 4

中国画基本绘画技法与示范
Basic Painting Techniques and Demonstrations of Chinese Painting

中国画拥有独特的绘画技法体系。这些技法能够丰富画面的表现力，使作品具有独特的艺术魅力。在这些技法中，中锋、侧锋、点、线、面最为基础。它们在绘画创作过程中扮演着至关重要的角色，直接关系到作品的整体质量和艺术效果的呈现。

Chinese painting possesses a unique system of painting techniques. These techniques can enrich the expressiveness of the picture and endow the works with unique artistic charm. Among these techniques, the center-tip technique, side-tip technique, dots, lines, and planes are the most fundamental. They play a vital role in painting creation and directly affect the overall quality and artistic effect of the work.

中锋是指在书写或绘画过程中，笔锋垂直于纸面并且始终保持在笔画的中心线上运行。通过这种方式，笔画能够呈现出圆润、饱满且富有立体感的视觉效果。中锋的运用在勾勒物象的轮廓和细节部分时尤为常见，能使线条更加细腻和精确。

The center-tip technique requires the brush tip to be perpendicular to the paper surface and maintain its position along the central line of the stroke during the writing or painting process, endowing the strokes with a visually round, full, and three-dimensional appearance. This technique is particularly common when outlining the contours and detailed parts of objects, making the lines appear more delicate and precise.

侧锋是指在行笔过程中，笔锋与纸面形成一定的夹角，笔锋在笔画一侧运行，而不是像中锋那样始终保持在笔画的中心线上。这种技法能够产生变化多端的线条效果，例如线条粗细、浓淡的变化，甚至可以创造出独特的纹理和质感。侧锋的运用在表现物体的质感和空间感方面尤为有效，它能够使画面更加丰富和层次分明，增强画面的视觉冲击力，使作品更具艺术表现力和深度。

The side-tip technique implies that the brush tip forms a certain angle with the paper surface during movement and moves along one side of the stroke rather than stay on the central line like the center-tip. This technique creates varied line effects, such as thickness and shade variation, and can even produce unique textures and tactile qualities. The application of the side-tip technique is particularly effective in expressing the texture and spatial sense of objects, making the picture visually richer and layered, enhancing the visual impact of the painting and thus endowing the work with greater artistic expressiveness and depth.

在中国画的创作过程中，点、线、面是构成画面的基本元素。点不仅仅是形态上的最小单位，更是情感与意境的浓缩。它们可以是山巅之上历经风霜的苔点，斑驳而富有生命力，象征着时间的流转与自然的坚韧；也可以是人物画中细腻勾勒的眉眼，一颦一笑间，尽显人物的神韵与情感。

In the creative process of Chinese painting, dots, lines, and planes are the basic elements that constitute the composition of the painting. The dot is not just the smallest unit of form but also a concentration of emotion and artistic conception. Dots can be the lichen spots atop mountain peaks, weathered by the elements, mottled yet full of vitality, symbolizing the passage of time and the resilience of nature; they can also be the delicately outlined eyebrows and eyes in figure paintings, expressing the charm and emotions of the characters with every smile or frown.

线是连接点与面的桥梁。在中国画中，"骨法用笔"的理念深入人心，线条的力度、节奏与韵律，无不彰显画家的功力与情怀。唐代画家吴道子，以其"吴带当风"的线条著称于世，他的线条流畅而有力，宛如行云流水般自然洒脱，既展现了物体的形态之美，又蕴含了丰富的情感与生命力。

The line is the bridge connecting dots and planes. In Chinese painting, the concept of "bone method of brushwork" has been deeply rooted in people's hearts. The strength, rhythm and cadence of the lines all manifest the painter's skills and emotions. Wu Daozi, a painter in the Tang Dynasty, was renowned all over the world for his lines characterized by the so-called "Wu's belts fluttering in the wind." His lines were smooth and forceful, as free and unrestrained as floating clouds and flowing water. They not only demonstrated the beauty of the forms of objects but also conveyed rich emotions and vitality.

作为由点与线构成的广阔领域，面在中国画中扮演着至关重要的角色。它不仅能够表现物体的体积与空间感，更能够通过墨色的深浅、浓淡与渲染技巧，形成丰富而细腻的层次与质感。元代画家黄公望的《富春山居图》便是对此的最佳诠释。层层叠叠的墨色变化仿佛是大自然的神奇笔触，将山水的神韵与意境展现得淋漓尽致。

As an extensive field composed of dots and lines, the plane plays a crucial role in traditional Chinese painting. It can not only convey the volume and spatial sense of objects but also create rich and delicate layers and textures through the variation of ink shades, density, and rendering techniques. The painting *Dwelling in the Fuchun Mountains* by Huang Gongwang, a painter in the Yuan Dynasty, is the best illustration. The overlapping changes of ink shades seem like the miraculous brushstrokes bestowed by nature, displaying the charm and artistic conception of the landscape vividly.

点、线、面的笔法技巧在中国画中占据着举足轻重的地位。它们各自承载着不同的艺术表现力与审美价值，又相互依存、相互融合，共同展现了中国画的独特魅力与韵味。

The brushwork techniques of dots, lines, and planes hold a pivotal position in Chinese painting. Each carries different artistic expressiveness and aesthetic value, yet they are interdependent and integrated, collectively showing the unique charm and flavor of Chinese painting.

中国画基础技法的练习方法和步骤主要包括以下几个方面。

The practice methods and specific steps for basic Chinese painting techniques mainly consist of the following aspects.

第一，了解中国画的基本特点和工具。中国画以其独特的意境、笔墨和构图著称，使用的工具主要是毛笔、宣纸、墨和颜料。掌握这些工具的使用方法是学习中国画的基础。

Firstly, it is crucial to get acquainted with the fundamental characteristics and tools of Chinese painting. Renowned for its distinctive artistic conception, brushwork, and composition, Chinese painting primarily employs tools like writing brushes, rice paper, ink, and pigments. Mastering the usage of these tools serves as the cornerstone for learning Chinese painting.

第二，学习基本的笔法和墨法。笔法包括点、线、面的运用，如中锋、侧锋、逆锋等。墨法则涉及干、湿、浓、淡的变化。学习者要通过反复练习熟悉各种笔墨的特性及其表现力。

Secondly, learn the basic brushwork and ink techniques. The brushwork encompasses the application of dots, lines, and planes, such as center-tip, side-tip, and reverse-tip painting techniques. Meanwhile, ink techniques involve the variations of dryness, wetness, thickness, and lightness of the ink. Through consistent practice, one can master the unique features and expressive power of brush and ink.

第三，练习构图和布局。中国画讲究画面的平衡与和谐，构图时要注意主次分明、虚实相生。学习者可以通过临摹经典作品来学习构图，逐步掌握安排画面元素的技巧。

Thirdly, practice the composition and layout. Traditional Chinese paintings attach great importance to the balance and harmony of the picture. When composing, one should pay attention to differentiating the primary and secondary elements as well as the interrelationship between the void and the solid. By copying classic works, one can acquire composition skills and gradually grasp how to arrange the elements in the picture.

第四，学习色彩的运用。中国画中的色彩不仅仅是自然色彩的再现，更注重意境和情感的表达。掌握色彩的搭配和渲染技巧，能够使画面更加生动和富有表现力。

Fourthly, learn the color application. In Chinese painting, colors are not merely a replication of natural hues but rather place more emphasis on the conveyance of artistic conception and emotions. Gaining proficiency in color matching and rendering techniques can make the painting more vivid and expressive.

第五，进行创作实践。在掌握了基础技法之后，学习者可以尝试创作一些简单的作品，逐步积累经验，通过不断练习和创作，提高自己的艺术修养和审美能力。

Lastly, engage in creative practice. Once the basic techniques have been grasped, one can attempt to create some simple works and progressively accumulate experience. Through continuous practice and creation, one's artistic cultivation and aesthetic ability can be enhanced.

在进行中国画创作时，除了毛笔、墨汁、宣纸和颜料这几种基础绘画材料外，还需准备一些辅助工具。比如，将毛毡铺在宣纸下面，能够有效防止墨水渗透，避免弄脏桌面；笔洗用来盛放清水，以便在绘画过程中随时涮笔，维持墨色的准确与稳定；笔帘或笔架便于毛笔的放置和取用；白瓷盘或调色盘则有利于颜料或墨色的混合调配，使取色更加迅速便捷；墨碟用来盛放墨汁；镇纸可以压住宣纸，防止其出现位移，保证绘画流程顺利开展；印章和印泥用于落款。在后续的绘画示范中，上述这些辅助工具将不再赘述，重点聚焦于毛笔、宣纸和颜料的使用。

When working on a Chinese painting, in addition to several basic painting materials such as brushes, ink, rice paper, and pigments, some auxiliary tools also need to be prepared. For instance, a felt mat is placed under the rice paper to avert ink seepage and keep the table clean. A brush washer is used to hold clean water, allowing for the convenient rinsing of brushes during the painting process to guarantee the precision and stability of the ink color. A brush holder or a brush stand facilitates the organized placement and easy access of brushes during the creative process. White porcelain plates or palette are conducive to the mixing and blending of pigments or ink colors, enabling a more rapid and convenient color selection. An ink palette serves the purpose of containing ink. Paperweights are used to secure the rice paper in place, preventing any unwanted movement and ensuring the seamless progression of the painting. Seals and seal paste are needed to sign the artwork. In the forthcoming painting demonstrations, these supplementary tools will not be elaborated upon further. Instead, the emphasis regarding the painting materials will be primarily placed on the choice and utilization of brushes, rice paper, and pigments.

1 绘制荷花
Painting Lotus

荷花，又名芙蕖、莲花，生于水中。花呈复瓣，以粉红及白色者为多，花色极为净洁明丽。翠叶如盖，亭亭玉立。荷花在中华文化中是纯洁、高雅和坚韧的象征，有着出淤泥而不染的高洁品性。在绘画艺术中，荷花是极为重要的题材。荷花是水生植物，气质圣洁高雅，有君子花、凌波仙子之美誉。在创作荷花绘画作品时，一定要把荷花"出淤泥而不染，濯清涟而不妖"的特性，以及它端庄的形态、飘逸如仙的神韵很好地表现出来。

Lotus, also known as Fuqu and Lianhua in Chinese, grows in water. Its flowers, with multiple petals, are mostly in pink and white, presenting an extremely pure, clean, and bright color. The emerald-green leaves, like covers, stand gracefully upright. The lotus, which is a symbol of purity, elegance, and tenacity in Chinese culture, possessing the noble quality of emerging unstained from the mud. In the art of painting, the lotus is an extremely important subject. The lotus, an aquatic plant with a holy and elegant temperament, enjoys the good reputations of "Gentleman's Flower" and "Fairy on the Water." When creating a painting work of the lotus, it is essential to well present the characteristics of the lotus that "out of the mud, yet unstained; bathed in clear waves, yet untainted," as well as its dignified form and the fairy-like charm.

荷花花头充满妙趣，在写意画中，画荷花花头的常用技法有双勾法、没骨法两种。双勾法是中国画技法中的一种重要方法。这种技法一般用线条勾勒物象的轮廓，这一过程称作"勾勒"。由于勾勒荷花花头时基本上是用左右或上下两笔勾成，不分方向（顺、逆）或单、复笔，故称为"双勾"。

The flower heads of lotus are abundant in allure. In freehand brushwork paintings, two techniques are commonly employed for painting them, namely the double-outline method and the boneless method. The double-outline method, an important approach in Chinese painting techniques, generally means outlining the contours of objects with lines. This process is known as "outlining." Since it is fundamentally formed by drawing two strokes either from left to right or from top to bottom, regardless of direction (forward or backward) or whether it uses single or multiple strokes, it is thereby designated as the "double-outline method."

扫描二维码获取双勾法绘制荷花花头教学视频
Scan the QR-code to get the teaching video of painting various forms of lotus flower heads drawn by using the double-outline method

用双勾法绘制的荷花花头
Various forms of lotus flower heads drawn by using the double-outline method

没骨法是一种直接用色彩或墨色描绘物象，而不使用墨线勾勒轮廓的绘画技法。"没骨"即"无骨"，强调以色彩和墨色的自然融合与晕染来塑造物体的形态、质感和神韵，使画面呈现出一种细腻、柔和、自然的艺术效果。没骨法同样适用于表现荷花花头的多样形态，诸如花苞、初放、含蕊、盛开等，以及其正面、侧面的不同呈现角度。

The boneless method, on the other hand, is a painting technique that directly depicts objects with colors or ink without using ink lines to outline the contours. "Boneless" literally means "without bones." It emphasizes depicting the form, texture, and charm of objects through the natural fusion and gradation of colors and ink, presenting a delicate, soft, and natural artistic effect on the painting surface. This method is also applicable to demonstrating various forms of lotus flower heads, such as buds, initial blooming, half-blooming (with pistils visible), and full blooming, as well as multiple presentations of their front and side views.

扫描二维码获取没骨法绘制荷花花头教学视频
Scan the QR-code to get the teaching video of painting various forms of lotus flower heads drawn by using the boneless method

用没骨法绘制的荷花花头
Various forms of lotus flower heads drawn by using the boneless method

荷叶与花秆在国画中呈现出多样姿态，荷叶包括半开叶、下垂叶、侧翻叶、正面舒展叶、残荷枯叶、下垂残叶、侧面舒展叶、荷尖小叶芽等；花秆则有浓墨实杆、空心虚杆等。

In traditional Chinese painting, lotus leaves and flower stalks present a variety of postures. Lotus leaves include half-opened leaves, drooping leaves, side-turned leaves, fully expanded front-facing leaves, withered leaves, drooping withered leaves, fully expanded side-facing leaves, and small leaf buds at the tips of lotus shoots, among others. As for flower stalks, there are solid stalks rendered in thick ink and hollow stalks painted in light ink.

扫描二维码获取荷叶绘制教学视频
Scan the QR-code to get the teaching video of painting lotus leaves

中国画中荷叶与花秆的不同姿态
Different postures of the lotus leaves and flower stalks in Chinese paintings

荷花绘画作品《碧池清影》

Lotus painting *Clear Shadows in the Blue Pond*

所需材料：一支兼毫大提斗；一支兼毫大楷笔；一支狼毫小楷笔；墨汁；生宣纸，建议尺寸为 52 厘米 ×96 厘米；曙红；胭脂。

Material needed: one large-sized Tidou brush with mixed hair, one large-sized regular script mixed-hair brush, one small-sized regular script wolf-hair brush, ink, raw rice paper (recommended size: 52cm × 96cm), Shuhong, and Yanzhi.

兼毫大提斗用于绘制荷叶和花秆；兼毫大楷笔用于绘制荷花花头；狼毫小楷笔用于绘制花蕊。

The large-sized Tidou brush with mixed hair is used for painting lotus leaves and stems. The large-sized regular script mixed-hair brush is used for painting lotus flower heads. The small-sized regular script wolf-hair brush is used for painting the stamens.

扫描二维码获取《碧池清影》绘画步骤与教学视频
Scan the QR-code to get the painting steps and teaching video of *Clear Shadows in the Blue Pond*

Exercises

1 **Answer the following questions.**

(1) Compare and contrast the center-tip technique with the side-tip technique in terms of the line effects they produce and their roles in expressing the texture and spatial sense of objects.

(2) Explain how the dot in Chinese painting can convey emotion and artistic conception.

(3) How can an artist use additional symbolic elements like a dragonfly, frog or fish to enrich the meaning and tell a more complete story of the lotus pond in a painting?

2 Choose the best answer to each of the following questions.

(1) Which of the following aspects does the boneless method in Chinese painting pay more attention to?

A. The natural fusion and gradation of colors and ink.

B. The accuracy of the outline.

C. Using thick ink to highlight the main body.

D. Depicting details with fine lines.

(2) Which of the following is NOT a characteristic of the center-tip technique in Chinese painting?

A. The tip of the brush is perpendicular to the paper surface.

B. It is commonly used for outlining contours and details.

C. The strokes are round, full, and three-dimensional.

D. The brush tip moves along one side of the stroke.

(3) Which statement about the double-outline method is correct in freehand brushwork paintings of lotus flower heads?

A. It uses colors or ink directly to depict the object without outlining the contours with ink lines.

B. It emphasizes the natural fusion and gradation of colors and ink to shape the form, texture, and charm of the object.

C. It is a painting technique that outlines the contours of objects with lines, usually forming two parallel or basically parallel lines along the outer edges of the object.

D. It is mainly used to depict the leaves of the lotus rather than the flower heads.

(4) Why is the lotus known as "Gentleman's Flower" and "Fairy on the Water"?

A. Common appearance.　　　　　　　B. Large size.

C. Holy and elegant temperament.　　　D. Easy cultivation.

(5) When painting the lotus, in addition to resembling the shape, what is more important to highlight?

A. The proportional relationship and size of the lotus in the painting.

B. The charm and unique temperament of the lotus.

C. The color selection and harmony for the lotus.

D. The background design and its interaction with the lotus.

2 | 绘制竹子
Painting Bamboo

竹有很多节，内部呈中空结构，外壁质地坚硬，可制器物，又可作建筑材料。在中国文化中，竹与梅、兰、菊并称"四君子"。即便在寒冷的冬季，竹子也屹立不倒，其深厚的根基和不屈的精神，常常被视为坚忍不拔、清廉高洁的象征。竹子作为中国传统文化的重要象征符号之一，备受人们的喜爱与推崇。竹是君子的化身，在画竹子时要彰显其气节。竹子虽不粗壮，却正直、坚韧挺拔，不惧严寒酷暑，万古长青。

Bamboo has numerous joints, is hollow in the middle, and has a hard texture. It can be used to make utensils and serve as a building material. In Chinese culture, bamboo together with plum, orchid, and chrysanthemum are known as the "Four Gentlemen." Even in the cold winter, bamboo can stand firm. Its deep roots and unyielding spirit are often seen as symbols of perseverance, integrity, and purity. As one of the important symbols in traditional Chinese culture, bamboo is highly favored and respected by people, and regarded as the embodiment of a gentleman. When painting bamboo, one should highlight its integrity. Although bamboo is not thick, it is upright, tough, and erect, not fearing severe cold or intense heat, and remaining evergreen all year round.

绘制墨竹的竹竿时，宜选用较为坚硬的兰竹笔。运笔时需经历起笔、行笔和收笔三个阶段。行笔速度不宜过慢，也不宜过快。采用中锋行笔法，画竹竿可以由下往上画，也可以由上往下画，起初笔画短小，随后逐渐变长，笔画之间相互衔接，笔意连贯，直至笔尖逐渐变短变细。

不同形态的墨竹竹竿
The bomboo stems of ink bamboo in different forms

When drawing bamboo stems of ink bamboo, it is best to choose a relatively hard Lanzhu brush. The brushwork should go through three stages: starting the brush, moving the brush, and lifting the brush. The speed of moving the brush should not be too slow or too fast. Using the center-tip method, you can start from bottom to top or from top to bottom. Initially, the strokes are short, and then they gradually become longer, connecting with each other with coherent brush intent until the brush tip gradually becomes shorter and finer.

古人在绘画时将竹节的形态总结为上弯乙字形、八字形和下弯乙字形。竹枝为互生，画时须注意出枝的长度、方向。画枝要挺拔劲健，行笔要快，笔意连绵。枝上又生小枝，小枝应自内向外画。

The ancients summarized the forms of bamboo joints in painting as upward-bending " 乙 " shape, " 八 " shape, and downward-bending " 乙 " shape. As bamboo branches grow alternately, attention should be paid to the length and direction when painting the emerging branches. Branches should be drawn upright and vigorous, with swift strokes and continuous brushwork. Small branches sprout from the main branches and should be drawn from the inside out.

扫描二维码获取竹竿、竹节和竹枝绘制教学视频
Scan the QR-code to get the teaching video of painting bamboo stems, bamboo joints, and bamboo branches

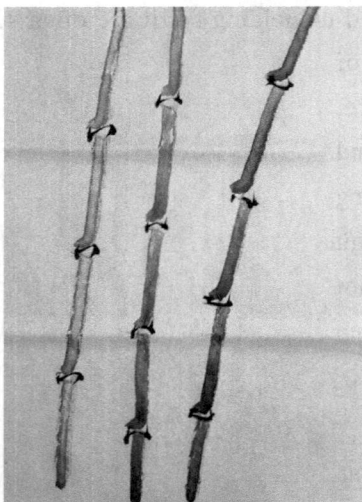

上弯乙字形、八字形与下弯乙字形的竹节画法
（从左到右）
Painting methods for the upward-bending " 乙 " shape, " 八 " shape, and the downward-bending " 乙 " shape of bamboo joints (from left to right)

竹枝
Bamboo branches

画竹叶时以中锋为主，中锋侧锋互用，要有起、行、收的过程。起笔宜轻，行笔爽利，实按而虚起，不可稍有迟滞，要画出竹叶流利的形态，这是画竹过程中要勤加练习的。同时要勤于观察竹叶的生长规律。竹叶通常三四片叶成组，并重叠交错。竹叶的组合主要有"人"字、"个"字、"介"字、"分"字的组合重叠，虽分类繁多，但都以"个"字为基础。此外，在画竹叶时，要有大小、长短、肥瘦、正侧、俯仰、浓淡等变化，以使画作更具深度和真实感。

When painting bamboo leaves, the center-tip painting technique should be predominantly employed, supplemented by the side-tip painting technique as needed, ensuring a proper progression of starting, stroking, and concluding. The initiation of each stroke ought to be gentle, followed by a crisp and fluid movement, applying firm pressure while lifting with a light touch, allowing no hint of hesitation. This is crucial for achieving the sleek and natural appearance of the bamboo leaves, a skill that demands persistent practice throughout the bamboo painting endeavor. Simultaneously, it is essential to be observant of the growth patterns of bamboo leaves. Typically, they cluster in groups of three or four, overlapping and intertwining in an orderly manner. The composition of bamboo leaves primarily consists of combinations and overlaps resembling the Chinese characters " 人 ," " 个 ," " 介 ," and " 分 ." Despite diverse arrangements, they all stem from the fundamental " 个 " shape. Moreover, when painting bamboo leaves, variations in size, length, thickness, front-facing or side-facing, upward or downward, and color intensity should be incorporated to add depth and realism to the painting.

《芥子园画谱·竹谱》展示了不同形态的竹叶画法，包括一笔片羽、一笔横舟、三笔飞燕、三笔燕尾、四笔惊鸦、四笔落雁、二笔鱼尾、三笔金鱼尾、三笔个字、四笔介字、一川、四笔交鱼尾、四笔分字、六笔叠个字、七笔介个相叠、一笔破分字、八笔叠介字、双人字，等等。

Mustard Seed Garden Painting Manual: Bamboo Manual shows the painting methods of various bamboo leaves, including following types: One-Stroke Feather, One-Stroke Horizontal Boat, Three-Stroke Flying Swallow, Three-Stroke Swallowtail, Four-Stroke Startled Crow, Four-Stroke Landing Goose, Two-Stroke Fish Tail, Three-Stroke Goldfish Tail, Three-Stroke Chinese Character "Ge" (个), Four-Stroke Chinese Character "Jie" (介), One-Stroke "Chuan" (川), Four-Stroke Intersecting Fish Tails, Four-Stroke Chinese Character "Fen" (分), Six-Stroke Overlapping Chinese Character "Ge" (个), Seven-Stroke Overlapping Chinese Characters "Jie" (介) and "Ge" (个), One-Stroke Breaking Chinese Character "Fen" (分), Eight-Stroke

扫描二维码获取不同形态竹叶绘制教学视频
Scan the QR-code to get the teaching video of painting various types of bamboo leaves

Overlapping Chinese Characters "Jie" (介), Double Chinese Character "Ren" (人), Overlapping and Intersecting, etc.

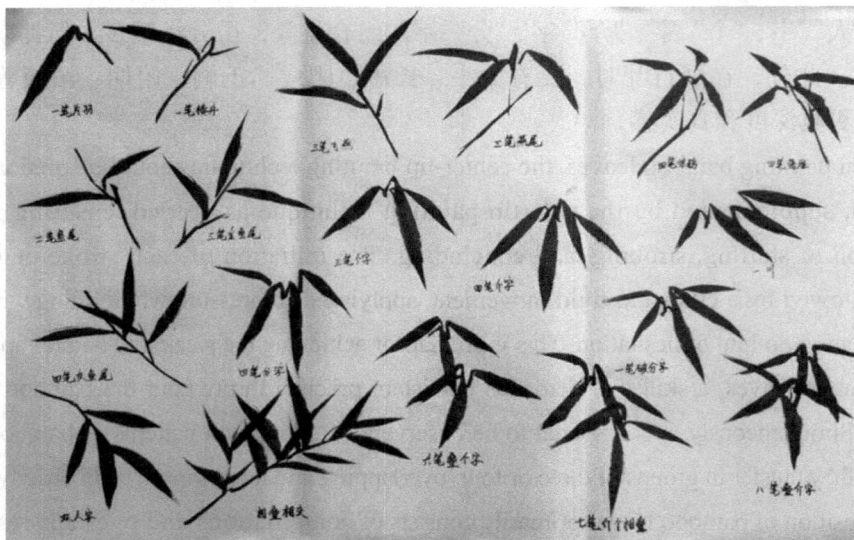

中国画中竹叶的不同形态
Different types of bamboo leaves in Chinese painting

竹子绘画作品《清韵图》
Bamboo painting *Qing Yun Tu*

　　所需材料： 一支兼毫大楷笔；一支大兰竹笔；墨汁；生宣纸。

　　Material needed: one large-sized regular script mixed-hair brush, one large-sized Lanzhu brush, ink, and raw rice paper.

　　兼毫大楷笔用于画竹竿，大兰竹笔用于画竹节和竹叶。

　　The large-sized regular script mixed-hair brush is used for painting bamboo poles and the large-sized Lanzhu brush is used for painting bamboo joints and leaves.

扫描二维码获取
《清韵图》绘画步骤
与教学视频
**Scan the QR-code to
get the painting steps
and teaching video
of *Qing Yun Tu***

3 绘制大熊猫
Painting the Giant Panda

　　大熊猫是中国特有物种，主要栖息地为四川、陕西和甘肃的山区。大熊猫皮肤厚，体型丰腴富态，头圆尾短，雄性个体稍大于雌性；脸颊圆，有大的黑眼圈，黑白相间的体色有利于其隐蔽于密林的树上和积雪的地面而不易被天敌发现。

The giant panda is endemic to China, with its primary habitats being the mountainous regions in Sichuan, Shaanxi, and Gansu provinces. It has thick skin and a plump body shape, featuring a round head and a short tail. The male individuals are slightly larger than the females. Their faces are round, and they possess prominent black eye patches. The black and white body coloration is advantageous for them to conceal themselves among the trees in the dense forest and on the snow-covered ground, making it difficult for predators to detect them.

大熊猫是中国的国宝，在中国的国际政治关系中充当和平使者的角色。其憨态可掬的外形和温顺的性格也使大熊猫深受人们喜爱。大熊猫的形象也经常出现在国画艺术中，非常适合用水墨画来表现。

The giant panda, China's national treasure, plays the role of a peace ambassador in China's international political relations. Its adorable appearance and gentle temperament have made it deeply beloved by people. The image of the giant panda also appears frequently in Chinese paintings, which makes it an ideal subject for ink wash painting.

大熊猫绘画作品《难得憨厚》
Giant Panda painting *Rare Simplicity*

所需材料：一支兼毫大提斗；一支兼毫大楷笔；墨汁；长方形生宣纸。

Material needed: one large-sized Tidou brush with mixed hair, one large-sized regular script mixed-hair brush, ink, and rectangular raw rice paper.

扫描二维码获取《难得憨厚》绘画步骤与教学视频
Scan the QR-code to get the painting steps and teaching video of *Rare Simplicity*

用兼毫大提斗画熊猫，用兼毫大楷笔画竹子。

The large-sized Tidou brush with mixed hair is used to paint the giant panda. The large-sized regular script mixed-hair brush is used to paint bamboo.

Exercises

1 **Answer the following questions.**

(1) Why do you think the bamboo has been highly regarded in Chinese culture and poetry?

(2) What role does the traditional Chinese painting style play in representing the beauty of bamboo and the giant panda?

Choose the best answer to each of the following questions.

(1) What are the "Four Gentlemen" in traditional Chinese culture?

A. Bamboo, plum, orchid, and lotus.

B. Bamboo, plum, orchid, and chrysanthemum.

C. Bamboo, plum, magnolia, and chrysanthemum.

D. Bamboo, peach blossom, orchid, and chrysanthemum.

(2) How should the branches of bamboo be drawn?

A. Branches should be drawn from the outside in.

B. Branches should be drawn curved and weak, with slow strokes.

C. Branches should be drawn randomly without considering the direction.

D. Branches should be drawn upright and vigorous, with swift strokes and continuous brushwork.

(3) What is the basic form of the combination of bamboo leaves according to the text?

A. The Chinese character "人" (Ren).

B. The Chinese character "介" (Jie).

C. The Chinese character "个" (Ge).

D. The Chinese character "分" (Fen).

(4) The black and white body coloration of the giant panda is beneficial for _____.

A. concealing from predators   B. withstanding cold weather

C. attracting mates   D. finding food easily

(5) Chinese people love pandas not only because of their rarity and appearance but also because _____.

A. they are very cute and gentle

B. their fur resembles the Tai Chi diagram

C. they can perform various shows

D. they are good at climbing trees

参考文献
Bibliography

曹海梅.手工时光.中国结 [M].北京：中国画报出版社，2017.

陈培仲.漫谈梅派艺术的传承与发展 [J].川戏剧，2016(2):131-136.

陈绥祥.国画讲义 [M].北京：文化艺术出版社，2017.

陈婷.浅谈我对京剧尚派的理解与认识 [J].中国民族博览，2015(11):131-132.

陈师曾.中国绘画史 [M].北京：中华书局，2014.

陈阳.中国结编织技巧分步详解 [M].南京：江苏凤凰科学技术出版社，2022.

程裕祯.中国文化要略（第 4 版）[M].北京：外语教学与研究出版社，2017.

封杰.勾勒京剧形成之路展现数位卓越功臣：简评《同光十三绝合传》[J].中国京剧，
　　2014(10):84-86.

方振宇.从"教育家精神"看程砚秋的艺术教育思想 [J].美育学刊，2024,15(4):115-
　　120.

郭超.中西戏剧的双向确认：程砚秋访欧与"国剧运动"的"写意"戏剧观 [J].戏剧艺术，
　　2024(4):160-170.

郭宇.梅派艺术的当代意义 [J].上海戏剧，2014(1):3-5.

国家汉办，孔子学院总部.中国欢迎你.学中国结 [M].北京：高等教育出版社，2016.

国家汉办，孔子学院总部.中国欢迎你.学剪纸 [M].北京：高等教育出版社，2016.

国家汉办，孔子学院总部.中国欢迎你.学脸谱 [M].北京：高等教育出版社，2016.

国家汉办，孔子学院总部.中国欢迎你.学书法·水墨画 [M].北京：高等教育出版社，
　　2016.

靳蓉，许明.中国文化翻译实践教程 [M].西安：西安交通大学出版社，2024.

蓝博艺站.国画基础教程 [M].北京：中国铁道出版社有限公司，2021.

李立新."中国结"在现代服饰中设计与应用的研究 [D].苏州大学，2006.

刘彦君.梅兰芳传 [M].河北教育出版社，1996.

梁燕.梅兰芳访美演出的传播策略 [J].戏剧艺术，2015(9):80-84.

潘天寿.中国绘画史 [M].北京：应急管理出版社，2023.

庞长华，庞昭华.一学就会的时尚编绳技法 [M].武汉：武汉大学出版社，2015.

史晓丽.由荀派艺术观探其艺术魅力 [J].中国戏剧，2016(8):56-57.

苏移 . 漫谈京剧流派 [J]. 中国京剧，2023(3):34−38.

汪惟宝，彭嘉，张健萍，等 . 色彩心理学在京剧脸谱及服饰设计中的反映与应用 [J]. 色彩，2023(11):103−105.

吴宇 . 京剧流派的传习模式 [J]. 中国戏剧，2024(3):60−63.

徐雯 . 中国结 [M]. 合肥：黄山书社，2015.

颜长珂 . 哪来的"同光十三绝"画像 [J]. 中国京剧，1999(12):55.

杨明 . 京剧的行当：旦行 [J]. 文史知识，1999(8):84−87.

于文青 . 尚小云的人格魅力 [J]. 中国京剧，2000(1):6−7.

伊丽达，海韵，萨仁，等 . 图说中国绘画艺术 [M]. 南京：江苏科学技术出版社，2013.

张正贵 . 京剧梅派表演艺术的美学内涵 [J]. 戏剧文学 2009(1):81−84.

郑午昌 . 中国画学全史 [M]. 上海：上海古籍出版社，2011.

郑钰 . 文武兼擅面面俱全：浅谈京剧尚派艺术特色 [J]. 影剧新作，2017(2):169−170.

仲万美子，郭艳平 . 梅兰芳赴日公演之时日本知识界的反应 [J]. 戏剧艺术，2015(2):52−63.

朱良志 . 中国书画概论 [M]. 北京：高等教育出版社，2021.

DILLON M. History of China: from earliest times to the last emperor [M]. Beijing: China Translation & Publishing House, 2017.

引用网站
Cited Website

https://www.beijing.gov.cn

https://www.britannica.com

https://www.ccdi.gov.cn

http://www.chinadaily.com.cn

https://www.chnmuseum.cn

https://www.dpm.org.cn

http://www.gansumuseum.com

https://www.hbww.org.cn

https://www.hebeimuseum.org.cn

https://www.hnmuseum.com

https://www.ihchina.cn

https://www.nationalgeographic.com

https://www.shanximuseum.com

https://www.sxhm.com

http://www.wenming.cn

http://www.xinhuanet.com

https://www.zgbk.com

https://apiwenwu.hebeimuseum.org.cn

http://en.chinaculture.org

http://ep.ycwb.com

https://govt.chinadaily.com.cn/

http://kaogu.cssn.cn

https://m.gmw.cn/

https://mp.weixin.qq.com

https://news.gmw.cn

http://paper.people.com.cn

http://wiki.china.org.cn

https://wlj.yuncheng.gov.cn